Concepts,
Theory, and Explanation
in the
Behavioral Sciences

Concepts, Theory, and Explanation in the Behavioral Sciences

Edited and with Introductions by

Gordon J. DiRenzo

RANDOM HOUSE New York

Acknowledgments

This volume represents the edited proceedings of a Symposium held at Fairfield University in April, 1964, under the auspices of the Social Psychology Laboratory of the Department of Sociology. The program was made possible by the encouragement and support of Reverend James E. FitzGerald, S. J., then President of Fairfield University. Assistance in the execution of this event was given graciously by my colleagues: Professors Thomas A. McGrath, Vincent M. Murphy, James P. Vail, and John Kenyon, now of the University of Illinois; and by my student assistants: James Davidson and Eugene Fappiano.

For the realization of this volume, I gratefully acknowledge the encouragement of Reverend James H. Coughlin, S. J., Dean of the College of Arts and Sciences, who has enthusiastically, and with keen interest, supported the undertaking from its inception to this conclusion.

We were fortunate, indeed, to have had the opportunity to bring together on our podium—and, now, in these pages—a number of renowned scientists from the behavioral disciplines. They addressed themselves most eruditely to the challenging issues of this Symposium. Whatever scholarly merits this volume may have, they are due in greatest measure to these distinguished symposiasts. To participate with them in this collaborative effort has been a greatly valued opportunity.

My appreciation is also extended to Professor Robert Bierstedt of New York University for his encouragement and kindness in reading Chapter I and whose own work on conceptual definition aroused my interest in this question.

Special thanks go to the editors and staff of Random House for their kind assistance and particular attention: Charles H. Page, Ted Caris, Estelle Fine, and especially Judith Hillery Higgins for the excellent job of copy-editing.

A particular word of appreciation is expressed to Mary K. Ryan, who provided much assistance to this project in many personal ways, and especially for her help in the preparation of the Index.

G. J. D.

Fairfield, Connecticut
May, 1966

Contents

General Introduction

Science reaches its zenith when it has produced an explanation for the phenomena that it studies. As yet, it has not completely realized this objective; and perhaps it never will—given the seemingly inexhaustible intelligibility of reality. Nevertheless, more and more of this mystery of reality is coming steadily within the comprehension of man. Basic to the endless course of discovery is that complex process known as *theory construction*. Theories are the explanatory statements or systems which are devised by man as descriptions and interpretations of the findings of his scientific investigation. Success in theory construction has been a matter of variability among the several disciplines.

A science is said to be mature if it has developed a solid and valid foundation for the construction of theory. This well-grounded formation consists of a set of properly defined and logically consistent concepts in terms of which the theories may be formulated. The behavioral sciences—sociology, psychology, and anthropology—have witnessed a marked growth in recent years. Yet, today, they remain characterized by much word-play. Each of these disciplines deals with many concepts that seem to have a certain vagueness, not only about their substantial referent, but also with regard to their methodological utility. All kinds of nomenclature and terminology have been devised by the researchers in these fields in their attempt to explain the phenomena of their investigations. These efforts have met with both success and failure in varying degree. The lack of precision which has existed in many such cases is the result of unclear thought. Unclear thought, in turn, is often a consequence of ambiguous and invalid conceptualization.

Concepts—scientific language—comprise the indispensable tools of science, and the irreducible element in the process of scientific explanation. Precision in this fundamental area is imperative for the successful production of significant theory. Yet, despite the centrality of concepts in the scientific process, there has been very little concern—relatively speaking—for the role of conceptualization in theory construction. Much more consideration has been devoted to a closely related, yet secondary, question—that of the empirical measurement of concepts.

Underlying this complex problem of explanation, and equally true for all scientific disciplines, is the question of the *epistemology of science*—the investigation of the process whereby science comes to know the phenomena of reality. This aspect of science has been left nearly exclusively to the philosophers. But even among them, one notes a similar paucity of concern for this question that only in recent years has begun slowly to make an about-face.

The contemporary stage in the behavioral sciences has an inevitably transitional character. Until rather recently, the philosophy of these sciences was discussed sparingly, and then only in very general terms. But today the language of these disciplines and the number of specialized methods of their investigations are rapidly accruing. Consequently, many matters need to be subjected to reinterpretation in the light of advances which have been made not only in the areas of the philosophy and the epistemology of science, but in each of the respective disciplines of behavioral science as well. Theoretical development in these disciplines has been handicapped in part by such problems that have yet to be resolved—or, at least, clarified sufficiently.

Our attempt in the pages that follow is intended to contribute primarily to methodological and epistemological questions that relate to the process of scientific explanation in the behavioral sciences. This volume is concerned fundamentally with the nature and the problems of theoretical explanation for human behavior and our world of socio-cultural reality, and with the modes of scientific investigation in the behavioral sciences. It represents essentially the proceedings of a Symposium on the theme of "Conceptual Definition in the Behavioral Sciences." Particular focus and emphasis are given to the formation, definition, and measurement of scientific concepts. Specifically, the reader will find an examination of such topics as the logical nature and the theoretical use of scientific concepts, particularly with reference to the role of probability inference in concept formation; the logic of scientific procedure, both theoretical and empirical; some discussion of techniques of empirical investigation; and an examination of certain sociological and psychological dynamics which are involved in the research process. Much reference is made to the use of models—particularly mechanical models and computer simulation—as theoretical devices in the behavioral sciences, with a special attempt to explain some of their logical and epistemological ramifications under these circumstances.

While our concerns in these pages are primarily methodological, there is, of course, considerable preoccupation with several substantive issues. Specifically, these considerations involve an exploration of the development of some conventional—as well as some original—concepts in the fields of sociology, psychology, and anthropology; and a respecification of several basic concepts in these respective disciplines. In a more general perspective, this volume provides a summarization of some of the dominant theoretical approaches in the behavioral sciences, such as the general theory of action, reference group theory, and those anthropological perspectives that are pertinent to the new field of culturology.

Obviously, the problems that are singled out for consideration are dictated by the selection—limited as it must be in a one-day symposium—which we have made for this program, as well as by the personal interests and concerns of the participating symposiasts. By no means do we cover all the topics—even the more salient ones—in the general area of research methodology of the behavioral sciences, nor even all the aspects of the few selected problems that are considered. The principal distinction of this volume is that it brings together outstanding figures in the three behavioral disciplines to discuss common issues involved in the problem of theory construction and scientific explanation. Our intent was to select a foremost theoretician and a distinguished methodologist from the disciplines of sociology and psychology, a major theorist from the field of cultural anthropology, and a distinguished figure from the area of the philosophy of science. Our results exceeded the limits of success; all of the principals represented in these pages are widely recognized as outstanding figures in their respective fields.

The order for the chapters that follow is that of the original presentation of papers at the Symposium. The first of these, on the problem of conceptual definition in the behavioral sciences, is intended to provide a frame of reference for those that follow. Each chapter is introduced by the editor with a capsule of its contents that is intended, first, to highlight the major points of the author's message, and, second, to provide some continuity of theme with regard to the focal consideration of conceptualization. These introductory comments will attempt to emphasize the continuities rather than the divergences of the several contributions. Following the individual presentations is a general discussion among the symposiasts in which they extend their remarks and exchange observations on each other's contributions. The concluding chapter by the editor offers a critical delineation of some of the common themes and issues which—in the light of these deliberations—seem to be involved in advancing toward theoretical explanation in the behavioral sciences.

The issues to which this volume addresses itself are, in many respects, perennial questions of science. Indeed, we do not intend to resolve the central problem of conceptual definition in the behavioral sciences through the proceedings of this Symposium. It is our hope, however, that this examination of the role of concepts and theory in scientific explanation will contribute to a clarification that may be of some significant benefit, not only to the behavioral sciences, but to all the other areas of scientific inquiry as well.

CHAPTER I

Conceptual Definition in the Behavioral Sciences

Gordon J. DiRenzo

Editor's Introduction

Conceptual definition is not a new problem. In fact, it may be described more aptly as a perennial scientific question that never has been, and perhaps in some respects never will be, put to rest because of its intimate relationship to the general nature of the scientific research process.

This chapter—which is intended to offer a context and a focus for those that follow—is concerned essentially with the nature and the refinement of scientific concepts, and with the development of a more precise scientific language. Perhaps no one in science today, at least in the behavioral sciences, is satisfied with the existing status of scientific terminology. Each discipline is handicapped in some ways by the lack of a universally shared and standardized vocabulary. It has not been possible to achieve a consensus on the definition for a single concept— nor in fact on even the very nature of either a definition or that of a concept.

Professor DiRenzo speaks of the problem of faulty communication which this situation presents, as much within as without science. He mentions the increasingly acute need for a common scientific language, especially in order to facilitate interdisciplinary research, which seems to be demanded by the nature of the phenomena under investigation in the behavioral sciences. The primary issue involved here, however, is not chiefly linguistic. It is one of much more profound significance, since semantic confusion often is bound inextricably to errors of a theoretical and explanatory nature.

Concepts are the indispensable and irreducible elements that comprise theoretical explanations. The development and the validity of theory is contingent upon the accuracy of the conceptual apparatus that is employed. Conceptual definition and theory formulation go hand in hand as necessary steps of one unified process of scientific explanation. The formation of concepts is but one phase of that complex procedure of scientific inquiry which culminates in the production of theory.

Conceptual analysis is a fundamental problem for all areas of scientific investigation. With the behavioral sciences it is even more of a problem for a couple of reasons. In the first place, the majority of the terms that are used in these areas may be described as *relational* or *functional,* rather than *classificatory* or *property* terms. In the second place, the subject matter of the behavioral disciplines is more complex than in other areas of scientific inquiry. In any case, for all scientific disciplines the general problem of conceptual definition is compounded by the failure to distinguish between generically different kinds of concepts: *substantive* or *phenomenal* concepts, which are concerned with the subject matter under investigation; and *methodological* or *procedural* concepts, which are concerned with the process of investigation. While both these two types of concepts are necessary for scientific explanation, they lead to generically different kinds of "theory."

DiRenzo discusses some of the attempts to resolve this issue by citing several types of definitions which have been devised, and concludes that the fundamental problem involves a distinction between *nominal* and *real* definitions. The crucial significance for theoretical relevance is not that there are different kinds of definitions and concepts. It is rather a question of validity as regards the truth claims of any given concept. Often the scientist, through a process of reification, confuses the methodological function of a concept with its substantive validity and consequently endows it with truth claims. What are the consequences of using false or faulty concepts? The answer is reflected in the fact that the world of the scientist is as real as the concepts by which he knows it.

Since science seeks to confront ontological reality, the question comes down to whether or not there is an affinity between scientific concepts and metaphysics. DiRenzo raises the question of the validity of the methodological techniques for the formulation and application of substantive or theoretical concepts in the behavioral sciences. He suggests that their verification should take a particular orientation based upon an epistemic empiricism of the pragmatic variety. Concepts, like the propositions which they form, to be meaningful must be capable of being brought into relation with experience as a test of their truth. They serve no theoretical function without empirical meaning. Any given concept, moreover, must make a significant difference. It must be productive of substantive theory and explanation.

Conceptual analysis is a crucially fundamental phase of scientific research. Its significance is seen in the fact that it may facilitate or impede the pursuit of scientific explanation. The maturity of a science is reflected in the accumulation of its theory. Theoretical development in the behavioral sciences—and hence, their maturity—rests upon the resolution of this problem of conceptual definition. The perspectives of this chapter will provide a theme for the introductions to those that follow.

Scientific investigation seeks to explain the phenomena it studies in our world of experience; by establishing general principles with which to explain them, hopefully, science can predict such phenomena. The principles of science are stated ultimately in what are known as theories. To explain the facts of reality, scientists require an organized system of concepts. A "science without concepts"[1] is an impossibility—as unthinkable as any form of rational activity without concepts would be. Yet, to say that concepts are indispensable to science is merely to presuppose or to make possible *the* problems, namely, the definition and formation of the required scientific elements.

Initially, in scientific inquiry, description of phenomena may be stated in non-technical vocabulary. The growth of a discipline soon involves the development of a system of speculation, more or less abstract, of concepts and corresponding terminology. Nevertheless, even after decades of definition, and redefinition, many of the fundamental terms in the sciences are far from being distinguished by a universally accepted definition—as much within as outside of particular disciplines. For example, to name just three of the pivotal concepts of the behavioral sciences, there are several denotations for "society," "culture," and "personality." How scientific and technical concepts are introduced and how they function in the scientific process are the central questions here.

Conceptual definition and theory formulation go hand in hand as necessary steps in one unified process of scientific research. The analysis of concepts is but one phase—a fundamental requisite—of that complex process of scientific inquiry which culminates in theory.[2] Concepts, thus, are the irreducible elements of theory or theoretical systems, as the term "theory" has come to be understood more particularly in the behavioral sciences. The more precise and refined the conceptual elements, the more precise and refined the theory.

The question to which we are addressing ourselves is a fundamental one for all areas of scientific inquiry. Often, however, particular disciplines have distinguishing problems. With specific regard to the behavioral sciences—here understood to include the disciplines of sociology, psychology, and anthropology—one particular problem is that the majority of the terms used may be described as *relational* or *functional* terms, rather than *classificatory* or *property* terms.[3] This precludes—or, at least, limits—the utility of the traditional Aristotelian formula for definition—namely, by means of the specification of reference to genus and differentia. Moreover, the problem of conceptualization is an especially crucial one for the behavioral sciences because the subject matter with which these disciplines deal is "more" non-mutually exclusive, so to speak, than it is in other areas of scientific inquiry.

The Problem of Communication in Science

There is, obviously, a communication problem involved in this issue of conceptual definition. It is in fact a two-fold problem of communication. One aspect exists among the scientists themselves; the other exists between scientists and laymen. We need not here elaborate on one aspect of the latter problem: the somewhat incessant—and usually unjustified—charges that are hurled at the behavioral scientist for his neologistic proclivities, the products of which the layman labels as "jargon." There is no denying that there is much truth in this accusation; yet, neologization is not to be totally unexpected, for reasons (both valid and not so legitimate) which need not be elaborated here.

That a communication problem exists between scientists and laymen should not surprise us when even the professionals working within the same discipline—and, more specifically, within the framework of common methodological orientations—frequently are unable to achieve successful communication with one another. This unfortunate situation becomes compounded when scientists of closely allied—not to mention the widely diversified—fields attempt to communicate. Often the same terms are used with several different meanings—each allegedly referring to the same phenomena.

An indication of the problem may be shown in the following examples. In the field of sociology, the concept of "social role" is sometimes used descriptively; sometimes evaluatively; sometimes prescriptively; and sometimes fusionistically, when all of these dimensions are involved. Similarly, in the field of psychology, much controversy has centered around the concept of "mind." In the psychological literature one will find that this concept has been defined variously as a substance, a process, or a neurological epiphenomenon. And, in the field of anthropology, the focal concept of "culture"—among others—has been defined idealistically, realistically, and nominalistically.

There is, thus, an increasingly acute need for a common scientific language in the behavioral sciences, particularly if interdisciplinary research, which seems to be demanded by the nature of the phenomena under investigation, is to be meaningfully effective in explaining more precisely much "more" of that reality which the behavioral sciences seek to discover. One hopeful outcome of this Symposium may be a further recognition of the fact that those arbitrary lines which delimit the separate disciplines must be transgressed whenever such boundaries restrict or tend to distort scientific inquiry. This problem of communication, however, should be seen as only a secondary focus of our concern. The primary issue involved is not chiefly linguistic, but one with much more profound significance—the validity of scientific concepts.

Preliminary Definitions

An old dictum offers the thought that one cannot define anything until one first understands the nature of the act of defining.[4] Perhaps to begin, then, one should determine— however tautological it may seem—the definition of a definition, as well as the definition of a concept. There is, of course, no agreement on these questions, either. It has been affirmed, on the one hand, that a definition is not definable; on the other hand, one finds a grand array of definitions. Robinson, for example, enumerates eighteen different species of definition.[5] Be that as it may, dictionary references suggest in a general sense that the term "definition" refers to the explanation of the meaning of a word—that is, to the determination of the precise signification of a word.

Cohen and Nagel have stated in *An Introduction to Logic and Scientific Method:* "A definition must give the essence of that which is to be defined. The definiens must be equivalent to the definiendum—it must be applicable to everything of which the definiendum can be predicated, and applicable to nothing else."[6] A "definition" according to Aristotle "is a phrase signifying the essense of a thing." By essence is meant that set of fundamental attributes which are the necessary and sufficient conditions for any concrete thing to be a thing of that type.[7]

The term "concept" usually means a rational representation of universal application which comprehends the essential attributes of a class or logical species of phenomena. Thus, the function of a concept is symbolic representation. The *logical* function and purpose of a definition is to ". . . lay bare the principal features or structure of a concept, partly in order to make it definite, to delimit it from other concepts, and partly in order to make possible a systematic exploration of the subject matter with which it deals."[8]

Thus, in one sense, concepts and definitions are not distinguished; rather, they are synonymous with each other. Both may refer fundamentally to essences—that is, to the real nature of phenomena. This situation, however, does not remain true at all times. The factor of determination involves the ontological and the epistemological realms of application. Each, as should become clear in our subsequent consideration, involves a different type of concept and definition.

Attempts to Resolve the Problem

Among the attempts in the behavioral sciences to face the need for increasing the specification and utility of scientific concepts, the following six may be mentioned. (1) *Verbal definitions* are simply descriptive definitions. (2) *Heuristic devices* attempt to use diagrams and other graphic forms to represent concepts as entities. (3) *Models* of one sort or another—and more particularly of late, mathematical and logical models—attempt to provide a general "theoretical" framework or orientation. (4) *Operational definitions*, whose introduction into the behavioral sciences was an attempt to find a means for differentiating between concepts corresponding to reality and those existing in the verbal realm, assign meaning by specifying the activities or "operations" that are necessary to measure a phenomenon, and thus equate the concept to the measurement. (5) *Ideal-type definitions*—introduced originally in the behavioral sciences—suggest a typological configuration or constructive gestalt. (6) *Concepts of postulation* may be defined as those "the meaning of which in whole or in part is designated by the postulates of the deductive theory" in which they occur.[9] Even these various types of suggested definitions, however, are neither conceptually clear nor consensually accepted. For example, very seldom do scientists distinguish between a description, a literal model, an image, a conception, and even a theory.

Obviously, there are various modes for the process of definition. This is not, however, the crucial issue. The fundamental problem of these many types of definitions is the question of their validity: what *is* "society," "culture," "social system," or "personality"? Are these things real or ideal? And in what sense are they real or ideal? For instance, is "personality" a description, a diagram, a model, a measurement, a process, a mental construct, an entity, or simply something else? And, then, what are the scientific limits of this concept when defined in each of these variations?

There exists a notion, not completely erroneous perhaps, that scientists create objects that have no existence in the external world. The question often arises whether such things as, for example, "attitudes" and "atoms" are real or merely imaginary. Legitimate or not, reification has been a prevalent modus operandi in many scientific quarters.

In any case, some type of conceptualization is necessary for scientific activity. It is imperative, however, to keep in mind that the scientist lives as much in a world of scientific cognitions as any layman lives in a world of non-scientific cognitions. Accordingly, the world of the scientist is as real as the validity of his cognitions. Given the fundamental dynamics of cognition, conceptual language influences scientific perceptions and, consequently, the total research process. The researcher, thus, often draws different consequences for and from empirical research as his conceptual apparatus and orientation change.[10]

The general problem of conceptual definition is often compounded by the failure to distinguish, wherever possible, between generically different kinds of concepts. Two such types in particular may be mentioned: (1) substantive or phenomenal concepts, which are concerned with the *subject matter* under investigation, such as the concepts of "social system," "personality," and "culture"; and (2) methodological or procedural concepts, which are concerned with the *process* of investigation, such as the concepts of "cause," "validity," and "theory." These two generic types of concepts are related to and lead to generically different kinds of "theory." As we shall see, truth may be said to be the test of one, while utility may be said to be the test of the other.

The Epistemological Question

Insofar as science seeks to explain reality, its subject matter must be defined in terms of real things, which are observable either directly or indirectly; science, thus, seeks to confront ontological reality. The question we are asking, then, comes down to this: is there an affinity between scientific concepts and metaphysics?

So long as we assume that certain knowledge of social reality can be had, then we must raise the questions of how we know, and do we know, and when do we know, that we have attained metaphysical certitude, and not simply logic in one form or another.

Logical reality, such as that inherent in concepts of postulation, does not necessarily imply metaphysical reality. The concepts of mathematics, for example, are not limited by existing reality. This is the meaning of Einstein's famous dictum: "Insofar as mathematics is about reality it is not certain; and insofar as it is certain, it is not about reality."[11] Perhaps we can understand this more clearly in Bertrand Russell's remark that the mathematician never knows whether or not what he is talking about is true. It is possible to develop all kinds of mathematics and logical systems based upon postulates that have nothing to do with the actual world. Both Euclidean and non-Euclidean geometries testify to this. Even noted physicists have declared that many concepts of modern physics are nothing but sets of mathematical formulas, though in saying this they overlook the fact that such formulas may acquire significance for physical science when related to observable phenomena.[12] Thus, the logical analysis of the meaning of synthetic propositions does not imply any reference to their validity, that is, to their truth or falsity. The theories in which concepts of this type are used must be verified before the concepts themselves can be accredited any reality or validity. To propose an unverifiable theory is to make no significant contribution to science.

We may seem to be biasing our presentation of the problem by suggesting a particular epistemological orientation. Yet, as Abraham Kaplan stated recently: "If science is to tell us anything about the world, if it is to be of any use in our dealings with the world, it must somewhere contain empirical elements."[13] This, of course, implies a sort of epistemic empiricism, which suggests that we cannot know without depending somewhere upon empiricism, and which further implies as well a semantic empiricism—all of which in turn implies that to be meaningful a proposition must be capable of being brought into relation with experience as a test of its truth.[14] Concepts without empirical meaning serve no theoretical function.

These would seem to be valid assumptions, given the fact that the behavioral sciences are empirical sciences. Kaplan suggests three variations of this epistemological orientation: logical positivism, operationalism, and pragmatism. None of what we have said is meant to imply necessarily all of these variations. Yet, certainly, we would choose one of these variations, namely pragmatism, as being particularly valid for and necessary to the behavioral sciences. That is to say, any given concept must make a significant difference; otherwise, it is not of any scientific use in serving to explain reality, and thus is contrary to the goal of science. Concepts must facilitate substantive theory. Any conceptual schema that cannot do so is a sterile one.

Of course, lest we be misunderstood, let us hasten to add that whether or not concepts have ontological significance does not imply that they have no scientific utility; methodological concepts would verify this.

The problem, then, is how to distinguish not only between types of meaningful concepts and types of meaningless concepts, but also between those concepts and types of concepts that correspond to real experience and those that represent purely verbal definitions. Legitimate definitions, we suggest, should connect the concept with reality. And, in so doing, they should show the relationship of that one segment of reality to, and its differentiation from, other segments of reality.

Words, obviously, serve a necessary function in the acquisition of knowledge. As such they may be defined conventionally. Therefore, they may be either true or false. Concepts, or the metaphysical referents for words, on the other hand, are quite a different matter. Their truth or falsity is contingent upon their logical type.

Real Versus Nominal Definitions

Without attempting to over-simplify this most complex problem, we suggest that the theoretical and methodological significance of the issue we are confronting can be focused—at least as a working frame of reference—upon the distinction between *nominal definitions* and *real definitions*. This is perhaps the oldest dichotomy of definitions. The several examples of concept types that we mentioned above may be classified rather easily into one or the other of these two categories.

A real definition is a "statement of the essential characteristics of some entity."[15] It is, therefore, a genuine proposition which must be either true or false. A nominal definition "is an agreement or resolution concerning the use of verbal symbols. A new symbol called the definiendum is to be used for an already known group of words or symbols—the definiens. The definiendum is thus to have no meaning other than the definiens."[16] It is, therefore, a convention that serves to introduce an alternative notation for a given linguistic expression.[17] The point is that a nominal concept, such an operational definition, has no meaning other than that given arbitrarily to it. Thus, a nominal definition has no inherent claims to truth. An analogy may be made to the symbol x in mathematics, which has whatever meaning may be ascribed to it operationally.

There is no question that at some point a real definition assumes not only logical but also ontological significance. As Robert Bierstedt points out: "Real definitions, in short, have ontological and not merely logical consequences; they have empirical and not merely rational implications; and it is these characteristics that give to the distinction itself a certain relevance to contemporary . . . theory."[18] Thus, as regards nominal definitions, the basic question is this: is there anything in the world of reality that corresponds to them?

The major problem is that nominal definitions are usually equated to the real and thus are treated and regarded as real definitions; this is perhaps as much a consequence of repeated use as of methodological commitment. Nominal definitions, therefore, may produce conceptual schemes and theoretical systems that may not be ontologically true. This temptation for reification in science should be regarded as a professional hazard.

The implication is not, however, that nominal definitions are of no value in scientific research; they are useful, and even necessary, for their methodological and epistemological functions. Science, as we said, inevitably involves the creation of new concepts. Obviously, one function of nominal definitions is that of introducing new terms into a language and, therefore, new concepts into scientific terminology.[19] More importantly, the adoption of precise and standardized nominal definitions—if this were possible—would be desirable for the purpose of providing a more specific focusing of the research process. Moreover, conceptual consensus—relative to whichever type of concept—should be demanded, if only to alleviate the problem of communication.

The adoption of uniform nominal definitions may or may not be realized. Nevertheless, conceptual consensus regarding real definitions is not something that remains to be decided arbitrarily. By their very denotata, real definitions, once achieved, must be accepted. Thus, we can now comprehend the intention of the statement that nominal definitions are judged by their utility, while real definitions are judged by their truth.[20] As Bierstedt claims, both types of conceptual apparatus are important; but they must be discerned as being significantly different. "In the one . . . we are constructing the instruments of inquiry and the categories of classification; and in the other, we are building substantive . . . theory."[21] Substantive theory—the goal of science—is assertive; and its propositions are assertions about the world of reality.

The Theoretical Significance

The distinction between these two types of concepts becomes critically significant in the matter of the development of theory. The more nearly a given theory resembles a collection of nominal definitions, the more likely it is that it has no necessary claims to truth; the more nearly it resembles a set of real definitions, the more likely it is that it can be recognized as a valid contribution to scientific knowledge and theory.[22]

There is, of course, a variety of methodological procedures that may be used in each of the behavioral sciences. Our basic concern, then, is the validity of the methodological techniques for the formulation and application of scientific concepts in the behavioral sciences—particularly as regards those concepts that are based, as are the great majority of concepts in the behavioral sciences, upon the indirect observation of phenomena. As the sociologist Alex Inkeles recently pointed out, one of the funda-

mental problems is ". . . that while the theorist may have defined the concept, he frequently gives no precise indication of
how one should go about trying to find out whether the thing
defined actually exists in the real world. A second, and even more
forceful, complaint is that the theorist frequently fails to indicate
what one can do with his concepts other than use them as labels
to replace the labels the same things already bear."[23] Concepts
need to have more than merely descriptive power; they need to
have explanatory power. Their validity in this respect is determined through empirical confirmation, and this requires, first of
all, an essential correspondence between the conceptual and the
phenomenal elements.

It often is held that the maturity of science is reflected in the
status of its theory. Given the fact that theoretical development
is contingent upon conceptual definition, the significance of
conceptual definition is obvious for the growth of the behavioral
sciences. The validity of their theory—and, thus, the hope of the
behavioral sciences—rest upon the resolution of this issue.

NOTES

1. See Herbert Blumer, "Science Without Concepts," *American
Journal of Sociology*, XXXVI (1931), 515–533.

2. In fact, as Merton points out, to make clear what is "the
character of data subsumed under a concept" is one fundamental
"theoretical problem." Robert K. Merton, *Social Theory and Social
Structure* (Glencoe: The Free Press, 1957), p. 90.

3. See Carl G. Hempel, "Fundamentals of Concept Formation in
Empirical Science," *International Encyclopedia of Unified Science*
(Chicago: University of Chicago Press, 1952), Vol. II, No. 7.

4. Richard Robinson, *Definition* (Oxford: Clarendon Press, 1950),
p. 3.

5. *Ibid.*, p. 47. See also F. Stuart Chapin, "Definition of Definitions
of Concepts," *Social Forces*, XVIII (1939), 153–160.

6. Morris R. Cohen and Ernest Nagel, *An Introduction to Logic
and Scientific Method* (New York: Harcourt, Brace and Company,
1934), p. 238.

7. *Ibid.*

8. *Ibid.*, pp. 231–232. This, of course, is not to be confused with the

psychological motives for definitions, such as the use of more familiar and simpler expressions.

9. F. S. C. Northrop, *Logic of the Sciences and Humanities* (New York: The Macmillan Company, 1947), p. 83.

10. See Merton, *op. cit.*, p. 91.

11. Quoted in Felix Kaufmann, *Methodology of the Social Sciences* (New York: Oxford University Press, 1944), p. 37.

12. *Ibid.*, pp. 35–37.

13. Abraham Kaplan, *The Conduct of Inquiry* (San Francisco: Chandler Publishing Company, 1964), p. 34.

14. *Ibid.*, pp. 34–36.

15. Hempel, *op. cit.*, p. 2.

16. Cohen and Nagel, *op. cit.*, p. 228.

17. Hempel, *op. cit.*, p. 2.

18. Robert Bierstedt, "Nominal and Real Definitions," in Llewellyn Gross (ed.), *Symposium on Sociological Theory* (New York: Harper and Row, 1959), p. 133.

19. For other functions, see *ibid.*, pp. 129–130.

20. *Ibid.*, pp. 141–142.

21. *Ibid.*, pp. 137–138.

22. *Ibid.*, p. 133.

23. Alex Inkeles, *What Is Sociology?* (Englewood Cliffs: Prentice-Hall, Inc., 1964), p. 100.

SUGGESTED READINGS

Adler, Franz. "Operational Definitions in Sociology," *American Journal of Sociology* (1947), 52:438–444.

Bierstedt, Robert. "Nominal and Real Definitions," in Llewellyn Gross (ed.), *Symposium on Sociological Theory*. New York: Harper and Row, 1959.

Blumer, Herbert. "Science Without Concepts," *American Journal of Sociology* (1931), 36:515–533.

Burt, Cyril. "The Structure of the Mind," *British Journal of Statistical Psychology* (1961), 14:145–170.

Chapin, F. Stuart. "Definition of Definitions of Concepts," *Social Forces* (1939), 18:153–160.

Cohen, Morris R., and Nagel, Ernest. *An Introduction to Logic and Scientific Method.* New York: Harcourt, Brace and Company, 1934.

Gross, Llewellyn (ed.). *Symposium on Sociological Theory*. New York: Harper and Row, 1959.

Hempel, Carl G. *Aspects of Scientific Explanation.* New York: The Free Press, 1965.

———. "Fundamentals of Concept Formation in Empirical Science," *International Encyclopedia of Unified Science.* Chicago: University of Chicago Press, 1952, Vol. 2, No. 7.

Inkeles, Alex. *What Is Sociology?* Englewood Cliffs: Prentice-Hall, Inc., 1964.

Kaplan, Abraham. *The Conduct of Inquiry.* San Francisco: Chandler Publishing Company, 1964.

Kaufmann, Felix. *Methodology of the Social Sciences.* New York: Oxford University Press, 1944.

Lazarsfeld, Paul F. "Problems in Methodology," in Robert K. Merton *et al.* (eds.), *Sociology Today.* New York: Basic Books, Inc., 1959.

Merton, Robert K. *Social Theory and Social Structure.* Glencoe: The Free Press, 1957.

———, *et al.* (eds.). *Sociology Today.* New York: Basic Books, Inc., 1959.

Northrop, F. S. C. *Logic of the Sciences and Humanities.* New York: The Macmillan Company, 1947.

Robinson, Richard. *Definition.* Oxford: Clarendon Press, 1950.

Wood, Ledger. "Concepts and Objects," *The Philosophical Review* (1936), 45:370–381.

CHAPTER II

The Concept
of "Social System" as a
Theoretical Device

Charles Ackerman
and Talcott Parsons

EDITOR'S INTRODUCTION

One of the more dominant theoretical concerns in the behavioral sciences today is the general theory of action. This has been responsible for introducing a host of new concepts into the vocabulary of several disciplines, as well as for providing theoretical direction in many respects. Foremost among the creators of this system of thought is Professor Talcott Parsons of Harvard University. In this chapter he and Professor Charles Ackerman offer a summary statement of the general theory of action, with particular emphasis on its application to sociological analysis.

This chapter is not a technical exposition of action theory; it contains only the most general outlines of this systemic explanation. What it does attempt is to communicate the basic concepts that are employed by the actionists and the purposes for which they are intended. More particularly, the chapter is a manifesto—a statement of position and policy—on behalf of the action theorists; its intention is to provide an exposition of the authors' epistemological orientation and methodological approach to sociological analysis. It is, in the words of E. C. Tolman, a description of their "cognitive map."

Ackerman and Parsons take the position that all analytical thought is mythologization since the scientific method, by virtue of its selective approach, invariably involves some distortion of reality. This position is presented as a *sine qua non*. The "facts" of science are myths, however imperative they remain for the scientific process. They always contain something of the analyst, his frame of reference. To that extent, facts are not merely encountered—they are created. Within this context, they demand a conscious recognition, on the part of the analyst in particular, of the general structure of the analyst's cognitive map—his "input" to his analysis—and his interaction with the analytical situation.

Action theory is generic in nature. The focus of this chapter, however, is confined to but one segment of action theory, namely, the concept of "social system," which is considered as a specific variant. This concept is offered as a "theoretical device" for the analysis of the interaction of individual actors, which, the authors contend, takes place under conditions such that it is possible to treat this process as a system in the scientific sense, and to subject it to the same order of theoretical analysis that has been applied to other types of systems in other disciplines. Within this framework, the authors offer definitions for a number of key concepts that relate focally to the concept of "social system." Their approach, which involves the metaphorical application of a cybernetic model, contains the main outlines of a conceptual scheme for the analysis of the structure and function of social systems.

The analytical model in the frame of reference of general action theory provides for three independent, irreducible, and indispensable elements: the social, cultural, and personality sub-systems. Each of these "primary abstractions" is an independent focus for the organization of the elements of the action system. No one sub-system is theoretically reducible to the terms of any one, or to a combination, of the other two. Yet, in the structure of a completely concrete system of action, the personality system of the individual actor and the cultural system are built into the action of the social system. Accordingly, the conception of the social system is defined and mediated in terms of the cultural system and the personality system.

The actionists show how these three sub-systems interact with, stimulate, and respond to each other, how they are linked and activated by the flow of energy, and how they are controlled and regulated by information. Particular stress is placed on the "connectedness" and "interaction" of these theoretical elements. The "how" and "why" of this connectedness is shown by two factors of organizational analysis, namely, *function* and *interpenetration* (of a system and its environment), which provide conceptual bridges between the sub-systems of the general system of action.

Connectedness is the emphatic element in this systemic orientation. Ackerman and Parsons contend that their conceptualizations of systemic analysis militate against scientific mythologization by possessing a built-in requirement to consider the interaction of elements by means of the concepts of "interpenetration" and "function." They claim that this theoretical conception of the social system escapes, as much as any construct can, the negative consequences of mythologization by warning us against, and thus postponing, closure and contradiction—the eventually inevitable consequences of abstraction. It is this interpenetration and interdependence which make systemic analysis substantively different from the kind of reasoning that derives one system from one or both of the others by a process of reduction.

Another pair of focal concepts are the following: (1) "the energic hierarchy of conditions," which is concerned with the goal-attainment mechanisms of the system, and is referred to as its "output" or as the "flow-out" of the delivering system; and (2) "the informational hierarchy of controls," which relates to the adaptive mechanisms of the system, and may be referred to as the systemic "input" or as the "flow-in" of the receptor system. These two hierarchies of the energic factor and the control factor are envisioned as interactive and as opposed in directionality.

Ackerman and Parsons consider some of the consequences of systemic operation as presented in their conceptual model. Social systems, as communication and decision systems, are inherently normative. "Alienation" and "anomie" are discussed as potential pathologies which stem from an inadequate respecification of the generalized norms and values of the differentiated system within its sub-systems. That is to say, they are not made meaningful within the sub-systems. These dysfunctions of the systems are presented as consequences of the nature and the inadequacy of the informational controls.

As is apparent, this chapter offers a systematic consideration of a number of concepts, particularly those that have been defined as methodological and nominal in nature. It demonstrates the manner in which this type of concept performs a legitimate and necessary role in scientific explanation. With regard to the preceding chapter, the reader should pay particular attention here to the references that Ackerman and Parsons make to "analytical boundaries" and to the significance that these have for the functionality—and, in their context, for the distortion—of concepts.

To some, our contribution to this Symposium may appear entirely too philosophical. We proceed, however, in our chosen fashion deliberately. We wish to chart (to such degree as we can briefly) the ground in which action-theoretical formulations and concepts are rooted, and we wish to discuss the relation of patterned elements of our approach to the analytical situation, indicating certain consequences of this approach. Whether consideration of ground and approach, and their consequences, are, as we believe, methodological or are rather to be called "philosophical" is a matter, perhaps, of merest labeling. It is certainly the case that the boundary between methodology and philosophy is both shifting and permeable.

The Analyst's Cognitive Map

Sociology is not a *tabula rasa* upon which things called "facts" inscribe their determinate and essential paths and shapes. No disciplined inquiry is. We approach our data as humans; and, as humans, we approach with differential receptivity and intentionality everything toward which we propose a cognitive orientation. In this respect one need only recall Tolman's famous and provocative concept of "the cognitive map." Data do not simply impose their structure on our inquiring and open minds: we *interact* with "facts." We are not naive, we are not innocent; and, as we shall argue, "no fact is merely itself": a completely open mind is a completely empty one. There is a formative input to analysis, the components of which are not born *ex nihilo* in or of the moment of encounter with "facts"; rather, they are grounded in the orientation and frame of reference of the analyst. Indeed, in major part we create, we do not merely encounter, facticity.

Two grand and ultimate models have traditionally (and, of course, differently) guided sociological conceptualization and research—the *mechanical* and the *organic*. In recent years a third has emerged—the symbolic-interaction or *cybernetic* model—synthesizing to some degree important aspects of the traditional two. The virtues and vices of these models are irrelevant to the point we want to make, which is, simply, that they have been, and are, for many theorists and researchers, generators of ideas, orientational devices guiding conceptualization, research, and explanation.

We are at least as intelligent as Tolman's thoughtful rats, and we take into the analytical situation—a situation, we repeat, of interaction with the data—a cognitive map. There may be more or less "goodness of fit" of our map to the data, and we may be more or less sensitive to this, more or less willing to "learn," to adjust our map; but our learning does not make us inhuman and we always have maps before we encounter the "facts." Our maps tell us what *are* the "facts." We select, and we ascribe importance; and we select and ascribe importance according to criteria that are not simply immanent "in" the data. Our criteria transcend the array of data under analysis.

We feel it appropriate that an analyst attempt conscious recognition of the general structure of his cognitive map, his "input" to analysis. *Hier stehe ich; ich kann nicht anders* (Here I stand; I cannot do otherwise). The statement frequently attributed to Luther is one of flamboyant self-assertion and the sound of hammering echoes in it still. Although flamboyance, self-assertion, and hammering are not appropriate to a scientific symposium, honesty, introspection, and the attempt to reveal standpoint are. The purpose of this paper is to make as explicit as possible—at least in silhouette—the grounding of our approach, our cognitive map, our orientation, our standpoint, and some of the consequences of all these.

Scientific Mythologization

The "facts" of science are myths.

This is not a new thought. It is, however, one whose implications for theory-building have not always been recognized; we believe that they must be.

We select from what William James called "booming, buzzing" reality; we establish boundaries, we ascribe limit. In order to deal with what we make concrete as "fact," we rip it from concrete *connectedness* and we pretend that it is a discrete particle. We select, we ascribe importance; and both our selection and our ascription of importance are in a sense unnatural since the array of reality itself does not supply the criteria for the selection or the ascription. Ultimately, no one is entirely guiltless of the fallacy of misplaced concreteness.

Unfortunately, by ripping our "facts" from their bed in connectedness we make them to some extent unreal. We put on the blinders of a drayhorse and we stare at what has become unreal by our concentration upon it. However, *Ich kann nicht anders* and neither can you nor anyone else: selection, the imposition of boundaries, the ascription of importance (that is, noting in each act, the way in which the act transcends its nexus)—these are aspects of thinking itself. As Alfred North Whitehead put it in his first 1937 lecture at Wellesley College: "A single fact in isolation is the primary myth required for finite thought."[1] That fact is *myth*, fiction, but we must have it; we must isolate in order to encompass.

Whitehead pointed out also a consequence of our mythologization of nature by thought. He said:

> Connectedness is of the essence of all things of all types.
> . . . Abstraction from connectedness involves the omission
> of an essential factor in the fact considered. No fact is
> merely itself.[2]

And he argued, therefore:

> Both in science and in logic you have only to develop your
> argument sufficiently and sooner or later you are bound to
> arrive at a contradiction . . . externally in its reference to
> fact.[3]

We exclude—and what we exclude haunts us at the walls we set up. We include—and what we include limps, wounded by amputation. And, most importantly, we must live with all this, we must live with our wounded and our ghosts. There can be no

Bultmann of science, pleading that we "de-mythologize": *analytical thought itself is mythologization.*

These are, as we have admitted, old thoughts; all of this is known. We bring up such morbid matters because we believe that consideration of them can tell us something about a primary requisite for theory-building and concept formation. Let us attempt to demonstrate this by addressing ourselves to the issue of the "social system as a theoretical device." Choosing to emphasize the term "device," with its connotation of "useful tool," we shall argue that the "social system" is a device that escapes, as much as any analytical construct can, the negative consequences of mythologization. It maximizes analytical attention to one form of connectedness, and it does so in a disciplined manner.

On the one hand, in order to think at all, we must abstract, ascribe differential importance, select and establish analytical boundaries. On the other hand, these very activities doom our formulations to eventual inadequacy. Several relevant questions, to which we want to direct attention, are involved in that qualification "eventual." When do we encounter the inadequacy, soon or late? When do we achieve closure and at what analytical level? How far can we push our formulations before they fail?

The "when" of closure and the range of our formulations depend, we believe, on where and how we start. It is the *primary abstractions* that matter: the fecundity, and the generality, of theory depend upon the nature of our primary abstractions. It makes a difference where we carve our boundaries, what we include and what we exclude. It makes a difference to what we ascribe how much importance. For example, do we study the "human group" or do we study the "social system"? These are not the same things and it makes a difference which we choose. Do we study "behavior" or do we study "action"? These are not the same things, and the difference makes a difference. Slice up "reality" *this* way—and your formulations quickly curl upon themselves and fail of generality. Slice it up this *other* way—and your formulations open up and spread broadly over a wide array. *A physics based on mass is a physics more fecund than one based on weight*, although, of course, "weight" appeals more to common sense and empiricism. So do the "human group" and "behavior."

Given Group X of primary abstractions, the theorist encounters premature closure; given Group Y of primary abstractions, the theorist can ride and goad them beyond the quotidian and the "middle range" toward general theory. It seems likely that one crucial discriminant between Group X and Group Y is the degree to which the latter may incorporate "correction mechanisms" continually opening the formulations. There is a class of primary abstractions which, like sticks in the mouth of a crocodile, hold open formulations by merely being there; and in the discussion to follow we shall attend in particular to three such primary abstractions which perform this function in action theory—*system, interpenetration,* and *function.* They are theoretical devices, or concepts, whose emphasis on connectedness mitigates the eventually inevitable consequences of abstraction by postponing our arrival at closure and contradiction.

System, Interpenetration, and Function

In some respects we are the ragpickers of sociological theory, having derived many of our primary concepts from other disciplines. For example, system, in our usage, implies to an important degree its origin in physiological theory. The nineteenth-century French physiologist Claude Bernard pointed out that systems are less randomly ordered than the environment in which they are embedded. Indeed, one very highly generalized way of conceptualizing a minimal aspect of a system might be to consider it *an area of relative non-randomness.* It is also the case that system boundaries are permeable: the system and its environment *interpenetrate* each other. A system is an ordered aggregate embedded in, and in interaction with, a fluctuating environment.

Given this conceptualization of system, the analyst immediately finds implications. He may ask such relevant questions as, for example, "How is the degree of order maintained 'against' environmental fluctuation?" and "How are the internal system components ordered vis-à-vis each other?" The analyst will consider *system problems*, for example, problems of boundary maintenance, problems of resource procurement and allocation, and problems of pattern maintenance. If he wants theory rather than empirical generalizations, he will define and identify these problems in generic terms, that is, in terms not specific to any class of action systems, but specifiable to all, in principle, isomorphically. He will be drawn toward attempting: (1) to define problems, and (2) to identify *mechanisms* that, however adequately or inadequately, "resolve" the problems, and (3) to state the conditions and consequences of adequate or inadequate resolution.

Consider, for an example, the "adaptive" problems *implied by* interpenetration and differential randomness. Not only must system boundaries, by some mechanism(s), be maintained in relative integrity, but by some mechanism(s) the system must both draw "sustenance" from the environment and "defend itself" against extreme environmental fluctuation. At the boundary of the system—permeable, open to environmental impingement and intrusion—there must be *filtration* mechanisms, accepting and rejecting possible environmental inputs, and *regulatory* mechanisms, minimizing environmental fluctuation either by direct action into the environment toward control of its relevant aspects or, at least, by neutralizing those effects of such fluctuation as cannot effectively be controlled.

Thus, at the start, by the implication of two of our primary abstractions—system and interpenetration—we are required to consider the "connectedness" of what we study. We are required to do so in a *generic* fashion: by the very nature of the case, our definitions of problems and identification of mechanisms cannot be specific to any given class of action system. We are, in other words, goaded toward general theory. Interpenetration and system are "sticks in the mouth of a crocodile": they force consideration and analysis of connectedness.

Connectedness is not *fusion*, however. Consideration of connectedness does not in any way negate our necessary insistence upon the analytical distinction to be maintained between system and environment. To state, for example, that the two action systems, "personality" and "social system," constitute environments each for the other and that there is an energic input to the social system from the personality system, these systems interpenetrating each other, is not to deny the analytical integrity and "separateness" of the two systems. "Personality" and "social system" are not, from our point of view, fused into *a* system, nor is one epiphenomenal to the other; rather, they constitute two analytically independent *sub-systems of a system* (the general "action" system) in interaction and interpenetration. In the same sense we distinguish between the personality system and the behavioral organism: well and good that through the Id (the adaptive sub-system of the personality) "resources" enter the personality system from the behavioral organism, but the fact that these systems are connected does not mean that they are fused or that such resources "cause" personality.

An analogy may be helpful. (We use it with trepidation, since too often analogies are taken as definitive; we intend this one to *evoke*, not to define.) Imagine that we itemize a vast number of "behavioral" variables, not knowing their labels (such as "physiological," "psychological," and so on), and that we build with these variables an n-by-n correlation matrix. We submit the matrix for factor analysis. The areas of (relatively) dense intercorrelation suggest factors, and these factors in turn constitute systems. There are, we contend, four such analytically independent factors or systems in the "behavioral" area: those of the "behavioral organism," the "personality," the "social" system, and the "cultural" system. To fuse these would be to ignore the fact of the patterning of the intercorrelations within the matrix: the analytical integrity of a factor is not denied or threatened by the fact that many of its constitutive variables may be correlated with variables external to the factor. Of course, components within each system are intercorrelated with components of another system; this is evidence of connectedness, interpenetration, and function.

Interpenetration is only one of two aspects of the external connectedness of systems. We mentioned previously that there is an energic input to the social system from the personality system, and we mentioned also that resources from the behavioral organism enter the personality through what has been called the Id. In general terms, we are describing a set of "input-receptor" relationships; and consideration of such relationships will, we feel, clarify the second aspect of external systemic connectedness—*function*. Simultaneously, we hope, two further concepts of action theory will be made clear—the energic hierarchy of conditions and the informational hierarchy of controls.

It is convenient to begin with a definition, in summary form, of function. *A function is an energic output of an action system into another system, controlled informationally by the adaptive mechanisms of that receptor system.* As output, what is delivered flows "outward-bound" across the goal-attainment boundary of the delivering system; as input, what is received flows "inward-bound" across the adaptive boundary of the receiving system. *The locus of function is the goal-attainment sector of the relevant delivering system.* (Of course, the analyst may be interested in intrasystemic interchanges; in such case, the term "subsystem" is substituted for the term "system." The categories and dynamics are isomorphic.)

Since there are many ways of using any term, it would be presumptuous of any analyst to insist that his usage be granted normative status; moreover, there seems to be little general agreement among sociologists about the meaning to be ascribed to the word "function." We can only state what *we* mean and hope that our intended meaning will be understood. From our point of view, function is a term most appropriately used in the context of "output" and "contribution." (Is it necessary to point out that this does not beg the questions of eufunction and dysfunction?) As one example of our usage, we would say: the primary function of the Ego as a sub-system of the personality is the articulation of the personality system with the social system, energizing the latter; this articulation and input of energy are accomplished at the adaptive boundary of the social system, that is, through the *role*. As a second example: the function of the economy is production, not profit-making, the latter being more properly considered analytically as an adaptive aspect of empiri-

cal organizations. And for a third example: the function of role is
to deliver motivational energy toward, and in a form suitable for,
collective action. (Here, of course, we are conceptualizing
wholly at the sub-systemic level, that is, within the social
system.)

In function there are always directionality and contribution: a
function delivers up and contributes to. It is an output of a
delivering system. As such, the concept is itself "functional" for
theory-building. Along with the concept of interpenetration,
function holds open our formulations, is a built-in correction
mechanism allowing us—*requiring* us—to avoid the premature
closure threatened by the establishment of analytical system
boundaries. Function and interpenetration are two conceptual
bridges between systems.

We have not yet discussed the two hierarchies mentioned,
namely, the energic hierarchy of conditions and the informational hierarchy of controls. We have, however, implied them by
pointing out that the concept "system" leads us to the further
concept of control mechanisms existing at the adaptive boundary
and adjusting possible environmental inputs. These control mechanisms are informational in the cybernetic sense, just as the inputs
are energic in the cybernetic sense. It is information which
guides, constrains, adjusts; it is energy which activates.

We conceptualize the energic factor as being a flow out of the
delivering system into the receptor system. It flows across an
output boundary of the delivering system and across an input
boundary of the receptor system; these boundaries are connected
and they are both external aspects of the two systems concerned.
Although in minimal (that is, undifferentiated) systems these
output-input boundaries may be empirically the same, they are
not analytically the same; and in differentiated systems they are
not empirically the same. (Analytical distinctions are not angels
either in or on pinheads. Analytical distinctions become empirical
ones eventually, as nature rewards us by its isomorphism to
thought.) From our point of view these input-output boundaries
are most conveniently conceptualized as "adaptation" (input
boundary) and "goal-attainment" (output boundary). We say,

therefore, that energic inputs flow into the system through the adaptive sector and flow out of the system through the goal-attainment sector, which is linked in turn to the adaptive sector of the next receptor system. Our use of the cybernetic concept "information" rounds out the analytical picture of these aspects of connectedness, as the energic flow into the system is controlled informationally by the adaptive mechanisms of that system and the energic flow out of the system is controlled informationally by the adaptive mechanisms of the next receptor system.

We should like at this point in our exposition to return momentarily to our earlier statement about the purpose of this paper. It is our intention, we said, to make as explicit as possible the grounding of our approach to analysis, our cognitive map. Our purpose, then, is not the technical exposition of general theory; rather, it is to describe most generally what we think we see from where we stand. Thus far *we have attempted, above all, to sketch a picture of vibrant systems in sensitive interpenetration of each other, stimulating and responding to each other, linked and made lively by the flow of energy, controlled and regulated by information.* This is, in barest silhouette, our vision and model; it orients us to the analytical situation. We cannot isolate *a* variable or *a* restricted set of variables, except for analytical emphasis. We can "bracket" (to use Husserl's term) what we do not choose to consider for short-run purposes; but ultimately we are forced to break our brackets. Although we, too, use what Whitehead called "the single fact in isolation," we know that its isolation is artificial, and our whole orientation leads us eventually to correct the artifice, or device, and to consider the connectedness of a network of looser and tighter areas of structure through which energy and messages flow.

In orienting us, our model guides our attention to specific and empirical issues. As we have mentioned, it causes us to search for the specific adaptive mechanisms controlling the energic inputs into the system in question. It also leads us to consider the degree to which they are efficient and the circumstances under which they might fail to control the energy, as well as to consider the circumstances under which the energic outputs of the delivering system might fail. Referring once again to the interpenetration of the personality and social systems, we are guided by our conceptual framework to ask: "Under what circumstances might the Ego withdraw from cathectic commitment to role occupancy—might it, in a word, become *alienated?*" Role occupancy is only one aspect of role in which pathological situations might be found; another is role performance. "Under what circumstances," we ask, "might the informational controls internal to the system itself become inadequate? Under what circumstances, that is, might the Ego find itself in an *anomic* situation?"

On the one hand, the existence of the social system depends upon energic inputs from the personality, that is, cathectic commitment to role occupancy. On the other hand, the existence of the social system depends equally upon role performance; and for role performance, information is essential, information adequate to the specificity of the occasion—situational contingency, in other words. Thus, in a most general way, we would perceive in our conceptual framework the problems referred to by the terms "alienation" and "anomie," the first with a strong cathectic primacy with reference to role occupancy, the second with a strong cognitive primacy with reference to role performance.

Other important inferences can be drawn from our conceptual framework. Certainly it leads us to reject any reductionism whatsoever, while giving us a convenient device for categorizing reductionistic attempts.

Our conceptual framework also implies two hierarchies, already mentioned—one of energy and conditions, one of information and controls. We visualize these as interactive and of opposed directionality. Those aspects of a system that are high in information (tightly structured) exercise control over those that are lower in information but high in energy; reciprocally, those aspects of a system that are high in energy but lower in information constitute the conditions for the activation and realization of informational purpose and maintenance. To use Freud's famous analogy of the horse and the rider, in the interaction system composed of the horse and the rider, the rider—low in energy relative to the horse—controls and guides, by superior information, the path taken by the horse-rider system. He may do so by the merest and most delicate outputs of energy at strategic points. *Of course*, for the system to move at all, the energy of the horse must be utilized; and it constitutes a condition for system action. An analyst interested in explaining either "how" or "why" the system has moved from one village to the next must refer to both the energy and the information, since it is the interchange of energic and informational factors which determines—as, in a sense, a vectored resultant—the sequential path of the system.

Most reductionistic attempts can be viewed as attempts to reduce "causality" either to energic factors or to informational factors. As an example of the former, Marx's superbly dramatic intellectual constructs can certainly suffice; undeniably, in its grossest aspects Marx's theoretical framework placed informational factors in an epiphenomenal category. (It is of course true that Marx in his later years and Engels in some of his letters attempted to redress this imbalance, but "orthodox" Marxists have tended to ignore this and to term such attempts on the part of others as "revisionism.") Although energic reductionism is the most usual reductionism, there is a sense in which aspects of the idealistic school of German nineteenth-century historical analysis and the conceptualization of historical process as the self-realization of a *geist* are examples of informational reductionism.

The Social System

Norms are evaluative predications to activity. Values are evaluative predications to state. Norms predicate "doing"; values predicate "being." Norms and values predicate the activities and state of roles and collectivities. Social structure is syntactic.

With these statements we arrive finally at a discussion of the *social* kind of system. Up to this point we have emphasized system as a generic concept, because social systems are first of all systems—ordered aggregates embedded in and in interaction with a fluctuating environment. The units aggregated are, however, of a particular sort; they are neither the "need-dispositions" of the personality system nor the "symbolates" of the cultural system.

Social systems are ordered aggregates in which specific aspects of humans "take account of each other" and "express to each other"; social systems are comprised of interactive *roles* with a *collectivity* referent, the interaction being ordered in its specificity by *norms* grounded in and oriented by *values*. The structure of the social system consists of the patterning of symbolic references among these four categories of units.

We have said "aspects of humans"; we might better say, "aspects of personalities." The social system is not a human group and the social system is not an aggregate of personalities; only *aspects* of humans and their personalities are "in" the social system. Humans are "in" the social system only to the extent that, and in the same manner as, actors are "in" a drama, and that is through role occupancy. The role is the social-systemic unit accomplishing intersection with the personality system.

In introducing this section of the paper, we mentioned "predications" and differentiated between norms and values on the basis of the objects of their predications. We have also mentioned "syntax" and "symbolic references." Implicitly, our model here is a linguistic one, and we find a metaphor useful: action is "speaking." *The components of a social system speak to each other:* roles, collectivities, norms, values speak, intend, mean, communicate, assess, decide, and refer. This is a crucial point, since communication of intention and meaning is effective only when definitions and syntax are shared by the communicating actors; *and definitions and syntax are inherently normative.* As a communication and decision system, as a set of patterned cognitive ("taking account of each other") and cathectic ("expressing to each other") references, the social system is inherently normative. Its structure is, relative to personalities, informational; its processes, although activated by energic factors and proceeding at a rate that is a function of energic factors, are controlled and guided by informational factors.

What might be the usefulness of this conceptualization of the social system as a *device?* Let us consider some consequences of *differentiation* in the light of our conceptualization of norms and values as predications. An example will be helpful. We wish to predicate (at first descriptively and then evaluatively) *point-motion within an inclusion.* So long as all points are moving at the same speed—let us say, one foot per second—our predication to activity can be quite specific. If, however, only some points are moving at one foot per second, while others are moving at ten feet per second, and if our predication to activity within the *differentiated* inclusion is to be a universalistic one (true for all included points simultaneously), then by the very nature of the case it must become "generalized," that is to say, it must lose specific content.

In the terms of the example, only four universalistic statements are syntactically possible: (1) point-motion is *either* ten feet per second *or* one foot per second; (2) point-motion is *between* eleven inches per second and eleven feet per second; (3) point-motion is *no more than* ten feet per second; and (4) point-motion is *at least* one foot per second. Note the increment in degrees of freedom in each successive predication: either/or, between, no more than, at least. Each of these predications is less specific than the predication of the undifferentiated inclusion and each is less specific than the one preceding it; further, in each there is an increment in the degree of freedom constraining and allowing point-motion. If a point (now considered as a sentient creature) were seeking guidance as to how fast to move, if it needed to be told how fast it *should* move, obviously the predication of the differentiated inclusion would give it more freedom (and less guidance) than the predication of the undifferentiated inclusion. To answer, "Move *at least* one foot per second," is to place only a minimal limit on the activity; it is not the equivalent of saying, "Move at one foot per second."

So long as an inclusion is maintained, we believe that, with differentiation, there take place universalization of norms and (we repeat, it is in the *nature* of the case) generalization. Accompanying generalization as a part of it are (1) increments in the degree of freedom and (2) decrements in the specific "guidance-value" of the norm. Empirically, then, we shall look for the emergence in differentiated social systems of sub-systems whose function is *respecification* of the generalized norms; the legal system and educational systems are examples of such sub-systems. We shall look for these, and recognize their purpose, because we are guided by the "social system" as a theoretical device; and our conceptualization of norms as evaluative predications of activity, taken with the empirically contingent process of differentiation, *implies* a "system-problem," that is, the respecification of generalized norms.

A possible pathology is implied, namely, *anomie*. In those sectors to which the generalized norms are not adequately respecified, the acting units do not receive an adequate answer to their question, "What shall we do?" We attribute to *anomie* cognitive primacy, since, in principle, an anomic situation represents a failure of informational controls and can be resolved by information. It is a pathological situation of the normative structure, or it is, in other words, the generalization of norms beyond an institutionalized capacity for their respecification.

Another possible pathology is implied, and that is *alienation*. In addition to (or instead of) asking, "What shall I do?" one might ask, "Why?" The first question evokes a normative response, a predication to activity; the second evokes a *value*, a predication to state: "You should do this because it belongs to the desirable state of the system." To ask the question "Why?" is to call into question the state of affairs, the *meaningfulness* of the defined order. Alienation is, ultimately, a threat to the system at the level of role occupancy, since no matter how adequate the answer to the question "What?" if the answer to the question "Why?" is inadequate, the best that one might expect from the questioner would be the role performance of an apathetic automaton and the worst, rebellion or total withdrawal of the personality from cathectic commitment to role occupancy.

It is noteworthy that both these pathological situations can be seen as functions of the informational components of the system, with no necessary reference to the energic ones. Given differentiation, the cost of the resultant freedom is potential anomie and potential alienation—*because of* what has happened to the norms and values: they have become generalized and they may or may not be adequately respecified and made meaningful. Alienation and anomie vary in their location within the system and in their rate with the nature and adequacy of informational controls, not with the amount, kind, or rate of energic components. It is also worthwhile to point out that both the threat to role performance and the threat to role occupancy represent potential *decrements* in the energic forces available for system action, and that these are, consequently, cases in which the energic level may be seen as *itself a function of* informational controls. Anomie and alienation are surely pathologies inexplicable by energic reductionism.

Conclusion

We have given only a few examples of the usefulness of the "social system" as a theoretical device. They may suffice, however, to indicate that we are more than a little justified in our belief that the concept of social system, along with what is implied by it, is a quite useful device.

At the level of general theory, we would maintain, our conceptualization of system allows us to mitigate the consequences of what we have termed "mythologization." Built into our conceptual framework is a requirement that we continually consider the connectedness of things; built into our conceptual framework are those "sticks in the mouth of the crocodile"—system, interpenetration, and function—which, in a disciplined manner, organize analysis of the connectedness of things. (It is not enough, we feel, to say with Whitehead that "connectedness is of the essence of all things": we must analyze *how* and *on what terms* and *with what consequences for each other* things are connected.)

At the level of empirical research into the "social system," our conceptual framework guides us to take note of specific system problems and to expect specific system mechanisms or, in their absence, specific system pathologies. The *where*, the *when*, and the *why* of anomie and alienation can be understood in this conceptual framework, along with the consequences they represent.

What more can be asked of a "cognitive map" but that it direct the attention of the analyst to relevant questions and to the *loci* of relevant problems while supplying a conceptual framework wherein "facts" and the answers to the questions and the solutions of the problems become meaningful?

NOTES

1. Alfred N. Whitehead, *Modes of Thought* (Cambridge: Harvard University Press, 1938), p. 12.
2. *Ibid.*, p. 13.
3. *Ibid.*, p. 14.

SUGGESTED READINGS

Parsons, Talcott. *The Structure of Social Action*. Glencoe: The Free Press, 1937.
———. *The Social System*. Glencoe: The Free Press, 1951.
———. "An Outline of the Social System," in Talcott Parsons, Edward A. Shils, Kaspar D. Naegele, and Jesse R. Pitts (eds.), *Theories of Society*. Glencoe: The Free Press, 1961.
———, and Bales, Robert F. "The Dimensions of Action-Space," in Talcott Parsons, Robert F. Bales, and Edward A. Shils (eds.), *Working Papers in the Theory of Action*. Glencoe: The Free Press, 1953.
———, and Shils, Edward A. *Toward a General Theory of Action*. Cambridge: Harvard University Press, 1951.
White, Winston. "An Alternative View," in Winston White, *Beyond Conformity*. Glencoe: The Free Press, 1961.
Whitehead, Alfred N. *Modes of Thought*. Cambridge: Harvard University Press, 1938.

CHAPTER **III**

Theoretical Analysis of the Individual-Group Relationship in a Social Situation

Muzafer Sherif

Editor's Introduction

Widely recognized as one of the principal, and pioneering, reference group theorists, Professor Muzafer Sherif has spent a considerable number of years in experimental work on the problem of intergroup relations. His latest work on the subject—at the time of this Symposium—was written in collaboration with his wife, Carolyn, an Associate Professor of Psychology at the Pennsylvania State University. Entitled *Reference Groups: Exploration into Conformity and Deviation of Adolescents* (Harper and Row, 1964), its conceptual formulations are to a large extent the basis for the paper that he presents in this chapter.

One might wonder at first glance whether a topic such as the one that Sherif has chosen is really not beyond the scope of the experimenter. Sherif's answer is an unqualified "no." The problem of theoretical consideration is inescapable for the experimenter, however consciously he may attempt to avoid it or perhaps be naive about it. There are always a number of selective processes in research activity, just as there are in the span of one's observations and apprehensions. Both research and one's everyday cognitions presuppose certain assumptions that amount to either an explicit or an implicit definition of the universe of discourse. In fact, argues Sherif, significant research problems can be formulated only after one has substantial familiarity with the universe of discourse in theoretical formulations. Such theoretical orientations define the research problem and guide the selection of methods and techniques for its analysis.

Whether there is need for conceptual orientation and theory is a "futile and wasteful" question for Sherif. There is no choice to be made between this and purely empirical research. Sheer empiricism, such as that expressed in maintaining that "the facts speak for themselves," is both naive and absurd. Facts cannot speak for themselves. They need interpretation. This is provided in the context of a theoretical orientation. All research work involves a theoretical orientation: it is encountered in the process of conceiving, formulating, and operationalizing research projects, and to some extent is usually a consequence of the theoretical orientations and conceptualizations that were utilized in previous research. Sherif describes some of the theoretical considerations of his own research in order to articulate by means of concrete examples this relationship between conceptual orientation and actual research.

Since there is no escape from conceptual and theoretical entanglements for the researcher, it would be more fruitful and productive, argues Sherif, if he were to make explicit and to evaluate the conceptual and definitional bounds that he utilizes. This sort of activity—which, in fact, *is* theorizing—avoids disjointed and incoherent research activity, since it relates the empirical process to a framework of fundamental orientations concerning significant problems within the particular discipline. There are, however, in Sherif's perspective, boundaries to theorizing. He cautions against undisciplined speculation and the lack of responsibility which lead to ignoring the limitations imposed by empirical data and, often, to neglecting to use such data to verify theoretical formulations. He takes to task in particular the followers of "grand scale theory," "the proponents of the current craze for 'models,' " and the provincial researchers.

In considering the relationship between theory and research, Sherif pays particular attention to the question of the isomorphism existing between theoretical analysis and the domain of events that such analysis purports to treat, and he discusses some current practices in theorizing, with specific reference to model-building. (The logical dimensions of model-building will be considered in Chapter IV.) Particularly with reference to the validation of models and the procedures involved, Sherif cautions against two dangerous practices: first, transferring into the behavioral sciences those attempts at formalization that have been used in other disciplines; and second, uncritically extrapolating models from the mathematical and physical sciences and adapting them in the behavioral sciences without checking their postulations and, especially, failing to consider the isomorphic problem. Researchers should pay special attention, says Sherif, to the often neglected principle that a system determines the nature of its parts.

Sherif disapproves of the narrow-minded and isolated approach of single-discipline research and calls for a more extensive interdisciplinary orientation. Mere discussions about the same or related problems on the part of scientists in different disciplines do not constitute interdisciplinary research activity. This lack of a unifying perspective accounts for the fact that only a relatively minimum number of generalizations characterize the behavioral sciences today. Human behavior cannot be studied in a socio-cultural vacuum. "Personality," for example, is not an isolated phenomenon, and "interaction" is not a pure process, devoid of content and context. Sherif wants to move from the nominal use of these concepts into real definitions by specifying their precise content. One of the more neglected problems in this respect, he contends, concerns the specification of the "social situation" wherein behavior transpires. Much sociological and psychological research fails to consider adequately the nature and the content of the social situation in which the human behavior under investigation is taking place. Sherif gives an indication of the significance of the organizational and normative aspects of a social situation and examines its constitution for the individual both in simply interpersonal relations and in group situations.

This chapter is, in a certain sense, an extension of the analytical scheme presented by Ackerman and Parsons. They delineated in an abstract manner the conceptual nature of the social system and the framework of action in which social behavior takes place. In a less abstract (but no less theoretical) manner, Sherif describes the concrete composition of the specific situation in which the human actor behaves, and to this he adds another specific element—that of the referential situation. He offers a classification of *sets* of factors that enter into any social situation, and which may, as a result, affect the social behavior therein and hence determine its variability. The constitution of the social situation is such as to make for a logical sequence of study and a procedure which thereby avoids reductionism: (1) the characteristics of the socio-cultural setting, (2) the prevailing values and norms, and (3) the behaviors and interaction processes of specific groups. It is important, maintains Sherif, to know the structure and composition of the social situation before one analyzes the behavior within it.

Sherif pleads for a framework of fundamental orientation for significant and persistent problems in the behavioral sciences, and for the development of new ways to link the study of human behavior, particularly that of small groups, to the settings in which it takes

place. He labels attempts to reduce all patterns of social organization
and culture to aspects of human behavior as an untenable solipsism; by
such logic, he argues, everything in science could be reduced to
psychological dynamics. Moreover, Sherif maintains that the sharp
dichotomy which traditionally has been drawn between the individual
and the group is a hopelessly naive position. There is, he would argue
in the terms of Ackerman and Parsons, an interpenetration of elements from the one into the other.

Sherif's fundamental affirmation is that theory should have a focal
and guiding role in all research activity. He concludes his paper with
an outline of a multi-faceted research program which exemplifies the
integrative orientations and methods that may be derived from analyzing the facets of the social situation and which indicates how research
problems may be formulated from such analysis. His discussion of the
research program involves some observation on how the various sets
of factors composing a social situation may be translated into research
operations, and as such entails implications of the relationship between
the substantive use of scientific concepts and the methodology of their
empirical measurement.

I will take the liberty of introducing my analysis of the individual-group relationship in a social situation by mentioning briefly a few thoughts that were triggered when I first received Dr. DiRenzo's invitation to participate in this Symposium. It was stated that the theme of the Symposium was "Conceptual Definition in the Behavioral Sciences"—in its particular relevance to construction of theories and to some persistent philosophical problems. My first reaction was a feeling of trepidation that such an assignment was beyond my depth as an experimental social psychologist. Nevertheless, I gave serious thought to the all-important problem of theory and its relationship to actual research, as I have whenever, inevitably, I have encountered this problem in conceiving, formulating, and operationalizing the various research projects that I have carried out over the past thirty years. Once again I realized that every one of these projects had a theoretical orientation which defined the problem and guided the selection of appropriate methods and techniques for data collection. Illustration of this common thread running through all the projects will lead to the main theme of this paper.

The Relationship Between Theory and Research

Our research in the mid-1930's, for example, on the experimental creation of social norms, utilizing the autokinetic phenomenon, was not conceived through concern over the psychology of vision, though vision was involved.[1] Rather, it was conceived in part on the basis of theoretical leads derived from Durkheim's conceptualization of *représentations collectives*, or norms, as emerging in interaction situations that are fluid, out of the ordinary, and not encountered in the humdrum of daily routine; and, for the other part, it was conceived from empirical facts and theoretical orientations derived from the fruitful line of research of the Chicago school of sociology under the seminal inspiration of Robert E. Park. The Chicago studies showed in different ways that individuals interacting under conditions that lack stable anchorages for experience do generate their own norms and that these norms become binding for the individuals over a time span.

The series of experiments on intergroup conflict and cooperation also had a theoretical orientation. They started with the necessity of defining the human group. Such a definition was needed because the then prevailing theories dealt with aggressive, pugnacious, and competitive intergroup behavior, without viewing such behavior within the framework of the membership character of the individuals within their respective groups.[2]

The same is true of a series of studies dealing with attitude assessment and attitude change, some of which were summarized in a joint book with the late Carl I. Hovland, entitled *Social Judgment*,[3] and also in our recent *Attitude and Attitude Change*.[4] This line of research, which is still continuing in several current projects, arose from the need for moving toward definitions that would be in line with an established body of research evidence on social perception and social judgment. Prior to this research, the dominant assumptions in the attitude-measurement field had been extrapolated from experiments on psycho-physical judgments devoid of motivational-affective components.[5]

Currently, our research program is confronted with problems of basic definitions on a wider scope; this is particularly the case with our ongoing research on natural groups in differentiated socio-cultural settings.[6] This research involves problems of the group, the place of individual members in it, and specification of the characteristics of the social situation and setting in which a group and its members operate. Therefore, in the last analysis, participating in this seminar with the particular topic of this paper does not leave me with the feeling of uncertainty about plunging into terra incognita.

In order to give concreteness, I have deliberately used my own research experiences as cases in point in order to articulate the relationship between conceptual orientation involving definitions and actual research. (This is perfectly legitimate, since the problem of this relationship is not unique to one researcher; it is representative of all those who devote themselves to research as a life work in social science.) For example, the point that my research illustrated concerning the relationship of theoretical orientation and actual research practice involving data collection is, as will become evident, fundamental for the discussion of my topic—analysis of the individual-group relationship in a social situation.

What stood out in this illustrative case can be summarized in a few sentences. The question of whether there is need for theory and conceptual orientation, or whether what is needed is more down-to-earth research unhampered by theoretical problems of the past, is both futile and wasteful. The pious contention "Let the facts speak for themselves" is an absurdity which cannot occur in actual practice, even in the case of empiricism in the raw. Facts are *there*, all right, whether they are studied or not. This is one thing. But it is altogether another thing to claim that facts speak for themselves. Without exception, there is always a selective process in the collection of data. The span of apprehension or observation has a limited scope—as any standard experimental psychology text, such as Woodworth's, will report, as the work of psychologists from William James, to Oswald Külpe, to Dwight Chapman will verify, and as is proven again and again in the psychology of testimony from Binet and Münsterberg to the present day.

For example, in data collection through observation or interview, the decisions about who will constitute the sample and the time period to be studied immediately determine, in part, the nature of data that will be obtained. Nor is the case of data collection in the laboratory an exception to the general rule of selectivity in the processing of what kind of data will be obtained. By the time the decisions are made about the kind of experimental set-up—subjects, procedures, and techniques selected from so many possible ones; the units of data determined; and units of analysis selected—a great deal of the game already is played. And all of these decisions presuppose the selectivity of the experimenter in deciding what belongs to the domain of the study, what is to be excluded, and into what categories events will be sliced.

Whether or not the researcher in the field or in the laboratory is conscious of the process of selectivity in which he is immersed, these inevitably selective processes in the conduct of research, experimental or otherwise, presuppose assumptions as to the nature of the problem as well as definitions of the universe of discourse (categorizing it into what belongs and what is to be excluded). Whether we are conscious of it or not, research is always guided by assumptions about the nature of the problem at hand and by conceptual orientations which amount to explicit or implicit definitions of the universe of discourse. In short, there is no escape from theoretical and definitional entanglements. This being the case, it will be more productive and fruitful for research if the conceptual or definitional bounds that the researcher utilized are made explicit. What is called theorizing, I suspect, involves this sort of activity, among other things.

On the other hand, the inevitable involvement of theorizing is not justification for unbridled and unfounded speculation. Especially when there exists an accumulation of empirical data—as is the case in the social sciences today—with literally thousands of research reports pouring in from the laboratory and field, it is the responsibility of the theorizer or systematist to take stock of the available data, to restrain his theorizing to that which he can legitimately advance, and to square his theorizing with the facts at hand, scattered though they may be. Of course, there is charm and even elegance in grand theorizing. But if it is speculative activity unmindful of the checks from accumulating data, one may find it preferable to satisfy himself with charm and elegance at their best in the works of such masters as Plato and Hobbes.

Nor are the proponents of the current craze for "models" based on the prestige of more established physical and biological sciences exempt from the responsibility to take account of empirical data. The uncritical and hasty extrapolation of models from the physical sciences is not different in character from the unbridled and grandiose speculation against which I have just raised a caution. To be sure, models are needed to formalize a discipline, to give it bounds, and to save it from an aimless proliferation of empirical facts in all directions. To be sure, precise and quantitative indices are essential in the process of formalization. And, of course, it is in line with the parsimony of formulation to have, for example, a few quantitative judgments as indices of the status hierarchy of an organization, instead of piles and piles of descriptive data. While it is thus undeniably true that formalization in terms of an internally coherent and consistent model and discovery of short-cut and precise indices (as the hairline of a needle indicates an electric charge) are necessary and desirable goals, nevertheless uncritical adoption of ready-made models without checking their assumptions against accumulated data is not the path that will lead to these goals.

First of all, there is the fundamental problem of the *isomorphism* between assumptions of the model and the properties of the universe of discourse it purports to represent and to formalize. In the past, there were serious attempts to use models from more established sciences. The model of "mental chemistry" of Wundt and Titchener in the early history of experimental psychology, which attempted to define clearly the psychological counterparts of chemical elements in the form of sensation and image units, utilizing refined instruments, is an example of the maladaptive use of a model that had at the time proved useful in another field. Probably the organic analogy of Herbert Spencer and his followers, whose works would fill a small library, is another case in point. In my opinion, the extrapolations from the so-called dynamic equilibrium models of fluid mechanics or thermodynamics, stemming from the works of Pareto, will suffer a similar fate.

Unfortunately, the problem of isomorphism between assumptions of a model and the properties of the domain it purports to handle is of only minor concern to those psychologists and social scientists who are caught up in the excitement of current fads. It is ironic that some mathematicians regard the problem of isomorphism as basic in scientific activity. Thus, in the very first chapter of a mathematics text for college freshmen, we find the following statement as the first principle of model-building:

"The first step in the study of any branch of science is that of observing nature. When enough facts have been collected, the scientist begins to organize them into some pattern."[7]

The opposite sequence, much more frequent in current attempts at formalization in the social sciences, is to find a model that has been successful in one of the more established sciences and to transfer it, often uncritically, to some problem area in the social sciences. In an invited address in 1955 to the sixty-third annual convention of the American Psychological Association, the physicist Robert Oppenheimer warned of the pitfalls of the latter sequence of science by analogy in the following words:

> . . . between sciences of very different character, the direct formal analogies in their structure are not too likely to be helpful. Certainly what the pseudo-Newtonians did with sociology was a laughable affair; and similar things have been done with mechanical notions of how psychological phenomena are to be explained. I know that when physicists enter biology their first ideas of how things work are indescribably naive and mechanical; they are how things would work if the physicist were making them work, but not how they work in life. I know that when I hear the word "field" used in physics and in psychology I have a nervousness that I cannot entirely account for. I think that, especially when we compare subjects in which ideas of coding, of the transfer of information, or ideas of purpose, are inherent and natural, with subjects in which they are not inherent and natural, that formal analogies have to be taken with very great caution.[8]

Further, Oppenheimer noted a possibility that makes the uncritical extrapolation of a model from the physical sciences an even greater exercise in futility: ". . . it seems to me that the worst of all possible misunderstandings would be that psychology be influenced to model itself after a physics which is not there anymore, which has been quite outdated."[9]

When model-building proceeds without concern for the problem of isomorphism, it may quickly degenerate into a game with no objective criterion for deciding when victory has been attained, much less one for whether it was a worthwhile game to play. An observation to this effect comes from a gratifying source—the presidential address to the Society of Engineering Psychologists by A. Chapanis at the American Psychological Association Convention in 1960. In the course of his paper on "Men, Machines, and Models," he commented:

> *Models are too often not validated* . . . or, if attempts are made to validate them, the procedures used are scientifically valueless. . . . I am sometimes frankly appalled by the faith which some model builders have in their own powers of analytical and synthetic reasoning when it comes to making models of human behavior. . . . I will state my bias on this score in no uncertain terms: I will gladly exchange one hundred well-informed guesses at any time for the results of one carefully executed experiment.[10]

"My final criticism of model building," Chapanis concluded,

> is that the modeler often becomes so intrigued with the formulation of his models that he constructs them for essentially trivial problems. Having at one's disposal a large electronic computing machine, for example, invites one to try out all kinds of things, because computers are such fun to play with. Considering the state of knowledge within psychology, however, the easiest problems to build models for are essentially unimportant problems.[11]

I have gone into the problems of formal model-building by analogy with the physical sciences because it is a very general problem in the social sciences and psychology and because the effects of uncritical analogy with mathematics and physical sciences have hampered exploration in certain problem areas. One such problem area is attitude research. Specification of measurement units and quantification of data are, I repeat, goals in every science. But they are not ends in themselves. As Oppenheimer said so clearly: "It is not always tactful to try to quantify; it is not always clear that by measuring one has found something very much worth measuring . . . and I would make this very strong plea for pluralism with regard to methods that, in the necessarily early stages of sorting out an immensely vast experience, may be fruitful and may be helpful."[12]

Attitude research in this country proceeded for over thirty years as though its major problem were simply the refinement of measurement models based on analogy with the equal-interval scales derived in psycho-physical judgment of neutral stimuli (weights, lengths, and so forth) or, more recently, with the cumulative scales so common in measurement of physical properties of objects. Consequently, the plentiful results from attitude studies had very little to offer toward clarifying theory, or even toward defining the properties of the attitudes that made their study significant for social science in the contemporary world, where one group is constantly competing with another to change attitudes in its direction. On the contrary, the whole effort of attitude research was directed toward assigning a single score to an individual so that his "attitude" could be ranked relative to others.

In association with colleagues and students, I have spent fifteen years trying to break through the mass of convention and sterile assumptions in attitude research. The results of this work are presented in our book on attitudes and ego-involvements.[13] Here, I can indicate only a few of the outcomes.

(1) The assumptions of equal-interval scaling, developed by Thurstone, can be satisfied provided that the individuals do *not* have strong attitudes—in other words, provided that we ignore the very problem that we are supposed to be studying.

(2) The assumptions of a cumulative scale, as stated in the Guttman model, can be satisfied by taking a very limited range of positions on an issue, and by ignoring others actually upheld by interested groups in society. If we do not choose to put on such blinders, however, then we find that many social dimensions are simply not "cumulative." It is true that six inches will always be included in a twelve-inch measurement, but it is not even typical for an individual who upholds an ardently pro-segregationist

stand to accept a mildly pro-segregationist statement. Similarly, devoted Republicans or Democrats do not, typically, accept a mild statement of support for their side; they are more likely to reject it. These are phenomena that simply cannot be investigated with a "cumulative" scale, because they violate its assumptions.

(3) A single score representing the positions acceptable to an individual is a most inadequate indicator of his attitude. Nonetheless, this single score is what the prevailing models, on the whole, seek to attain. Much greater predictability of actual behavior can be obtained if we assess an individual's attitude in terms of the range or latitude of positions he accepts, rejects, and toward which he remains non-committal. These findings have led us to define attitude in terms of a set of evaluative categories slicing the relevant stimulus world into a latitude of acceptance, a latitude of rejection, and a latitude of non-commitment. As it turns out, the latitudes of rejection and non-commitment are even more useful in predicting behavior than the single score of acceptance or even the latitude of acceptance. These measurement concepts were not derived from a pre-existing model, but from laborious study of actualities of psycho-social scales in social life.

As Einstein and Infeld stated in discussing major advances in physics, and as Wolfgang Köhler stated in discussing needed developments in psychology: the first, major step toward a breakthrough in any science is a result of formulating pertinent and significant problems, not in thin air, but on the basis of the actualities of the universe with which we are dealing. Operationally, the issue boils down to evaluating the isomorphism between the *facts* in a universe of discourse and the theoretical scheme or model we propose, as well as the appropriateness of the techniques that we use in gathering data to evaluate our theory.

No model, no theoretical scheme is "right" or "correct" in its own right, no matter how much fun it is nor how intellectually intriguing. No procedure and no technique for data collection are powerful or effective in their own right. The theory should be the *guide* for fruitful research. The techniques are powerful tools for data collection, if—*and only if*—they are appropriate in terms of the nature and characteristics of the *problem*. And significant *problems* can be formulated only *after* gaining substantial familiarity with the universe of discourse, and not before.

An Analysis of the Social Situation

Now I shall pursue this discussion by asking a question fundamental to the entire problem of the individual-group relationship, a question whose answer necessarily determines the conception of that relationship: "What constitutes the social situation for the individual, represented in his interpersonal and group relations?"

One of the most thriving activities in social psychology today is what passes under the name of "small group research." The more I study this thriving activity and the resulting host of publications, the more convinced I become that they are doomed to be a collection of disjointed and incoherent artifacts so long as they are not related to a framework of fundamental orientations concerning significant and persistent problems. An analysis of what constitutes a social situation is certainly among these fundamental orientations. Because of the absence of a unifying orientation, established generalizations in social psychology today are only a tiny fraction of the total output of publications from the universities and the military and industrial establishments, whereas there are hundreds of studies published that are labeled as studies of two-person, three-person, or *n*-person groups, studies of decision-making, and studies of coalition formation.

These are, of course, perfectly legitimate topics of study. But can they be studied adequately without first raising the question, "What is the social situation?" For example, is it just that the number of individuals varies—and so we have dyads, or triads, or quartets? Experiments have shown that the number of people is an important factor, but it is not the only significant factor. More important for the behavioral outcome may be such considerations as the prevailing relationships among the individuals as friends, or as enemies, or as collaborators for mutual benefit in a temporary crisis situation. The degree of ego-involvement that individuals have in the problem or task at hand can also be more important than the number of individuals participating.

To take another illustration: is a social situation characterized by the task or problem at hand, for example, as it is introduced by an experimenter in the laboratory? Can the experimenter even adequately describe the task or problem as an isolated factor? Here the evidence is contradictory and even conflicting, as one might expect. The task or problem introduced is always a task or problem for individuals with particular experiences, particular involvements, and particular skills.

In the study of any social situation—whether the problem is the effects of the number of individuals, whether the problem is the setting or the task, or whether it is the decision-making process—the factors under study have to be taken as parts of the social situation at hand. The need for considering different aspects of a social situation as part-processes within their appropriate framework is a problem of cardinal significance and not only in social psychology. It is also of cardinal importance in the study of all psychological problems, including those traditionally considered most basic and most elemental, such as psychophysics. The point was illustrated well by Harry Helson in his address in Philadelphia in 1963 upon receiving the APA Distinguished Scientific Contribution Award:

> Let me begin by recalling an episode in the early 1930's when I gave a demonstration before the Optical Society of America of the inadequacy of the CIE (Commission Internationale de l'Eclairage) method of color specification. In this demonstration, although the stimulus *qua* stimulus did not change with change in surround, its color could be made anything we pleased by appropriate choice of the luminance and hue of the background color. In the discussion that followed, the late Selig Hecht, perhaps the leading worker in visual science at that time, arose and said: "Why do you complicate the problems of color vision by introducing background effects? Why can't you wait until

we have solved the simpler problems before we go on to the more complicated ones?"[14]

Helson continued his address with a list of subsequent discoveries in color vision that were possible only because he did *not* wait for the solution of so-called "basic" problems, but continued investigating the problems that he had formulated as basic—the problems of background and illumination in color vision. This work led him to develop a "frame of reference psycho-physics" with a fruitful line of experiments.

Helson's point is of great relevance to our present discussion. Let us pose the question: If there is a necessity, as demonstrated by Helson and his co-workers, for studying visual perception of a single patch of color within the context of its background, how much more compelling is the same principle in studying social behavior. How much more important it becomes to consider the social situation for a two-person or *n*-person group beyond the sheer presence of the two persons or the *n*-persons.

What is the background and the stimulus context for individual behavior in a social situation? Obviously the most concrete aspect is the presence of other individuals in face-to-face relations, and for some social psychologists, as we have said, their domain of study consists only of the study of person-to-person relations in face-to-face interaction. Of course these are important.

However, persons cannot be studied in *isolation*. At no time are persons in a socio-cultural vacuum, even in their moments of greatest intimacy. They have peculiar customs of inhabiting certain places and having certain histories. If we restrict our concept of the social situation to consist only of other persons here and now, we commit a fundamental error. There is a long tradition in experimental psychology that we specify the independent variables or experimental conditions. We take it for granted that an experiment on vision or audition will specify the light and sound frequencies presented, their intensity, and whether the experimental set-up permitted other light and sound frequencies to enter. We would severely criticize an experiment on learning as a function of drive and reward that did not specify how many hours the organisms were deprived and the quantity and kind of reward to be found in the goal box, as well as the dimensions of the paths leading to the goal object.

Applying the same standards, how can we possibly say that we, as social psychologists, are interested only in "personality" variables and that this is all we shall consider? We may temper this statement by saying that "sociologists" or "anthropologists" will study the rest of it, and that we are sophisticated enough to know that there are "variations." This amounts to saying: "I know that the behavior I am studying is affected by influences that are not apparent to my naked eye nor detected by my instruments and which I, as a researcher, am not controlling. But I am only interested in what *I* see and detect here and now." Unfortunately, much of the theory and research on social interaction among different combinations of individuals is about as nearsighted as this statement suggests. It is usually justified as being a study of "basic" features of personality or "pure" interaction process.

Unfortunately, however, personality is not an isolated phenomenon; "interaction" is not "pure process" devoid of *content*, devoid of *context* and background. Person-to-person interaction must be placed in a context and background, in turn. Interpersonal relations, among friends, or lovers, or enemies, do not take place in a vacuum. They take place in a restaurant, a bedroom, or an office, or a church, or a convention hall, or on a city street; or they take place in a psychological laboratory. In recent years, our attention has been called to the fact that the subject's appraisal of a situation and the setting can affect the outcome even of a psychological experiment.[15] In any culture and in any specific situation, every social situation forms a pattern or context for individual behavior. What is being done to specify this context in contemporary psychology?

One of the noteworthy developments is the simple awareness of the variety of factors that may affect social behavior. Saul Sells has emphasized the point by his attempt to list the stimulus factors that may contribute to behavior variance under general headings; he has tried, in other words, to indicate the possibility of a taxonomy of the stimulus situation. His published volume of papers on this topic, *The Stimulus Determinants of Behavior*,[16] provided, in my opinion, a sorely needed contribution to our field. But the sheer bulk of his listings is sufficient to show us that a "taxonomy" in the form of a syllabus is not a solution to the problem, valuable as it may be as a methodological device. At latest count, there were *over* 250 factors in his list. I do not think that his purpose in compiling it was to suggest that we should permute these 250-odd factors in *factorial* research designs.

Therefore, instead of a syllabus, I venture to repeat a simple classification of *sets* of factors that, as *sets*, enter into any social situation, even though particular sub-sets and their members may be present or absent in different cultures, and even though the *range* of the sets may differ in different cultures (which, in fact, it does). Here are the sets of factors in brief form.

(1) The set of factors pertaining to *individuals who participate* in the social situation. These include:

(a) The characteristics of the individuals, such as the number of persons, their ages, their sex, their educational, occupational, economic, and social attainments.

(b) The composition of the total participants in the social situation in terms of their similarities and differences in age, sex, homogeneity and heterogeneity as to religion, class, and so on.

(c) Relations among the participating individuals. Are they strangers, friends, rivals, and in what combinations? To what extent are their relations stable or subject to change? This is a crucial sub-set of factors. To dramatize it, we may note that it makes a big difference whether a distribution of opinions—say, 40 per cent pro, 50 per cent con, and 10 per cent undecided—represents a collection of unrelated individuals or the member ship of two well-organized groups and potential adherents.[17]

(2) The set of factors pertaining to the *task, problem,* or *activity* at hand. Man's activities are, after all, of some importance to the study of his behavior. Is his task new or familiar, simple or

complex, habitual or calling for creative efforts? Is it structured or unstructured in some degree in the structured-unstructured gradation?

(3) The set of factors pertaining to the *setting and the circumstances* surrounding it. These include the place, the material culture of that place, the objects and tools available, the facilities, the presence or absence of other people not involved in the task or problem at hand, and notably they must include the cultural and value orientations of the setting. There are, after all, appropriate settings for work, for problem-solving, for religious conversions, and for romance. These cannot be defined apart from a background of cultural values and status and role relationships.

(4) The set of factors pertaining to *each individual participant's particular relation to the above three sets of factors*. These include, among other things, his proficiency in the task or problem at hand, the degree of his enduring involvement in the problem, his attitudes toward other participants, his feelings of ease or discomfort in the situation, and so on.

One way of attempting to deal with these four sets of factors would be to vary the components of each set. If you are prepared to undertake this venture, you also should be aware that the relative *weights* or contribution of each to the behavioral outcome may vary in the following ways:

(1) The relative weights of different sets of factors may vary in different cultures. In fact, in different cultures the number of different factors and the range of different factors do vary.

(2) Within any given culture—including within the microculture of the psychological laboratory—the weights of different factors may vary. Thus, the task may be very important if the individuals are strangers and unfamiliar with the task; on the other hand, it may be a minor detail if they are comfortable companions and if the task is within the range of their experience.

(3) Finally, the relative weights, or significance, of the individuals participating, of the task or problem, and of the setting in which events take place vary according to the *temporal sequence* of events. This is a problem that we, as social psychologists, have

left to the developmental area. But it is equally crucial in terms of the development of interpersonal, intergroup, and intercultural relationships. What may be crucial today—the old patterns of interaction and the old conceptions of tasks—may be "old hat" tomorrow. The problems of getting acquainted among strangers, for example, may give way to the efforts of interested parties and rivals to gain the day. Unlike "pure interaction" or "pure psychological process," the patterning of social life, and thus the patterning of the social stimulus situations for its participants, do not stay put with fixed and immutable weights.

I have, quite deliberately, concentrated so far on the various sets of factors and their variable weightings in social situations, because the overwhelming tendency among psychologists has been to over-simplify the context in which the individual-group relationship takes place. The traditional and sharp dichotomy between individual versus group appears hopelessly naive when we engage in the effort of analyzing the context of the social situation.

However, I should not like to leave the impression that the variability of the social situation means that no regularities are exhibited, nor the impression that prediction of behavior is therefore impossible. On the contrary, the social sciences have already, even in their infancy, demonstrated that certain variables are persistently weighty ones and that knowledge about these variables has striking predictive value for the student of individual behavior. Here I shall mention only two such variables and associated concepts. One pertains to the first set of factors that I have listed, namely the individual's place or position relative to others who, perceptually or conceptually, *count* for him. The second refers to factors included in the third set, especially the characteristics of the setting and its socio-cultural background.

Let me illustrate the first variable concretely. When several strangers meet, by coincidence or circumstance, their presence does affect the behavior of each in some way, no matter what the task or setting. A thousand times over, it has been demonstrated in the psychological laboratory that the mere presence of other persons does affect experience and behavior in definite and measurable ways.

Now, let us define the presence of several individuals who are unacquainted and who are not related by any past history of association as a *togetherness* situation. Think now of what happens over a period of time if these individuals are faced by some common problem, some dilemma, or seek a common goal that requires their joint participation. We have replicated this situation experimentally a number of times, and the results are in accord with numerous field studies. Over a period of time, relationships develop among these former strangers. And, if the problem or activity is of any consequence at all to the individuals, they do develop modes of procedure, customs, private jokes, and other shared products which are, to some extent, respected and even cherished by each individual.

In short, under these circumstances over a period of time, a human group will take shape. When it does, the properties of the group provide a powerful basis for predicting the behavior of individual members. But, suppose that you are doing research starting with unacquainted individuals, and that you must decide when you have a group, and not just a togetherness situation in which the variations among individuals, in the task, and in the settings produce profound shifts in behavior. How can you decide when you have a group?

We must have a definition, and the definition must specify certain units for assessing whether the definition is met. Cutting a very long story of study and research very short, let me give you a definition of a group that does resemble groups in real life, and that does help to predict the behavior of individual members: a group is a social unit that consists of a number of individuals who (1) at a given time, stand in status and role relationships to one another, stabilized in some degree; and who (2) possess a set of values or norms of their own, regulating the behavior of individual members, at least in matters of consequence to the group.

Status positions in a group can be measured in terms of observed differences among the individuals with respect to the *effectiveness* of their initiative over a time span. Role relationships are more complex, and require a composite measure relative to the activities of the individual and the personal contributions of members in interaction. The second major property, values or norms, can be measured by defining the limits within which behavior is acceptable to group members, and beyond which some form of disapproval or punishment occurs—in short, by observing when sanctions are invoked.

To sum up, the organizational and normative aspects of a human group are, invariably, weighty determinants of individual behavior. Knowledge of them does permit prediction of individual attitude and action. Together, these organizational and normative aspects of a human group, along with any tools and procedures that it may develop, constitute its culture. These aspects are analytically separable, but they are all part-processes in the group's culture. The separation of the organizational and cultural, or the social and non-social aspects of culture, is tenable only for purposes of closer analysis of part-processes.

The second, and more comprehensive, set of factors that lend regularity to the social situation, and individual behavior within it, pertains to the socio-cultural background. Since Professor White will inform us on its patterned properties in a later chapter, I shall not dwell on them. Instead, I shall simply emphasize that social organization, cultural values, and the man-made arrangements of the material environment do have distinctive properties that must be included in any adequate account of a social situation.

But let me articulate further one of the points just made. It is the social structure, the organization or social system of the group, and also it is the norm or value system which, together with other group products, constitute the *culture* of the group. Both social organization and norm systems, along with the other material and non-material products, are of the group. If we subscribe to the notion that sociology is primarily concerned with organization or social systems, and cultural anthropology with other cultural products, it will be puzzling to make sense of one of the major preoccupations of cultural anthropologists, which has been with kinship systems.

In social psychology, there is a widespread assumption that any influences of the socio-cultural setting are revealed in immediate situations, here and now, through the words and actions of individuals. This may ultimately prove true, but certainly not unless the investigator is prepared to study socio-cultural influences and has a prior grasp of their patterned properties.

The attempt to boil down the patterns of social organization and cultural products to items of individual behavior is one form of "reductionism." It is still strong in psychology and in the larger trend in social sciences which adopts, by preference, the label "behavioral sciences." The reduction of social organization and culture to a question of individual behavior is, ultimately, an untenable solipsism. By the same logic, everything in science could be reduced to psychology, including chemistry and physics. To be sure, if there were no human beings to interact, there would be no culture, no social organization, no means of communication or transportation or production. But once such social products come into existence, they do become significant parts of the social situation in which any individual functions. Man makes machines; we can also say that machines, in turn, make man. Man creates social organization; we can also say that social organization recasts man. Man is the beginning of all of these social things, but his products are not man himself. His products do have properties that are patterned and distinctive and that cannot be studied with sole reference to the behavior of single individuals.

This account of what constitutes a social situation, and of the significance of its organizational and normative aspects, suggests a *sequence* of study that is most appropriate for assessing the individual-group relationship. If we do not know anything about the perceptual and conceptual relationships among individuals in a social situation, we are like blind men trying to understand their actions. In brief, the first—not the last—step in research is specifying the properties of social organizations and their cultural patterns, within which the situation is a part-process. Then, and only then, are we in a position to specify the importance of the immediate situation and the individuals within it, including their uniquely personal characteristics, in as great detail and shading as possible.

Analysis of the Factors in a Social Situation

With such questions in mind as, "What constitutes a social stimulus situation?" we initiated in 1958 a project to study the behavior of individuals as a function of their group membership in differentiated socio-cultural–socio-economic settings. We have reported the formulation and summary of the first five years of this research in a book entitled *Reference Groups: Exploration into Conformity and Deviation of Adolescents*.[18] Here, of course, I can only hope to indicate in a general way how the various sets of factors composing a social situation have been translated into research operations.

(1) First, different socio-cultural settings are selected. Here we encounter problems still not solved in social science. How "low" is "lower class" and how "high" is "upper class"? What do these designations mean for individuals growing up and living their lives in these settings? We have used indicators developed by sociologists (particularly Eshref Shevky and Wendell Bell) that can specify the rank of urban areas as low, middle, or high in terms of socio-economic level, urbanization, and ethnic composition. These indicators have the great advantage that they permit comparisons in terms of gradation of low and high, rather than merely arbitrary divisions into lower, middle, and upper ranks. In addition, we have studied the settings through local data and block surveys, in order to specify what it means to live, work, be educated, and play in a setting of a particular social rank.

(2) Within the areas designated as low, middle, or high social rank—in terms of indicators that are specified and can be checked —we have surveyed the prevailing patterns of values and goals among representative samples of high-school boys who are similar to the boys of high-school age whose behaviors are to be

studied intensively over a period of time. Therefore, the indices of value orientations—labeled "Self-radius" and "Goals" indices—are obtained from the normal high-school age-mates in the same urban areas as the members of the natural groups of boys, whom we study intensively.

These Self-radius and Goal indices of the representative group serve as the *baseline* against which the self-picture, the attitudes, and behaviors of the members of the intensively studied group are evaluated.

(3) Within each of the areas, the behaviors of individual members belonging to groups of their own choosing are studied intensively over a period of time ranging from six months to a year. These groups are reference groups for the individuals. The intensive study of small groups is carried out under field conditions, and it is the focal aspect in the study. Yet it is fruitless and meaningless without the background and context of the ecological and socio-cultural situation specified in the previous two phases of the research design.

In studying behavior as a function of membership in informal groups, and as a function of groups in different settings, we have developed procedures to avoid arousing the individual's awareness of himself as being a research "subject." At the same time, through careful specification of a sequence of observation, through introducing independent observers, and through adapting measurement techniques to the field situations, we have found it possible to combine the validity of facts in our universe of discourse with the precision and reliability associated with the psychological laboratory. The study focuses, successively, on organizational and normative properties of the group and then upon particular individuals within it.

This research program attempts to *integrate:* (1) the study of the characteristics of the socio-cultural setting; (2) the study of prevailing values of the comparable age-mate population in the same neighborhood, which serves as a baseline for evaluating the behavior of particular individuals; and (3) the intensive study of behaviors and interaction processes among individuals within groups chosen by the members. This intensive study involves specifying the characteristics of each interaction episode, and through them, the characteristics of the particular groups.

This multi-faceted research program exemplifies the integrative research orientations and methods that can be derived from the analysis of the facets of the social situation.

Concluding Remarks

I began my analysis of the individual-group relationship in a social situation by pointing out that an active researcher cannot help seeking conceptual and theoretical orientations to guide his research operations. This led to a consideration of the relationship between theory and research, with emphasis on the all-important problem of isomorphism between theoretical analysis and the domain of events that analysis purports to treat.

What kind of theorizing serves to provide effective conceptual tools? What kind is ineffective and futile in the conduct of fruitful research? These questions led to a brief consideration of some current practices in theorizing and model-building.

Then, an analysis of the individual-group relationship proceeded by placing the analysis within the framework of the social situation. The problem of what constitutes a social situation is a sorely neglected one. Yet experimental psychology definitely has established that a single item of individual experience or behavior has very little significance unless it is considered as part of the context and background within which it takes place. As the context and background of individual behavior, the social situation was analyzed in terms of interdependent sets of factors. Among these, the presence or absence of stabilized reciprocities among individuals, conceived in gradations from mere togetherness to group situations, and the socio-cultural setting within which interaction takes place, were singled out for special articulation.

The analysis of the social situation has inescapable implications for psychology, sociology, and interdisciplinary efforts—which should supplement one another instead of being a source of bickering over the prerogatives of the various social sciences.

Articulation of the sets of factors in the social situation points to a definite and orderly sequence in the study of individual-group relationships. It eliminates a sharp dichotomy between individual and group.

The conceptualization of a social situation provides for due emphasis on the socio-cultural setting for interaction. It provides for the analysis of groups as groups, without falling into the pitfall of "reductionism" which is prevalent, on the whole, in what are given the blanket label of "behavioral sciences." At the same time, the analysis places proper emphasis on the unique individual or personality characteristics, which can be studied in as fine detail of idiosyncratic factors and their shadings as can be desired by proponents of personality nuances.

The sets of factors that should be included in analysis of the social situation (and that therefore constitute the framework of the individual-group relationship) were indicated in broad outlines, making place for socio-cultural, group, and idiosyncratic personal factors. The last section of the paper was devoted to a brief summary of our research program since 1958, whose aim is to operationalize the theoretical analysis of the individual-group relationship in a multi-faceted research design and in concrete research procedures carried out in successive phases.

NOTES

1. Muzafer Sherif, *The Psychology of Social Norms* (New York: Harper and Brothers, 1936; and Harper Torchbook Series, 1966).

2. Muzafer Sherif and Carolyn W. Sherif, *Groups in Harmony and Tension* (New York: Harper and Brothers, 1953); Muzafer Sherif, B. J. White, and O. J. Harvey, "Status in Experimentally Produced Groups," *American Journal of Sociology*, LX (1955), 370–379; Muzafer Sherif, O. J. Harvey, B. J. White, W. R. Hood, and Carolyn W. Sherif, *Intergroup Conflict and Cooperation: The Robbers Cave Experiment* (Norman, Oklahoma: University Book Exchange, 1961).

3. Muzafer Sherif and Carl I. Hovland, *Social Judgment* (New Haven: Yale University Press, 1961) paperback edition, 1965.

4. Carolyn W. Sherif, Muzafer Sherif, and R. E. Nebergall, *Attitude and Attitude Change: The Social Judgment–Involvement Approach* (Philadelphia: W. B. Saunders Company, 1965).

5. L. L. Thurstone and E. J. Chave, *The Measurement of Attitude*

(Chicago: University of Chicago Press, 1929); Carl I. Hovland and Muzafer Sherif, "Judgmental Phenomena and Scales of Attitude Measurement: Item Displacement in Thurstone Scales," *Journal of Abnormal and Social Psychology*, LIV (1952), 257–261; and Muzafer Sherif and Carl I. Hovland, "Judgmental Phenomena and Scales of Attitude Measurement: Placement of Items with Individual Choice of Number of Categories," *Journal of Abnormal and Social Psychology*, XLVIII (1953), 135–141.

6. Muzafer Sherif and Carolyn W. Sherif, *Reference Groups: Exploration into Conformity and Deviation of Adolescents* (New York: Harper and Row, 1964).

7. C. B. Allendoerfer and C. O. Oakley, *Fundamentals of Freshman Mathematics* (New York: McGraw-Hill Book Company, 1959), p. 19.

8. R. Oppenheimer, "Analogy in Science," *American Psychologist*, XI (1956), 133–134.

9. *Ibid.*, p. 134.

10. A. Chapanis, "Men, Machines, and Models," *American Psychologist*, XVI (1961), 130.

11. *Ibid.*, pp. 130–131.

12. Oppenheimer, *op. cit.*, p. 135.

13. Sherif, Sherif, and Nebergall, *op. cit.*

14. Harry Helson, "Current Trends and Issues in Adaptation Level Theory," *American Psychologist*, XIX (1964), 26.

15. M. T. Orne, "On the Social Psychology of the Psychological Experiment: With Particular Reference to Demand Characteristics and Their Implications," *American Psychologist*, XVII (1962), 776–783; R. Rosenthal, "On the Social Psychology of the Psychological Experiment: With Particular Reference to Experimenter Bias," paper read at the 1961 Annual Convention, American Psychological Association, New York City; and B. L. Kintz, D. J. Delprats, D. R. Mettee, C. E. Persons, and R. H. Schappe, "The Experimenter Effect," *Psychological Bulletin*, LXIII (1965), 223–232.

16. S. B. Sells (ed.), *The Stimulus Determinants of Behavior* (New York: The Ronald Press, 1963).

17. Muzafer Sherif and B. Koslin, "The 'Behavioral' vs. 'Institutional' Controversy in Social Science with Special Reference to Political Science" (Norman, Oklahoma: Institute of Group Relations, University of Oklahoma, 1960). Mimeographed.

18. Sherif and Sherif, *Reference Groups: Exploration into Conformity and Deviation of Adolescents*.

SUGGESTED READINGS

Allendoerfer, C. B., and Oakley, C. O. *Fundamentals of Freshman Mathematics*. New York: McGraw-Hill Book Company, 1959.

Chapanis, A. "Men, Machines, and Models," *American Psychologist* (1961), 16:113–131.

Helson, Harry. "Current Trends and Issues in Adaptation Level Theory," *American Psychologist* (1964), 19:26.

Hovland, Carl I., and Sherif, Muzafer. "Judgmental Phenomena and Scales of Attitude Measurement: Item Displacement in Thurstone Scales," *Journal of Abnormal and Social Psychology* (1952), 54:257–261.

Kintz, B. L., Delprats, D. J., Mettee, D. R., Persons, C. E., and Schappe, R. H. "The Experimenter Effect," *Psychological Bulletin* (1965), 63:223–232.

Oppenheimer, R. "Analogy in Science," *American Psychologist* (1956), 11:127–135.

Orne, M. T. "On the Social Psychology of the Psychological Experiment: With Particular Reference to Demand Characteristics and Their Implications," *American Psychologist* (1962), 17:776–783.

Rosenthal, R. "On the Social Psychology of the Psychological Experiment: With Particular Reference to Experimenter Bias." Paper read at the 1961 Annual Convention, American Psychological Association, New York City.

Sells, S. B. *The Stimulus Determinants of Behavior*. New York: The Ronald Press, 1963.

Sherif, Carolyn W., Sherif, Muzafer, and Nebergall, R. E. *Attitude and Attitude Change: The Social Judgment–Involvement Approach*. Philadelphia: W. B. Saunders Company, 1965.

Sherif, Muzafer. *The Psychology of Social Norms*. New York: Harper and Brothers, 1936; Harper Torchbook Series, 1966.

———, Harvey, O. J., White, B. J., Hood, W. R., and Sherif, Carolyn W. *Intergroup Conflict and Cooperation: The Robbers Cave Experiment*. Norman, Oklahoma: University Book Exchange, 1961.

———, and Hovland, Carl I. "Judgmental Phenomena and Scales of Attitude Measurement: Placement of Items with Individual Choice of Number of Categories," *Journal of Abnormal and Social Psychology* (1953), 48:135–141.

———, and ———. *Social Judgment*. New Haven: Yale University Press, 1961.

———, and Koslin, B. "The 'Behavioral' vs. 'Institutional' Controversy in Social Science with Special Reference to Political Science,"

Norman, Oklahoma: Institute of Group Relations, University of Oklahoma, 1960 (mimeographed).

——, and Sherif, Carolyn W. *Groups in Harmony and Tension.* New York: Harper and Brothers, 1953.

——, and ——. *Reference Groups: Exploration into Conformity and Deviation of Adolescents.* New York: Harper and Row, 1964.

——, White, B. J., and Harvey, O. J. "Status in Experimentally Produced Groups," *American Journal of Sociology* (1955), 60:370–379.

Thurstone, L. L., and Chave, E. J. *The Measurement of Attitude.* Chicago: University of Chicago Press, 1929.

CHAPTER **IV**

Models and Explanations in the Behavioral Sciences

Alan Ross Anderson
and Omar K. Moore

Editor's Introduction

Much reference has been made in the preceding chapters to logic and to philosophy. The present chapter is intended to provide us with contributions from the philosophy of science that are relevant to the topics of this Symposium.

One of the duties of the philosopher is to inquire into the language that is used by the scientist and to interpret the concepts that are developed and presented by the separate sciences. Another is to examine the assumptions of the individual disciplines for the purpose of determining their validity. These two objectives of making clear what is happening in scientific thinking are accomplished in the following pages with regard to the use of "models" in the behavioral sciences.

This chapter is the collaborative effort of a philosopher, Professor Alan Ross Anderson, and a behavioral scientist, Professor Omar K. Moore. These men have joined forces in much work that spans the disciplines of sociology, psychology, anthropology, and the philosophy of science—and much of which bears upon logical and epistemological problems. Anderson's main field of interest is the philosophy of mathematics and science. He has been concerned in particular with the use of "models" in mathematical logic—an interest that has become so extensive that a "model theory" is recognized now as a subspecialty within this sphere. In this chapter, however, the particular concern of Anderson and Moore is with mechanical models, or the simulation of human behavior by means of the electronic computer. It is an expository attempt to clarify in some detail the logician's general notion of "model" as it relates to the behavioral sciences. Anderson and Moore feel that, unfortunately, the work in this area has been confined nearly exclusively to dialogues among the logicians themselves. Very few attempts have been made to explain what these logicians are attempting to do in a manner that would be comprehensible to the behavioral scientists—the majority of whom, while hopefully logical, are not logicians.

As Sherif pointed out in the preceding chapter, the behavioral sciences are witnessing considerable interest of late in "models"—not only in the more traditionally mathematical ones, but also, and increasingly, in "machine models"; these latter are an extension of the concern with mathematical models since they are based upon mathematical language and symbolic logic. Anderson and Moore perceive two assumptions as underlying much of the current work of applying computer technology to the analysis of problems involving human beings: (1) that computer programs—or more likely, the behavior of programmed computers—are in some sense models of the human behavior to which they are intended to be analogous; and (2) that these models in some manner enable the scientists to understand human behavior—that is to say, that they constitute theories or explanations of their human analogues. Extrapolation from the behavior of the programmed computers to the behavior of human beings in experimental situations would seem to constitute the goal of the scientist in utilizing these mechanical models.

Anderson and Moore consider the logic of these assumptions and suggest criteria for assessing the explanatory power of such models. The relations among such models, theories, and explanations are not the direct concern of these authors. Consequently, they do not attempt directly to solve the attendant methodological and philosophical problems. The authors' intention, rather, is to make some observations about the nature of finite automata on which human behavior, such as thought processes, is to be simulated. Their observations are placed in the context of the "theory" of such machines, particularly as developed in the pioneering work of A. M. Turing.

Electronic computers are based upon mathematics in their internal engineering. That is to say, they are programmed mathematically, and usually, if not always, their machine language is founded upon Boolean algebra. Accordingly, these machines, and therefore the mechanical models which they produce, are subject to whatever limitations characterize mathematics. The literature on the unsolvability of mathematical problems by constructive or effective methods has become quite extensive. These unsolvable problems raise one question about the limitations of mathematical models. Another, of course, concerns the validity of such models, since there is a lack of empirical verification in mathematics.

It is impossible, maintain Anderson and Moore, to build a computer that will tell accurately which classes of problems are solvable by machine and which are not. Yet, human beings have shown that some of these problems cannot be solved by machines. This would seem to put the scientist ahead and to allay any fear, at least for the time being, that he will be replaced by the computer. Nevertheless, given the machine limitations, the question remains of how precisely human behavior can be simulated. This question leads us, in turn, to the inevitable question, "Can the computers be made to think?"

Turing's answer was a qualified affirmation. Producing "intelligent machines" was for him an asymptotic function of time. Many scientists saw in this possibility the makings of an explanation for human behavior and pursued the problem of computer and model construction with zealous anticipation. Anderson and Moore contend, however, that mechanical simulations are not explanations of the behavior that they simulate. Moreover, it is doubtful that mechanical explanations should be regarded as models in the absence of further evidence —if "model" is intended to mean anything other than "a machine that roughly will reproduce the same net results." Computer programs are models for human behavior only in the sense that they achieve the same or a similar end by means of a different set of mechanics.

The answer which Anderson and Moore offer for the second assumption concerning the application of computer technology to the analysis of human behavior should be obvious. Is it possible to extrapolate from the similarity of behavior (same net results) to the similarity of structure? That is to say, can a case be made for the position that mechanical models constitute theories or explanations of human behavior? The dangers here are rather apparent. First of all, the assumption is that human beings and their mechanical models are structured the same, and thus, for example, brains are wired like electronic computers. Yet, as every structural-functionalist theorist knows, similarity of function does not imply a similarity of structure. Each of several structural alternatives may yield the same manifest function—along with a considerable variation in other types of consequences.

Anderson and Moore are not critical of efforts toward the mechanical simulation of human behavior. They caution only against the temptation to take these mechanical analogues as models for some a priori reason, and then to endow these models with explanatory power. There is, in other words, a confusion of the methodological function and the substantive nature of models. Models have scientific value in that they may generate an explanation in some way, but they themselves do not constitute explanations. What is needed is a theory, or an explanation of some kind, for both the original behavior and its simulated model. The crux of the authors' argument is that mechanical models have only heuristic—and not theoretical or explanatory— value. They have as such no truth claims. Theories or explanations make assertions; mechanical models do not. Their scientific utility lies in the fact that they may suggest a kind of theoretical problem which, if solved, will explain both the original behavior and that of its mechanical analogue.

Since the logical analysis is the same, the notions developed by Anderson and Moore should apply with similar validity to other types of models, especially mathematical ones. The scientific value of models, however substantial, is heuristic. Only in this methodological manner do they have theoretical relevance. The reader should perceive an interesting parallel, though somewhat imperfect, between models and nominal definitions. Both are methodological devices in the service of scientific analysis; but neither constitutes a substantive or theoretical explanation.

One of the most fascinating offshoots of recent developments in computer technology—from the point of view of many behavioral scientists, at any rate—has been the attempt to apply computer technology to the analysis of psychological or sociological problems, that is, to problems characteristically involving human beings and human intelligence. There is no dearth of examples. To quote Paul Armer:

> The mounting list of tasks which can now be carried out on a computer but which we normally consider requiring intelligence when performed by humans, includes such things as:
> proving theorems in logic and plane geometry
> playing checkers and chess
> assembly line balancing
> composing music
> designing motors
> recognition of manual Morse Code
> solving calculus problems[1]

Apart from the intrinsic interest involved in all these projects (and the fun, which we think is itself a sufficient justification for them), there seem also to be involved two implicit (sometimes explicit) assumptions concerning the application of such research. (1) The computer programs (or perhaps the behavior of the programmed computers) are in some sense *models* of the human behavior to which they are analogous. (2) These models in some sense enable us to understand human behavior or intelligence; that is, they constitute *theories* or *explanations* of their human analogues. In other words, we may hope to be able to extrapolate somehow from the behavior of the programmed computers to the behavior of human beings in experimental situations.

Research leading to this paper was supported in part by the Office of Naval Research, Group Psychology Branch, Contract no. SAR/Nonr–609 (16).

Now clearly the relations among such *models, theories,* and *explanations,* are in fact understood in many ways by many people—sometimes luminously, sometimes darkly. While we hope to be able to drop a few helpful hints *ambulando,* we have no intention here of attempting a wholesale solution of the attendant methodological or philosophical problems. Our intent is rather to consider the two assumptions mentioned above, which underlie much current work in the computer simulation of "human higher-order problem-solving," and in the course of the examination to suggest criteria for assessing the explanatory power of such mechanical models.

The Limitations of Machines

We begin by making some observations about the nature of the finite automata (hereafter "machines") on which the human behavior, and perhaps "thought processes" are to be simulated. As an example, one may think of an IBM 7040, or some other commercial electronic computer. A typical machine of this sort consists of a black box (we will not stop to analyze its entrails), into which a program is fed. Into the resulting programmed box is then fed an input, typically a request to compute the value of some function for given arguments; the machine then provides us with an output, typically the value of the function for the arguments specified. All this is of course familiar.

Now the general theory of such machines was developed long before our technological resources permitted their realization, notably by Herbrand–Gödel,[2] Post,[3] Church,[4] and A. M. Turing.[5] Of these only Turing looked at matters explicitly from the point of view of ideal machines; the others were thinking of the matter rather in the context of abstract mathematics. But the several theories just referred to, all developed around 1936 from different points of view, were in the end shown to be equivalent. Therefore we may, without loss of generality, restrict attention to Turing's approach and, in particular, to (what have come to be known as) "Turing Machines."

All existing examples (and presumably all possible examples) of digital computers are machines in Turing's sense, or are at least representable as such, disregarding differences in detail which are not differences in principle. And it is well known that such machines suffer from severe limitations, some of which we shall describe briefly by way of motivating further consideration of the mechanical "modelling" of human intelligence.

The limitations stem from a fundamental theorem of Gödel[6] which we may state roughly, for machines, as follows. Consider a machine designed to answer "yes-or-no" questions in elementary arithmetic, that is, to answer such questions as, "Is 64 a power of 2?" or, "Is there, for every prime number x, another prime number y greater than x?" Gödel's theorem says roughly that *every* such machine must in principle be in a certain sense defective, namely: it will either be *inconsistent*, in the sense that it will sometimes produce a wrong answer, or else it will be *incomplete*, in the sense that it will sometimes fail to give a "yes" answer, even though the correct answer is in fact "yes."

It should be emphasized that this defect in such machines stems solely from abstract mathematical considerations and has nothing to do with lack of space or time on the machine's part or with failure of human ingenuity in designing the machine. Construction of a machine which is *both* complete and consistent is simply a mathematical impossibility—in much the same way that it is mathematically impossible to square the circle with straightedge and compass in plane Euclidean geometry.

It follows, by an argument which, while not altogether trivial, is perfectly straightforward, that elementary arithmetic is *undecidable*, in the sense that there is no *effective* procedure (guaranteed to terminate with an answer in a finite number of steps) for determining whether or not a given statement of elementary arithmetic is provable, or even whether it is true or false.

The implications of this argument have been extended in many directions. In fact the literature on unsolvability of mathematical problems by constructive or effective methods has grown so vast in the past twenty-eight years that the topic is now considered a sub-specialty in the field of foundations of mathematics and mathematical logic. We mention two examples of unsolvable problems: (1) the question of whether an arbitrary formula is a theorem in the first-order quantification theory (Church's theorem), a question which is *much* less sophisticated than the same problem for elementary arithmetic; and (2) the question of whether an arbitrary algebraic polynomial equation with integral coefficients has roots in the integers.

Before returning to mechanical models of higher-order problem-solving, we should like to indicate as clearly as possible the relevance of these technical results to the problem at hand. The point is this: it can be shown by rigorous mathematical methods that once one takes the *first* natural step toward extending the very simplest of our logical structures (essentially a two-element Boolean algebra), we run into situations with which machines are in a sense unable to cope. It is impossible even to build a machine that will tell us accurately which classes of problems are solvable by machine and which are not. But *we* (human beings) have been able to show that at least some sets of problems are unsolvable (in the required sense) by machines. And this would seem, at first blush anyway, to put human intelligence forever one-up, vis-à-vis machines.

Rosenbloom has drawn the moral, somewhat extravagantly, that these developments, dating from the 1930's, provide a rigorous proof of the usefulness of brains (or, at any rate, of the brains of mathematicians):

> Church's theorem has sometimes been interpreted pessimistically as a proof that there are absolutely unsolvable problems. . . . But optimistically speaking, it is a rigorous proof that brains are indispensable, and that should be comforting to anyone who hopes that he can solve problems which a moron cannot.[7]

Turing's View

It was, presumably, such considerations of machine limitations which, at least in part, motivated Turing to discuss at length, in a classic paper of 1950, the question, "Can machines think?"[8] Put in the context of more recent research, his question may be regarded as meaning, "How closely can we 'model' human intelligence, mechanically?" or, "Can we tell our friends from the robots?"

Without going into details of his account of the matter, we can say that Turing's answer to, "Can machines think?" was, "Yes, with one qualification." Though he did not say so explicitly, it is clear from what he wrote in the article in question (and also elsewhere) that he thought of the solution to the problem of producing intelligent machines as being an asymptotic function of time (to state it pretentiously, as Turing would *not* have). Put more simply, there seems to be no intrinsic limit on the amount of storage capacity a machine can have (beyond the fact that it must, like human beings, be spatio-temporally finite), and there seems equally to be no intrinsic limit to the amount of sophistica-tion* which can be built into a program.

The qualification in Turing's belief that we probably could approximate human intelligence mechanically was, of course, that the question, "Can machines think?" is vague, and that in addition we do not quite know what to mean by "approaching it asymp-totically." Granted these obvious truths, it is interesting to note that Turing then exhibited two tendencies characteristic of a mathematical or logical approach to such problems: (1) he simplified the problem, so as to get some control over it; and (2) he specified some criteria for telling whether or not his problem had been solved.

(1) The simplification involved reducing the question, "Can X think?" to the question, "Can X play a (certain specified) game?" Turing described the rules of the game, and it seemed clear to him on the face of it that an entity that could play this game would properly be said to be capable of thought.

(2) The criterion for the success of his "mechanical model" was simply this: if one of the players were replaced by a

* Just how to measure "sophistication" is of course not known; but there is no reason to believe that it is impossible in principle to do so, in view of the fact that we can all recognize clearly that an IBM 7040 is in some sense more sophisticated than a tape adding machine. We could tell the difference between hot and cold long before we could *measure* the differences.

machine, the machine could win about as often as a human player could. (Actually, Turing specified "about as often" as being "more than 70 per cent of the time"—but in the context of the article this was clearly a joke, inessential to the argument.)

The simplification, and the specification of the adequacy criterion, seem to us of interest, methodologically, and they raise problems in their own right. But even more interesting is the fact that Turing nowhere said that such a development would *explain* anything or that it should be regarded as a *theory*. In fact, he did not even suggest that such a model would necessarily be relevant to an explanation of human behavior. The question he considered was simply and solely whether or not a machine could serve as a "model" of human intelligence, *in the sense that* it could play *this particular game* as well as a human being could.

Machines as Models of Human Behavior

In spite of the fact that Turing was not interested in explanations or theories of human behavior—nothing could have been further from his intent—his simplification of the problem leaves him open to some difficult questions. Their general tenor may be put briefly, and perhaps brutally, as follows.

Suppose we select some set of human activities that are sufficiently clearly delineated so that we have criteria for success or failure. We return to the list cited at the outset as examples:

proving theorems in logic and plane geometry
playing checkers and chess
assembly line balancing
composing music
designing motors
recognition of manual Morse Code
solving calculus problems.[9]

We might expand the list a little by adding:

opening doors
multiplying two five-digit numbers
driving a horse and buggy.

All these activities meet the two conditions just mentioned: they are characteristically human (no other species performs them as a matter of course), and in all cases we can tell whether the job was done well or ill. Moreover, both the original list and the second one mention activities that were originally undertaken by human beings without the help of machines, and again in the case of both lists we subsequently developed mechanical devices that produce the same net results as the original.

Let us take up the last three cases. First, presumably nobody would want to regard an electric eye as a model of a doorman, or as an explanation of a doorman's behavior, in *any* sense of "explanation." In the second case, it is at best doubtful whether or not one would want to consider the behavior of a 7040, in multiplying two five-digit numbers, as a *model* of similar activity on the part of a human being; and it would certainly not be thought of as explanatory of human behavior. And finally, we doubt that one would want to call an automobile a model of a horse and buggy, in spite of the fact that they achieve similar net results (and in spite of the fact that the term "horseless carriage" carries a suggestion that one is a mechanical model of the other).

It is equally doubtful whether mechanical simulations of human problem-solving should be regarded as models either, at least in the absence of further evidence—*if*, that is, the term "model" is intended to mean anything more than simply "a machine which will produce roughly the same net results." And if the term "model" *is* intended to mean something more than this, the additional meaning should be specified, in order to make the claim clear; this has not to our knowledge been done in the literature.

So as regards the first of the two assumptions we began to consider at the outset of this paper (namely, that the programs, in operation, provide *models* of higher-order human problem-solving), it thus appears that they are models, if at all, only in the same sense that a bicycle is a model of a horse, or a dish-washing machine is a model of a housewife.

Models as Explanations of Human Behavior

We turn now to the second of the assumptions mentioned at the outset, namely, that we can in some way extrapolate from similarity of behavior to "similarity of structure," and that therefore the models constitute *theories* or *explanations* of human behavior. And here it seems to us that the dangers are obvious.

One might be misled, by the analogy between a horse and buggy and a horseless carriage, into thinking that a horse contains an internal combustion engine. One might equally be led (or perhaps misled) into thinking that since a programmed machine can play checkers, there must be important structural similarities between the wiring diagram, or the program, and the central nervous system. But of course this need not at all be the case. To quote Keith Gunderson, whose elegant article on the topic suggested some of these ideas:

> In the end the steam drill outlasted John Henry as a digger of railway tunnels, but that didn't prove the machine had muscles; it proved that muscles were not needed for digging railway tunnels.[10]

The Value of Models

We hope it has been quite clear that at *no* point in the foregoing discussion have we been critical of the efforts of those who are actively engaged in problems of mechanical simulation of human higher-order problem-solving. We have been concerned *only* with the assumptions (1) that such machine analogues can for some a priori reason be taken seriously as "models," and (2) that if they are, the models can be considered as explanatory. In fact we think that attempts at the construction of mechanical models are of great value, but their value is *heuristic*, rather than explanatory. To elucidate this remark, we adopt an example suggested to us by Paul Armer's paper quoted earlier:

While it is true that man wasted a good deal of time and effort trying to build a flying machine that flapped its wings like a bird, the important point is that it was the understanding of the law of aerodynamic lift (even though the understanding was quite imperfect at first) over an airfoil which enabled men to build flying machines.[11]

The point Armer had in mind is not quite the same as ours, but the example serves equally well as an illustration. The explanatory importance of the attempt to construct a controlled-flight machine lay *not* in the fact that the mechanical model (airplane) of the original (bird) *explained* anything about birds or their behavior. It lay rather in the fact that the attempt to make a mechanical model of a bird provided problems of a practical sort, which led heuristically to a solution of the theoretical problems. As a consequence we were led to develop the theory of aerodynamics, which is relevant *both* to the flight of the bird *and* to the flight of an airplane. And it is by virtue of the fact that both birds and airplanes are models (in an entirely different sense of the word now—a sense more like that to be found in the literature on mathematical logic) of the *same* abstract formal theory, that one can be said to be a mechanical model (in the sense that we have been using throughout this paper) of the other.

Put more succinctly, if we have a gadget G, which imitates the behavior of an organism O, and if, moreover, we have a *theory* that explains the behavior of both G and O, then (and *only* then) can we say sensibly that G is a mechanical model of O. (And, as we have argued elsewhere,[12] it is only with the advent of the theory of games of strategy that we are in a position to say that social games are models—"folk-models"—of the serious social interaction which occurs in the market place.)

Conclusion

The virtue of attempts at mechanical simulation is that they *may*, with luck, suggest the kind of theoretical problem which, if solved, would explain both the original behavior and that of the mechanical analogue. But theories, or explanations, make *assertions;* mechanical models do not.[13] To say that they do, suggests that if a child asked us how a bird flies, and if we then pointed to a flying airplane and said, "Look! *That's* how it's done"—that under these circumstances the child would say, "Ah. *Now* I see." And this clearly will not do.

NOTES

1. Paul Armer, "Attitudes Toward Intelligent Machines," in E. A. Feigenbaum and J. Feldman (eds.), *Computers and Thought* (New York: McGraw-Hill Book Company, 1963), p. 396.

2. See S. C. Kleene, "General Recursive Functions of Natural Numbers," *Mathematische Annalen,* CXII (1936), 727–742.

3. E. L. Post, "Finite Combinatory Processes—Formulation 1," *Journal of Symbolic Logic,* I (1936), 103–105.

4. Alonzo Church, "An Unsolvable Problem of Elementary Number Theory," *American Journal of Mathematics,* LVIII (1936), 345–363; and "A Note on the Entscheidungsproblem," *Journal of Symbolic Logic,* I (1936), 40–41.

5. A. M. Turing, "On Computable Numbers, with an Application to the Entscheidungsproblem," *Proceedings of the London Mathematical Society,* Ser. 2, XLII (1936–37), 230–265.

6. K. Gödel, "Über Formal Unentscheidbare Sätze der Principia Mathematica und Verwandter Systeme I," *Monatshefte für Mathematik und Physik,* XXXVIII (1931), 173–198.

7. P. Rosenbloom, *The Elements of Mathematical Logic* (New York: Dover Press, 1950), p. 161.

8. A. M. Turing, "Computing Machinery and Intelligence," *Mind,* LIX (1950), 433–460.

9. Armer, *op. cit.,* p. 396.

10. K. Gunderson, "The Imitation Game," in A. R. Anderson (ed.), *Minds and Machines* (New York: Prentice-Hall, Inc., 1964), pp. 60–71.

11. Armer, *op. cit.,* p. 398.

12. See our articles "Autotelic Folk-Models," *Sociological Quarterly,* I (1960), pp. 203–216; and "The Structure of Personality," in O. J. Harvey (ed.), *Motivation and Social Interaction* (New York: The Ronald Press, 1963), pp. 167–186.

13. Nor do computer programs, in spite of those who write to the contrary. See an interesting article by A. Newell, J. C. Shaw, and

H. A. Simon, "Elements of a Theory of Human Problem Solving," *Psychological Review*, LXV (1958), 151–166. They propose there to *identify* an explanation (or a theory) with a programmed computer: ". . . an explanation of an observed behavior of the organism is provided by a program of primitive information processes that generates this behavior" (p. 151). But a programmed computer is simply a block of hardware, and the program is simply a flock of numbers. Neither of these makes any assertions at all; hence, neither is an explanation of anything.

SUGGESTED READINGS

Anderson, Alan R. (ed.). *Minds and Machines.* New York: Prentice-Hall, Inc., 1964.

————, and Moore, Omar K. "Autotelic Folk-Models," *Sociological Quarterly* (1960), 1:203–216.

————. "The Structure of Personality," in O. J. Harvey (ed.), *Motivation and Social Interaction.* New York: The Ronald Press, 1963.

Armer, Paul. "Attitudes Toward Intelligent Machines," in E. A. Feigenbaum and J. Feldman (eds.). *Computers and Thought.* New York: McGraw-Hill Book Company, 1963, pp. 389–405.

Church, Alonzo. "An Unsolvable Problem of Elementary Number Theory," *American Journal of Mathematics* (1936), 58:345–363.

————. "A Note on the Entscheidungsproblem," *Journal of Symbolic Logic* (1936), 1:40–41.

Feigenbaum, E. A., and Feldman, J. (eds.). *Computers and Thought.* New York: McGraw-Hill Book Company, 1963.

Gödel, K. "Über Formal Unentscheidbare Sätze der Principia Mathematica und Verwandter Systeme I," *Monatschefte für Mathematik und Physik* (1931), 38:173–198.

Gunderson, K. "The Imitation Game," in Alan R. Anderson (ed.). *Minds and Machines.* New York: Prentice-Hall, Inc., 1964.

Harvey, O. J. (ed.). *Motivation and Social Interaction.* New York: The Ronald Press, 1963.

Kleene, S. C. "General Recursive Functions of Natural Numbers," *Mathematische Annalen* (1936), 112:727–742.

Newell, A., Shaw, J. C., and Simon, H. A. "Elements of a Theory of Human Problem Solving," *Psychological Review* (1958), 65:151–166.

Post, E. L. "Finite Combinatory Processes—Formulation 1," *Journal of Symbolic Logic* (1936), 1:103–105.

Rosenbloom, P. *The Elements of Mathematical Logic.* New York: Dover Press, 1950.

Turing, A. M. "On Computable Numbers, with an Application to the Entscheidungsproblem," *Proceedings of the London Mathematical Society* (1936–37), Ser. 2, 42:230–265.

———. "Computing Machinery and Intelligence," *Mind* (1950), 59:433–460.

CHAPTER V

Definitions and
Conceptions of Culture

Leslie A. White

EDITOR'S INTRODUCTION

Professor Leslie A. White is recognized as one of the world's foremost cultural anthropologists. For many years he has devoted much of his time and energy to the clarification of the nature of culture and to the establishment of a distinct discipline for its study— culturology. The concept of "culture" is a focal one, not only in the field of anthropology, but also in the other behavioral disciplines. This chapter is concerned with a further analysis of both the concept and its denoted phenomena.

Ackerman and Parsons spoke of the "social system" as involving three sub-systems: the social, the personality, and the cultural systems. Sherif provided a specification of the "social situation" by delineating its composition in more concrete terms. White offers here a specification of the "cultural system." Unlike Sherif, however, he continues in somewhat the same scheme as Ackerman and Parsons, since it is apparent that he envisions culture as an organized and integrated system. In fact, the cultural system is for him one of three sub-systems of the cosmic reality of man, the other two being the biological and the physical.

Despite their parallel lines, however, the views of White and those of Ackerman and Parsons have much dissimilarity. One may wonder, for example, if "society" (social system) and "culture" are in any sense synonymous since White elsewhere has defined a "socio-cultural system" as the culture possessed by a distinct group of people. Obviously, for him culture becomes the focal system, with society as a sub-element; this is substantially different from envisioning the three parallel sub-systems in the general action view of Ackerman and Parsons. White rightly argues that culture, and not society, is the distinctive feature of man; culture is uniquely human.

Behavioral scientists seem much in agreement on the fact that culture is acquired by man through the process of social interaction, but they disagree sharply with regard to its essential nature and functions. A definition of culture offered in 1871 by the British anthropologist Edward B. Tylor traditionally has provided the anthropological meaning that has been at the base of this controversy. The real issue, however, is not an essentially historical one. It seems to be rather a metaphysical controversy that has remained unsettled for only the past few decades. After the 1920's, the term "culture" was disseminated into several other disciplines and underwent considerable scrutiny, especially in regard to its essential nature and distinguishing characteristics. White describes the consequences of this examination as a "conceptual jungle of definitions."

Anthropologists A. L. Kroeber and Clyde Kluckhohn in 1952 reviewed the usage of the term "culture" and found over three hundred definitions for it. Of these, they speak of three major uses for the term: (1) cultural realism—an external, existential reality in the super-organic realm; (2) cultural nominalism—simply a logical construct, with no ontological reality; and (3) cultural idealism—ideal norms and patterns of behavior which have only a mental existence and as such do not constitute actual behavior. The dominant anthropological position today appears to be that of cultural nominalism, whereby the concept is considered as a purely descriptive device.

White argues for cultural realism. It is unfortunate, he contends, that so much preference has been given to "culture" as an abstraction. An amazing state of affairs results from this situation for those who deny the reality of culture, namely, that the cultural anthropologist finds himself without a subject matter—without a real one, that is. Anthropologists thus survive as analysts of mere abstractions.

White recovers "culture" for the anthropologists. Culture for him has ontological reality. He defines it in this way: "Culture is that class of phenomena, dependent upon symboling, which is considered and interpreted in an extra-somatic context." Culture thus is made up of things and events that depend upon the ability of man to use symbols—a uniquely human phenomenon. Things and events that are dependent upon the act of symboling for their existence are termed "symbolates"—another Whitean neologism. Analyzing symbolates in terms of their relationship to one another, and not to the human organism, constitutes the scientific objective of culturology.

Opponents of this view argue that *real culture* is behavior and that to find elements of causation in culture is to make behavior the cause of behavior. For them, this is to assert self-causation—to say, in other words, that an inference is the cause of that from which the inference is made. But the referent of "culture" is a real one for White. Symbols are things—real things. They are as real as the things that comprise human behavior. In fact, they are the same things in one respect. Culturology and human psychology have the same subject matter— the same material object. But because they deal with it in different contexts—the one in the somatic context, the other in the extra-somatic context—they have different formal objects. Thus culture is not human behavior—it is not people or their actions—but another distinct order of phenomena. And therefore culturology is not directly concerned with people. White's striking example of the scientific study of a class of non-biological phenomena without reference to the human beings who are its carriers is that of linguistics, widely regarded as one of the principal divisions of cultural anthropology. Its dynamics are explained culturologically.

Through symboling man has created a new environment. Yet, culture, once in existence, has its own laws. The elements of culture interact with one another in accordance with their own principles. Culture cannot be explained by anything except culture, but culture does not explain all behavior. Both psychology and culturology are essential for a comprehensive interpretation of human behavior. In order to avoid confusion, however, it is necessary to know and to respect the proper boundaries and perspectives of each. White's position is that the distinction between the subject matter of psychology and that of the science of culture need not be drawn along the lines of real versus unreal behavior. His argument involves a realization of which aspect (such as culture) is taken as a constant, and which is taken as a variable (as human beings are, in the perspective of culturology). Cultural anthropology has a real, substantial, and objective subject matter. And so it must have, declares White, for no science can exist without real things and real events as its subject matter.

Cultural phenomena can be explained as cultural phenomena only when treated *as if* they had a life of their own, quite apart from organisms—just as a physicist must treat a falling body *as if* there were no atmospheric friction. There is nothing mystical in doing this, contends White. One is simply applying the traditional technique of science to cultural phenomena. People, of course, are necessary. The individual is a catalytic agent for the interactive cultural process and a medium of expression for it. The analytical focus for culturology, nonetheless, remains on the product of this behavior.

White, however, in confronting the question of the ontological referent for the concept of "culture," takes a curious, and somewhat paradoxical, epistemological position. There seems to be one discrepancy in his argument. He accords real existence to culture, but at the same time he maintains that it is a collective term. In its collective sense, culture appears to be only a mental construct, a nominal definition, which White offers as a methodological or descriptive device, much as Ackerman and Parsons speak of the "social system." Moreover, he suggests that the question of definition is not so much one of precision as of usefulness or fruitfulness. White argues, using the terms of Whitehead, that "culture" is a technical term, and as such is assigned arbitrarily. There is no question of right or wrong in such a matter. Now this to be sure is true as far as the *term* or *word* "culture" is concerned, but the *concept* of "culture"—the ontological or metaphysical referent for this—is another matter. It is not determined arbitrarily, but either given or not given in nature. White, it would seem very clearly, is fundamentally a realist. Yet, when he maintains that culture should be treated *as if* it were real, he seems to suggest that it actually is not real, and that to perceive it as such is to indulge in a scientific and methodologically created fiction. There seems to be a contradiction or a distortion implicit in the juxtaposition of these two premises.

Another important question is raised by White's paper. Ackerman and Parsons described their conceptual scheme in terms of human societies. Yet, the same type of analysis applies to non-societal systems. It is interesting to speculate on the question of whether or not non-societal systems have culture—in the same or in a different sense than that presented by White. For example, Sherif spoke of the "micro-culture" of a research laboratory; and in Chapter VI references will be made to the culture of a mental hospital. In similar instances in the fields of sociology and psychology, the term "social organization" is often used with the essential denotation of "culture" when referring to non-societal culture. White's definition and usage of "culture" would seem to be applicable and equally appropriate in both societal and non-societal contexts, especially because the criteria of definition would appear to be "symbolates" in both instances. Yet, neither he nor any other anthropologist seems to make any reference to a non-societal context for culture—except perhaps in the nature of a "sub-culture." Probably this is a consequence of the focal role which "culture"—rather than "social system"—has in the anthropological perspective. This distinction may be only a question of terminology among the disciplines; nevertheless, it would seem to be crucial in respect to theoretical analysis, especially of the type that has been suggested in the previous chapters, and even of the type that White offers with reference to the discipline of culturology.

White's paper is of much significance for the theme of this Symposium. Concentrating as it does on the analysis of a single concept—a crucially pivotal one for all areas of the behavioral sciences—it demonstrates the elusive and laborious problem that the fundamental issue of conceptual definition presents for the scientist. Furthermore, his examination of the concept of culture reveals the central importance of conceptual definition, not only in determining the nature of the subject matter and hence the very existence of a particular discipline (in this instance, cultural anthropology), but for the entire scientific process as well.

Primitive—that is, preliterate—peoples of the modern world have been quite aware of differences in language, custom, and belief among themselves, and no doubt their predecessors for ages past have had the same awareness. The ancient Greeks, as exemplified by Herodotus, also were well aware of differences between Greek and "barbarian," but they did not possess, as far as I have been able to discover, a conception of culture that was equivalent to the anthropological conception of the last century in the Western world. It might perhaps be said that something approximating our modern conception was implicit in *De Rerum Natura* of Lucretius, in which a sketch of the evolution of man's ways of life is presented. The modern conception of culture was adumbrated in the works of some social philosophers, such as Ibn Khaldun and Montesquieu, over a period of centuries following the collapse of the Roman state. But it is not until we come to the German culture historians of the eighteenth and nineteenth centuries that we reach something close to the modern conception.

A. L. Kroeber and Clyde Kluckhohn, in their monograph, *Culture*,[1] discuss the early use of the word culture, in the sense of "cultivation." But we are not so much interested in the past use of a word as we are in the origin of a conception of a distinct class of things, namely, languages, customs, and beliefs. The modern conception of culture was not derived from early uses of the word culture. Rather, a certain class of phenomena came eventually to be called by the term culture.

Edward Burnett Tylor (1832–1917), the great pioneer in British anthropology, is usually credited with the first "scientific" definition of culture. In the opening words of his *Primitive Culture* (1871), he defines culture "or civilization" as "that complex whole which includes knowledge, belief, art, morals, law, custom, and any other capabilities and habits acquired by man as a member of society."[2] In other places, notably in his *Anthropology* (1881), he emphasizes man's uniqueness in the animal kingdom, which had the effect of making culture the possession of man exclusively. And Tylor distinguishes between man on the one hand (in Tylor's words, "tribes" or "nations") and culture ("the condition of knowledge, religion, art, custom, and the like") on the other. Finally, he entitles Chapter I of *Primitive Culture* "The Science of Culture," not the science of man; nor is it an account of the progress of the human mind after the manner of Condorcet, for example.

But Tylor had leaned upon and borrowed much from Gustav Klemm (1802–67), the great pioneer in German anthropology. Between 1843 and 1852, Klemm had published, in ten volumes, his *General Culture History of Mankind* (*Allgemeine Cultur-Geschichte der Menschheit*); and, in 1854–55, his *General Science of Culture* (*Allgemeine Culturwissenschaft*) was published.

Thus it appears that our present anthropological conception of culture was derived via Tylor from the tradition of the German culture historians, some of whom, like Klemm, aspired to make culture the subject of scientific study as well as of historical record. And, as we have said before, it was culture, culture as a distinct order of phenomena, and not man, that was to be the object of scientific study and interpretation.

The Tylorean definition, or conception, of culture served anthropologists well for many decades. They knew what they meant by it, and it brought them no difficulties. An ethnologist went out to a tribe. He studied their customs and beliefs. He collected myths, pottery bowls, and textiles. He was, as he would put it, studying and recording their culture. Similarly, the archaeologist excavated mounds or camp or village sites. The artifacts dug out of the ground, together with such social structure and religious ceremony as could be inferred from the artifacts, constituted the culture of the site, or of the people who had occupied it. In 1920, Robert H. Lowie began his *Primitive Society*[3] by quoting Tylor's definition of 1871. And nine years later Ruth Benedict[4] used the same definition in "The Science of Custom."

But during and after the 1920's, culture, as an anthropological term, spread to allied disciplines: to sociology, psychology, history, and so on; it even found its way into a syndicated comic strip. The dissemination of the term "culture" was accompanied by considerable reflection upon the concept. What *is* that class of phenomena of which the particular things listed by Tylor— "knowledge, belief, art, morals, law, custom"—are expressions? What is the nature of culture? What is its distinguishing characteristic? Some anthropologists wanted to know what culture basically *is*.

These reflections upon the distinctness and nature of culture led to a great multiplication and diversification of definitions of culture, or at least of ways of saying what culture *is*. In Part II of their monograph, *Culture*, Kroeber and Kluckhohn have "cited one hundred sixty-four definitions of culture."[5] But in a footnote they state that they have assembled almost three hundred definitions. The range of variation is great. Culture is behavior; it is learned behavior; it is behavior mediated by social symbols. Culture is a design for living, a logical construct, an abstraction, a precipitate of social interaction, a stream of ideas, a psychic defense system. Culture is m social responses to n social signals. And so on.

It is not surprising, in view of this conceptual jungle of definitions, to learn that at least one anthropologist came to the conclusion that it is impossible to define culture. In 1949 Douglas G. Haring published an article entitled "Is 'Culture' Definable?"[6] and, as I understand him, answers this question in the negative.

Kroeber and Kluckhohn, too, seem to be confused with regard to the problem of defining culture. Is it like the problem of determining the chemical composition of the sun? Or is it analogous to deciding what forms of life are to be embraced by the term "bug"? Kroeber and Kluckhohn appear not to see this distinction clearly.[7] Sometimes they seem to lean in one direction; at other times, in the other. On the whole, however, they seem definitely to prefer the "determination of the chemical composition of the sun" method of defining culture. They tell us, for example, that they "hope to assist other investigators [*sic*] in reaching . . . greater precision in definition."[8] They also tell us what culture "basically *is*."[9] Some anthropologists speak of "the ultimate reality of culture,"[10] as one might speak of the ultimate reality of matter or energy. (Just what "ultimate reality" means is not quite clear to me.) Linton[11] tells us that "the ultimate realities of culture are still hidden from us," while Herskovits[12] avers that "the ultimate reality of culture is psychological."

Investigators are indeed needed to determine the chemical composition of the sun, and the concept of precision is certainly relevant to their observations and measurements. But we do not need to resort to any investigation whatever to decide whether or not we wish to include spiders in the category "bug." Bug-ness is not a thing in or an attribute of the external world, whose nature we have to discover through investigation, as we do the chemical composition of the sun. And so it is with culture. Culture is not something "out there" in the external world, whose structure is so complex, it being so ineffable, that it cannot be defined at all or can be defined only after prolonged and laborious investigation. "Culture," like "bug," *is a word* that we may use to label a class of phenomena—things and events—in the external world. We may apply these labels as we please; their use is determined by ourselves, not by the external world. "It cannot be too clearly understood," says Whitehead, "that in science, technical terms are *names arbitrarily assigned*, like Christian names to children. There can be no question of the names being right or wrong. They may [however] be judicious or injudicious. . . ."[13]

As for "precision of definitions," definitions are not more or less precise in the sense that measurements of the velocity of light are more or less exact. A definition of "bug" that includes spiders is neither more nor less precise than one that does not. "Culture is learned behavior" is precise enough. Some patterns of behavior are acquired by learning; others are not. And one is perfectly justified in arbitrarily labeling the learned patterns "culture." The question of definitions raised here is not so much one of precision as of usefulness, or fruitfulness.

The conception of culture preferred by Kroeber and Kluckhohn is that it is an abstraction. This conception is held by many other anthropologists also. Unfortunately, no one makes clear what he means by an abstraction. Does he mean something abstracted from something else, a part from a whole, as one might abstract planets from other heavenly bodies? Does he mean a statistically typical thing, such as a typical American? Or does he mean something akin to Freud's Id? To turn to Kroeber and Kluckhohn directly, they say: "Culture being basically a form or pattern or design or way, it is an abstraction from concrete human behavior, but is not itself behavior."[14] Their meaning is not wholly clear, at least to me. They seem to be saying that culture is *form* rather than *substance*. They also seem to conceive of culture as something "out there" when they tell us what it "basically is"—like the chemical composition of the sun.

In another place Kroeber and Kluckhohn tell us that "even a culture trait is an abstraction . . . an 'ideal type' because no two pots are identical nor are two marriage ceremonies ever held in precisely the same way."[15] Here we seem to have the statistical conception of culture: all pots may be represented by a type.

And still further, they tell us that the patterns, at least of the "implicit culture," are "purely inferential constructs. They are thematic principles which the investigator introduces to explain connections among a wide range of culture content and form. . . ."[16] Here we seem to have something comparable to the Id of Freudian psychology, namely, a concept introduced as an explanatory device.

It is very unfortunate, it seems to me, that contemporary anthropology has given so much preference to the definition of culture as an abstraction. It would be difficult to find another word that would bring as much confusion into the situation as this tricky noun. But confusion is not the worst of the consequences of this definition; there is more to this sad story.

Those who think of culture as an abstraction tell us that we cannot perceive culture. According to Ralph Linton, "culture . . . is intangible and cannot be directly apprehended even by the individuals who participate in it."[17] In their textbook, Beals and Hoijer state that "the anthropologist cannot observe culture directly."[18] And an anthropologist in the imaginary symposium reported by Kluckhohn and Kelly[19] suggests that culture cannot be seen at all: "one can see" individuals, he says, but "has anyone ever seen 'culture'?"

Well, if culture is intangible, if those who live within a culture cannot apprehend it directly, if one cannot "see" culture, is it really there? Does it exist? This question has indeed been raised, and in all seriousness. "Do cultures actually exist . . . ?" asks Linton in *The Study of Man;*[20] and later he remarks, "if it [culture] can be said to exist at all."[21] Radcliffe-Brown says flatly that the word culture "denotes, not any concrete reality, but an abstraction, and as it is commonly used a vague abstraction."[22] Eventually a definitive verdict was reached by Melford E. Spiro in 1951: ". . . culture has no ontological reality."[23] Thus we observe the consequences of defining culture as an abstraction: (1) it is intangible, (2) you cannot perceive it, (3) does it then exist? (4) no, it is not real.

Thus an amazing state of affairs was created: a science—nonbiological anthropology—had defined its subject matter out of existence. And, equally astounding, no cultural anthropologist seemed to be in the least disturbed to learn that as a scientist he had nothing to work with—nothing real, that is. Other scientists had to have real stars, real mountains, real cells, real mammals; but the cultural anthropologist would have to content himself with abstractions that had no "ontological reality."

How are we to explain this bizarre situation, this pathetic comedy of errors enacted as a consequence of a definition? A number of factors may be involved, but we believe that Kroeber and Kluckhohn have hit upon the principal one: if the anthropologist defines culture as behavior then he must surrender it to the psychologist because behavior is the proper subject matter of psychology. Culture was long defined as behavior because it seemed so reasonable and realistic to do so. Obviously, Navaho culture was the way the Navaho Indians behaved; Hopi culture was the way the Hopi behaved. But, said Kroeber and Kluckhohn, "behavior is the first-hand and outright material of the science of psychology, and culture is not . . . [therefore] it is natural that psychologists and psychologizing sociologists should see behavior as primary in their field, and then extend this view farther to apply to the field of culture also."[24] Their reasoning was flawless; the threat was real. What should be done about it?

The solution proposed by Kroeber and Kluckhohn was ingenious but extremely unfortunate, at least for non-biological (that is, cultural) anthropology. They would give behavior to the psychologists; this was their right. They would keep abstractions of behavior for themselves. They would also keep abstractions of pottery bowls, too, because a culture trait is an "ideal type" and "no two pots are identical."

But in this rendering unto Caesar, Kroeber and Kluckhohn gave the psychologists the better part of the division, for they surrendered to them real things and events, locatable and observable, directly or indirectly, in the external world, in terrestrial time and space, whereas they kept for anthropologists only intangible, imponderable abstractions that "have no ontological reality." But, at least, they now had a subject matter of their own, no matter how imperceptible and unreal it might be.

This authoritative verdict, handed down by two of America's most distinguished anthropologists, might have caused acute embarrassment or distress in certain quarters had the persons involved been aware of the significance of the ruling. Ethnographers had long thought that they were studying the culture of the tribes they visited and lived with. Archaeologists believed that the potsherds and projectile points they excavated were culture. And museum curators were under the impression that they were cataloguing, storing, and exhibiting elements of culture brought to them from the field. Now they were to learn that behavior, even of primitive peoples, and products of their behavior, belong to the province of psychology, and that, as anthropologists, they were merely the students and custodians of abstractions—and these abstractions were not real. Fortunately for the peace of mind of the ethnographers, the archaeologists, and the museum curators, the philosophic distinction drawn by Kroeber and Kluckhohn proved to be a trifle too subtle for their comprehension and therefore left them unscathed. And in this bizarre world of dialectic and definition, it is not out of place to ask, "What would a museum curator do with an abstraction of a pottery bowl?" Well, he might catalogue it with an abstract number. And a Navaho woman might stew an abstraction of a sheep in her abstraction of a pottery bowl. When one has passed *through the looking glass* and entered the domain of the White Knight and the Jabberwock, one premise or conclusion makes as much sense as another.

But we do not need to go through the looking glass. The world we find there is fascinating and delightful, at least in the hands of a Lewis Carroll. But it is not science. And the distinction between the subject matter of psychology, on the one hand, and the subject matter of the science of culture, on the other, need not be drawn along the line of real behavior versus unreal culture. To do this would be fatal for a science of culture, for, as we have noted before, no science can exist without real things and events as its subject matter. And the curious thing about this whole situation is that anthropologists, and scholars in other disciplines, have been making good culturological studies for decades. To be sure, Kroeber and Kluckhohn knew this. But when they tried to rationalize their position they became lost in the woods of philosophy and dialectic. As a matter of fact, Kroeber himself has presented us, in his *Anthropology*,[25] with both a sketch of the evolution of writing and a history of the diffusion of the alphabet. Both are concerned with real things and events, and they are not presented as the behavior of human organisms.

To be sure, the evolution of writing and the diffusion of the alphabet could not have taken place without human organisms and their behavior. But human organisms are not necessary for an explanation of the evolution of writing. Neither could we have analytical geometry were it not for respiration, but one does not need to introduce this physiological process into an explanation of the evolution of mathematics. We have culturological accounts of the evolution of the steam engine, of clan organization, and of parliamentary government; we have studies of the structure and function of kinship systems, tribes, and chiefdoms, which are, as Tylor put it long ago, matters of custom, institution, ceremony, and belief, *not* of people. The science of linguistics is, perhaps, the best example of the scientific study of a class of non-biological phenomena without reference to the human beings who are their carriers. The linguistic scientist is concerned with the behavior of words, or languages, not with the behavior of people. Thus we have had a science of culture with us for many decades, and it definitely is not a science of the behavior of human organisms.

In order to make clear what the culturologist has been doing, and to distinguish his work from that of the psychologist, I wrote an essay a few years ago which I entitled "The Concept of Culture."[26] I will present a brief résumé of this article here.

Man is a unique animal. Only man has the ability to "symbol"—that is, to originate, determine, and bestow, freely and arbitrarily, meanings upon things and events in the external world.[27] These meanings cannot be grasped and appreciated with the senses. Holy water, or articulate speech, are good examples. Symboling is trafficking in non-sensory meanings.

And here we come to a most remarkable fact. Science has no name for one of the most fundamental classes of phenomena in the sciences of man, namely, things and events that are the result of symboling. Believing that it should have a name, I have suggested the term "symbolates": if an isolate is the product of isolating, could not a product of symboling be properly called a symbolate?[28]

Next, a thing is just what it is. There is no act which is, in and of itself, a moral act, or an economic act, or an erotic act. It becomes a moral, economic, or erotic act only when it is placed in a moral, economic, or erotic context for purposes of interpretation. A Navaho rug is a work of art in one context, a scientific specimen in another, and an article of commerce in another.

Symbolates have been interpreted in two fundamentally different contexts for many decades. (This is a matter of fact, of historic record, not a matter of theory or definition.) On the one hand, they are considered and explained scientifically, in their relationship to the human organism. So treated, they constitute behavior and are the proper subject matter of psychology. On the other hand, they have been treated, not in terms of their relationship to the human organism, but in terms of their relationship to one another. In this context they constitute culture and are the subject matter of culturology.

Let us illustrate with the example of the mother-in-law taboo, which is composed of acts, concepts, and attitudes. When we consider these in terms of their relationship to the human organism—how one feels, acts, and so on—we are dealing with behavior and we are doing psychology. But to explain the origin of the taboo we must relate it to other customs and institutions, such as form of marriage, place of residence of the newly married couple, and division of labor between the sexes. Here we are dealing with culture, and our science is culturology. And the things and events that constitute culture are as real as those that comprise human behavior. Indeed, they are the same things and events. Human psychology and culturology have the same subject matter; they simply deal with it in different contexts—one the somatic, the other the extra-somatic.

We would, therefore, define culture as follows: culture is that class of phenomena, dependent upon symboling, which is considered and interpreted in an extra-somatic context.

Thus we have rescued non-biological anthropology from the limbo to which Kroeber and Kluckhohn consigned it by their distinction between real behavior and abstract, unreal culture. Once again cultural anthropology can hold up its head within the family of sciences, for again it can have (as it traditionally has had) a real, substantial, objective subject matter. And we no longer need to wrestle with the question of abstractions of pottery bowls, what they are or what to do with them.

NOTES

1. A. L. Kroeber and Clyde Kluckhohn, *Culture: A Critical Review of Concepts and Definitions* (Cambridge: Harvard University, Papers of the Peabody Museum of American Archaeology and Ethnology), Vol. XLVII (1952), No. 1.

2. Edward B. Tylor, *Primitive Culture*, fifth ed. (London: John Murray, 1913, reprinted 1929), p. 1.

3. Robert H. Lowie, *Primitive Society* (New York: Boni and Liveright, 1920).

4. Ruth Benedict, "The Science of Custom," *The Century Magazine*, CXVII (1929), 641–649.

5. Kroeber and Kluckhohn, *op. cit.*, p. 149.

6. Douglas G. Haring, "Is 'Culture' Definable?" *American Sociological Review*, XIV (1949), 26–32.

7. Leslie A. White, Review of *Culture: A Critical Review of Concepts and Definitions*, by A. L. Kroeber and Clyde Kluckhohn, *American Anthropologist*, LVI (1954), 461–468.

8. Kroeber and Kluckhohn, *op. cit.*, p. 4.

9. *Ibid.*, p. 155.

10. Cora Du Bois, "Some Psychological Objectives and Techniques in Ethnography," *Social Psychology*, VIII (1937), 286.

11. Ralph Linton, *The Study of Man* (New York: D. Appleton-Century Company, 1936), p. 303.

12. Melville J. Herskovits, "The Processes of Cultural Change," in Ralph Linton (ed.), *The Science of Man in the World Crisis* (New York: Columbia University Press, 1945), p. 163.

13. Alfred N. Whitehead, *Introduction to Mathematics* (New York: Henry Holt and Company, 1911), pp. 87–88. Emphasis ours.

14. Kroeber and Kluckhohn, *op. cit.*, p. 155.

15. *Ibid.*, p. 169.

16. *Ibid.*, pp. 169–170.

17. Linton, *The Study of Man*, pp. 288–289.

18. Ralph L. Beals and Harry Hoijer, *An Introduction to Anthropology* (New York: The Macmillan Company, 1953), p. 210.

19. Clyde Kluckhohn and William H. Kelly, "The Concept of Culture," in Linton (ed.), *The Science of Man in the World Crisis*, pp. 79, 81.

20. Linton, *The Study of Man*, p. 288.

21. *Ibid.*, p. 363.

22. A. R. Radcliffe-Brown, "On Social Structure," *Journal of the Royal Anthropological Institute*, LXX (1940), 2.

23. Melford E. Spiro, "Culture and Personality," *Psychiatry*, XIV (1951), 24.

24. Kroeber and Kluckhohn, *op. cit.*, p. 155.

25. A. L. Kroeber, *Anthropology* (New York: Harcourt, Brace and Company, 1948).

26. Leslie A. White, "The Concept of Culture," *American Anthropologist*, LXI (1959), 227–251.

27. Leslie A. White, "Symboling: A Kind of Behavior," *The Journal of Psychology*, LIII (1962), 311–317.

28. White, "The Concept of Culture," p. 231.

SUGGESTED READINGS

Beals, Ralph L., and Hoijer, Harry. *An Introduction to Anthropology*. New York: The Macmillan Company, 1953.

Benedict, Ruth. "The Science of Custom," *The Century Magazine* (1929), 117:641–649.

Du Bois, Cora. "Some Psychological Objectives and Techniques in Ethnography," *Social Psychology* (1937), 8:285–300.

Haring, Douglas G. "Is 'Culture' Definable?" *American Sociological Review* (1949), 14:26–32.

Herskovits, Melville J. "The Processes of Cultural Change," in Ralph Linton (ed.), *The Science of Man in the World Crisis*. New York: Columbia University Press, 1945.

Klemm, Gustav. *Allgemeine Cultur-Geschichte der Menschheit*. 10 vols. Leipzig, 1843–52.

———. *Allgemeine Culturwissenschaft*. 2 vols. Leipzig, 1854–55.

Kluckhohn, Clyde, and Kelly, William H. "The Concept of Culture," in Ralph Linton (ed.), *The Science of Man in the World Crisis*. New York: Columbia University Press, 1945.

Kroeber, A. L. *Anthropology*. New York: Harcourt, Brace and Company, 1948.

———, and Kluckhohn, Clyde. *Culture: A Critical Review of Concepts and Definitions*. Cambridge: Harvard University, Papers of the Peabody Museum of American Archaeology and Ethnology (1952), Vol. 47, No. 1.

Linton, Ralph. *The Study of Man*. New York: D. Appleton-Century Company, 1936.

——— (ed.). *The Science of Man in the World Crisis*. New York: Columbia University Press, 1945.

Lowie, Robert H. *Primitive Society*. New York: Boni and Liveright, 1920.

Radcliffe-Brown, A. R. "On Social Structure," *Journal of the Royal Anthropological Institute* (1940), 70:1–12.

Spiro, Melford E. "Culture and Personality," *Psychiatry* (1951), 14:19–46.

Tylor, Edward B. *Primitive Culture*. London: John Murray, 1871; fifth ed., 1913, reprinted 1929.

———. *Anthropology, an Introduction to the Study of Man and Civilization*. London: Macmillan and Company, 1881; London and New York: D. Appleton and Company, 1916.

White, Leslie A. *The Science of Culture*. New York: Farrar, Straus and Company, 1949.

———. Review of *Culture: A Critical Review of Concepts and Definitions*, by A. L. Kroeber and Clyde Kluckhohn, *American Anthropologist* (1954), 56:461–468.

———. *The Evolution of Culture*. New York: McGraw-Hill Book Company, 1959.

———. "The Concept of Culture," *American Anthropologist* (1959), 61:227–251.

———. "Symboling: A Kind of Behavior," *The Journal of Psychology* (1962), 53:311–317.

Whitehead, Alfred N. *Introduction to Mathematics*. New York: Henry Holt and Company, 1911.

CHAPTER VI

Intraception:
Evolution of a Concept

Daniel J. Levinson,
Myron R. Sharaf,
and Doris C. Gilbert

Editor's Introduction

The authors of this chapter include among their current interests the development of a social psychology that combines dynamic personality theory with sociological and anthropological elements. One of the books along these lines which they have in progress concerns "intraception," or what they refer to as "psychological-mindedness." In this chapter they consider the nature, and particularly the development, of this conception and its relevance for social psychology.

Henry A. Murray invented the term "intraception" as an attempt to refine and to systematize some earlier psychological distinctions—particularly James's concepts of the tender- and tough-minded personalities, and Jung's concepts of introversion and extroversion. The authors define "intraception" as "the disposition, expressed via various modalities, to emphasize and to differentiate psychological aspects of oneself and of the external world." They discuss intraception at length in a somewhat psychoanalytical perspective. Referring to the fundamental role that "intraception" had in the development of the now-classic social psychological study *The Authoritarian Personality*, the authors consider in particular its antithetical form—"anti-intraception"—as a central and pervasively manifested aspect of authoritarianism.

By way of concrete illustration, the authors speak of the role of "intraception" as a cardinal element in the social psychology of the mental hospital, and its emergence therein at several levels of theoretical analysis, such as the culture, social structure, and occupational roles of the organization, as well as the personality structures of the hospital's personnel. This consideration of the authors' research in the setting of the mental hospital exemplifies the "new" social psychology with which they are concerned.

The authors perceive a growing importance in our scientific and cultural world for this psychological element, particularly as man seeks to cope with the hazards of an affluent—and an increasingly automated—society. In line with their emphasis on social psychology, they stress the role of personality in social life and cultural dynamics.

They would contend that there is, in the conception of the actionists, an "interpenetration" involved between personality and socio-cultural dynamics, and that more consideration should be given to the analysis of this interpenetration.

One of the major attempts of the authors of this chapter is to present a developmental perspective of conceptualization. Their presentation, like most of the others, is primarily analytical. It has the distinct feature, however, not only of confining itself to a single conceptual element as did two of the others, but also, by so doing, of attempting to describe the process and the dynamics whereby concepts develop and come to be, as well as the consequences (both practical and theoretical) which result thereby. The authors state clearly that concepts are not mechanically or electronically produced. Each is conceived necessarily by human progenitors, and in its evolution is nourished through a very complex process which involves, among many other things, a host of sociological and psychological dynamics and processes that rarely are acknowledged in treatises on scientific theory and methodology. Among such factors that go into hindering or facilitating the evolution of a concept as a step in the process of theoretical explanation are the values, motivations, and implicit assumptions of the theorist, and the rules of academic etiquette.

These authors, in elaborating on some of the notions introduced in the preceding chapters, present a social psychology of conceptual work. Concepts, theories, and explanations arise in a particular ideological climate, and the nature of the prevalent conceptual and theoretical orientations will determine in part the evolutionary course for a specific concept. More specifically, they speak of, and ask for consideration of: (1) the socio-cultural milieu in which the scientific enterprise is carried forward, and whether or not the intellectual climate either favors or opposes the psychological and sociological perspectives; (2) the continuing interplay of a specific concept with the broader theoretical context in which it is employed—in other words, the fads and vogues of the time in which it originates, such as a period of "intraceptive" or "extraceptive" thinking and theorizing; and (3) the modes of research by which it is studied.

One of the points stressed in this chapter is the relationship between the process of conceptualization and that of measurement for a particular concept. These authors contend that it is better to begin the theoretical process with clearly defined concepts as opposed to operational definitions, then to find ways of translating these into terms that facilitate empirical observations and measurements, and next to maintain a continuing dialectic between the concept and its findings. Theoretically, they maintain, one moves back and forth between concepts and sets of empirical variables, while methodologically (in the case of intraception, for example) one moves between the intuitive analysis of clinical materials and the use of structured tests measuring specific variables. These authors feel that conceptualization for too long has been conceived predominantly in terms of measurement, which has outstripped the work on conceptualization. This scientific measurement, moreover, has been concerned to a greater extent with the reliability rather than the validity of its techniques as well as of its referents. Chapter VII, as we shall see, will offer a position in contrast to these views.

The term "intraception" was invented by Henry A. Murray. It is first described in his seminal work, *Explorations in Personality*—a book that offers one of the few imaginative, comprehensive, and distinctively American theories of personality, and one that has helped to define and to legitimize the field of dynamic psychology in our academic establishment. In this book, published in 1938, Murray briefly defines "intraception," gives it a lengthy theoretical formulation, describes various techniques for its measurement, and presents some data on its relations to other variables.

We see in Murray's *Explorations*, then, the birth of the concept of intraception. We use the metaphor of birth deliberately. A concept is not produced mechanically (nor even electronically, despite the prevalence of this metaphor in many current writings) by an impersonal intellectual apparatus. A concept is *conceived*, and nourished, and in time presented to the outside world, by a procreator who is fully human. Its creation is a complex matter in which many psychological processes are involved. Every concept has near-relatives and ancestors extending far back in our intellectual history. It goes through numerous vicissitudes of development, and, if it has sufficient vitality and luck, it will generate conceptual progeny of its own. Its evolution is influenced by psychological and socio-cultural factors that are rarely acknowledged in treatises on scientific theory or methodology.

We shall attempt here to examine the concept of intraception from a socio-psychological point of view. Clearly, our interest goes beyond the explicit focus of this Symposium. We are concerned in part, but only in part, with the conceptual definition of intraception. For one thing, it is more appropriate to use the plural, to speak of conceptual definition*s*. Since the definitions are modified over time, and among different investigators, it is instructive to take a developmental perspective. We must take into account the continuing interplay of the specific concept with the broader *theoretical contexts* in which it is used, with the *modes of research* by which it is studied, and with the *cultural* *climate* in which the scientific enterprise is carried forward. In the process of conceptual evolution we may expect to find evidence of reason and unreason, scientific principle and academic etiquette, the constructive and the distorting effects of human values, and, hopefully, the slow emergence of more adequate theory and more valid findings. To begin, let us turn to Murray.

The Initial Formulation of Intraception

Murray[1] offers the following brief definition of "intraception": "The dominance of feelings, fantasies, speculations, aspirations. An imaginative, subjective human outlook. Romantic action." Intraception encompasses a variety of more specific characteristics such as psychological-mindedness, self-awareness, and empathy. In contrast, "extraception" is "the disposition to adhere to the obviously substantial facts. A practical, 'down-to-earth' skeptical attitude. . . ."

Murray tells us that he is trying to refine and to systematize distinctions made earlier—for example, William James's concepts of "tender-minded" and "tough-minded,"[2] and Jung's concepts of "introversion" and "extroversion."[3] He finds great value in the distinction between introversive and extroversive tendencies, but he is critical of the notion that the introvert and the extrovert are fundamental and dichotomous types. Murray suggests that several independent tendencies are involved here, and that we shall do better if we shift from the overly inclusive and simplistic typology to a more careful analysis of these independent tendencies. Intraception is one of them.

While offering intraception as a narrower and more manageable concept than introversion or tender-mindedness, Murray acknowledges that it, too, poses serious definitional problems. He makes clear that he himself is not satisfied with his conceptualization. It is remarkable how few efforts have been made to advance upon his promising start, even by those who have subsequently developed new measuring devices. We find here a recurrent theme in American psychology: the work on measurement—

with emphasis more upon reliability than validity—tends to outstrip the work on conceptualization.

In Murray's over-all scheme of personality, intraception is listed as a trait. The term "trait" is used so diversely in the psychological literature that we shall not use it here. Let us use another of Murray's terms and speak of intraception as a "disposition," a relatively generalized and enduring tendency that is reflected in various modes of psychological functioning. The intraceptive disposition is expressed in the individual's outlook on life and in his specific attitudes; it is evidenced in his ways of thinking, apperceiving, feeling, valuing, judging, and acting. To conceive of it solely as an attitude, or solely as a mode of action, is to be overly narrow and to overlook its operation as a more central, organizing disposition.

Murray points to many facets of intraception.[4] The highly intraceptive person is subjective, imaginative, sensitive, intuitive, and psychologically penetrating. His subjectivity, and his interest in the subjective states of others, may lead him to err grossly in his apperceptions.

> The intraceptive person who becomes conscious and critical of his own psychology may learn to correct for the projections which commonly occur, and by constant practice his interpretations of others may become reasonably reliable. The extraceptive person, on the other hand, by not using the process of [empathic] "participation," permits it to remain in an undeveloped state. . . . He will be deficient in his interpretation of the more irrational phases of human experience: dreams, fantasies, the play and perversities of children . . . the poetical and metaphysical utterances of adults, the vagaries of neurotic and psychotic patients.[5]

The extraceptor is not tuned to his own or others' inner life. He tends to explain human events "in terms of bodily appetites, economic pressures and social custom."[6] He prefers the tangible, the concrete, the practical. The intraceptor, by contrast, tends "to explain physical occurrences as resultants of energic processes and to interpret human action in terms of motivating forces."[7] The behavior of the intraceptive person is often a catharsis or a self-dramatization, which is not always adapted to the imagined goal, though it may have considerable inner value. . . . [He] cannot abide a cold, indifferent human climate. . . . Being more aware of his feelings than the extraceptor, he is quick to realize what is humanly wrong in existing social conditions. Thus he is apt to sympathize with the individual rather than with the group (authorities). His temperament is that of an artist and at some point one can always find tenderness, wonder and reverence.[8]

We shall speak, then, of the *intraceptive syndrome:* a structure having motivational, affective, cognitive, valuational, and other aspects. Murray has given the outlines of this structure and has pointed out many of its specific features, but he has not identified its primary components. Nor has anyone else. The components are, it may be supposed, dynamically related factors that inter-correlate significantly but imperfectly. We conceive of intraception as a more or less unified disposition, possessed to different degrees by different persons, while at the same time exhibiting diversity and variation in its internal character. We can say that one person is more intraceptive than another. We can say also that two persons, similar in over-all degree of intraception, nonetheless differ in particular components—one being, perhaps, more empathic in his relationships with others, while the second is more able to express esthetically his own dimly experienced moods and fantasies. An analogy may be drawn to intelligence, which varies both in degree and in patterning.

These thoughts about intraception as an ego structure or syndrome lead us beyond the work of Murray. Before moving on, however, we offer the following comments concerning the social psychology of conceptual work.

(1) Intraception was an important idea to Murray partly because of the conflicts emerging in the thirties between intra-ceptive and other viewpoints in psychology. The dominant ori-entation in American psychology in 1930 was a singularly extra-ceptive—indeed, anti-intraceptive—form of behaviorism. The thirties witnessed the initial development and the legitimation of

more intraceptive orientations. These included dynamic personality theory (stemming primarily from psychoanalysis),[9] Tolman's cognitive learning theory, and, to a lesser extent, the renewed interest in the earlier views of men such as James and McDougall, who had been largely swept aside in the upsurgence of extreme behaviorism during the twenties.

Murray's conceptualization of intraception can be seen from several perspectives. Viewed one way, it was a contribution to personality theory. In another way, it represented the personal efforts of a highly creative psychologist to orchestrate his own intraceptive talents within a more scientific, rigorous approach to theory and research. Finally, it enabled him, and then others, better to understand the nature of psychological theories; Murray's distinction between "centralist" and "peripheralist" theories, in which intraception and extraception are key concepts, played a major part in ending the monopoly of "peripheralism" and in broadening the horizons of psychology during the late thirties and forties.

(2) It is clear that Murray made a great effort to prevent the personal meaning and value that intraception had for him from complicating his formulation of it. In this effort he was largely but not entirely successful. For example, he includes as intrinsic features of intraception, personal characteristics such as religious-metaphysical interests, idealism, esthetic sensitivity, and social non-conformity. To include these as components of intraception is to over-extend and diffuse the concept. They are more properly regarded as independent variables whose relation to intraception merits study. Murray, placing a strong value on intraception, has "built in" to his definition of it certain virtues that may not in fact belong. The influence of the theorist's wishes, values, and implicit assumptions on his theorizing is a general problem in psychology, including fields far removed from personality theory. We call attention here not to a special phenomenon, but rather to the unusual opportunity that Murray affords us, by his openness, to further our understanding of this problem. We, too, place a strong value on intraception. We try to keep this preference from becoming bias by holding in mind the dilemmas, the

costs as well as the gains, of having this disposition to a high degree.

(3) In the almost thirty years since Murray first wrote about intraception, its social and psychological salience has increased remarkably. The mid-twentieth century has been variously described as the "post-Freudian age," "the age of anxiety" (or, at least, the age in which man is trying to confront his anxieties more directly), and the age in which the image of *psychological man* is superseding earlier and more restricting images of economic and political man. It is no doubt an over-simplification to characterize any period so monothematically. Still, it seems clear that the rise in intraception represents one of the major themes in the socio-cultural revolution of our times. Witness the rapid growth of dynamic psychology and psychiatry, and of the "mental health" professions. Witness the development of psychologically more sophisticated viewpoints in education, penology, industry, international relations, the Peace Corps, and in the Supreme Court decisions against segregation. And witness the cultural developments in such fields as literature, music, and philosophy.

Anti-Intraception and Authoritarianism

Let us move on now to further work on intraception. The next major development is to be found in the *The Authoritarian Personality*,[10] a study carried out during the period 1943–48 and published in 1950. It is commonly recognized that this study was strongly influenced by psychoanalytic theory and by the clinical formulations of Reich[11] and Fromm.[12] Its debt to Murray is less well known and understood. His personological approach, his concepts, and his multiform methodology in personality assessment were of fundamental importance.

Despite the widespread use of the Authoritarianism (F) Scale in recent years, very little interesting work has been done on the nature and development of authoritarianism. One reason for this is that the contemporary climate of research does not foster the Murrayan methodology in which extensive measurement of personality variables is combined with intensive clinical study of single cases.

Intraception appears in its obverse form in the theory of the authoritarian personality. A primary component of authoritarianism is *anti-intraception*, that is, active rejection of an intraceptive orientation. This is by no means the same thing as extraception. A person may be extraceptive in the sense, say, that he does not resonate to the subtleties of private experience and emotional life, and that his preferred dimensions of experience and action are more physicalistic, impersonal, or rationalistic. To be anti-intraceptive, however, implies something more: an anxiety when confronted with deep passions and feelings, a motivated objection to looking within oneself or others, a fear that immediately beneath the surface of conscious experience and rational behavior lurk tendencies that must at all costs be kept out of awareness.

Anti-intraception was revealed, as part of a broader authoritarian syndrome, by various clinical methods including the semi-structured interview, the Thematic Apperception Test, and the Projective Question Test. It is represented, at an ideological level, in the tendency to hold an overly idealized view of some individuals, groups, and institutions, and an overly deprecating view of many others. The highly anti-intraceptive person finds it difficult to acknowledge, indeed to conceive of, moral ambiguity and motivational conflict. He can hardly imagine that a "good" person should have "evil" desires, that a child can feel both love and hate toward a parent, or that a "rational" being can, for purposes both serious and playful, engage in fantastic imaginings.

The relation between intraception and anti-intraception is not a simple one. A low degree of anti-intraception is not necessarily associated with a high degree of intraception. In our research on psychiatric residents, for example, we found that most residents in our sample earned low scores on measures of anti-intraception and authoritarianism.[13] At the same time, they varied considerably in their capacity for empathy with patients, in their ability to grasp a psychodynamic approach, and in the extent and depth of their self-awareness.

Thus, it is apparent that intraception and anti-intraception are not bipolar opposites of a single, uni-dimensional continuum. Intraception is inhibited by anti-intraception, but it does not necessarily flourish when anti-intraception is lacking. Between the active wanting and seeking out of intraceptive modalities, and the active rejection of these, lies a wide range of indifference, ambivalence, and preference for other modes of experience and knowledge. Intraception, like other dispositions, is of special importance only in some personalities.

We need not pursue the concept of anti-intraception further, except to mention that its place as a central and pervasively manifested aspect of authoritarianism has been confirmed by much recent research.

Intraception in the Mental Hospital and in the Mental Health Occupations

Our interest in intraception was given impetus several years ago by our research on the mental hospital as a social organization and on its various component groupings such as psychiatrists, nurses, and patients.[14] The *Zeitgeist* of the modern mental hospital is strongly permeated by the theories of psychoanalysis and dynamic psychiatry, and by the personality characteristics commonly found in those who espouse such theories. Intraception is a key element in the social psychology of the hospital. It emerges at several levels of theoretical analysis: culture, social structure, occupational role, and personality. A brief comment on each of these must suffice.

(1) By the term *culture* we refer to the basic, integrating values of a collectivity, values that underlie its specific norms and practices. In the culture of the mental hospital, *intraceptive values* are of central importance. Heavy emphasis is given to empathy, psychological perceptiveness, warmth, and insight. The psychological meaning of behavior is often considered more important than its concrete form or effects. Hospital policies and ward practices are evaluated primarily in terms of their psychological value for patients and staff. The most valued therapeutic goals are those involving greater self-understanding and self-

expression by patients. Similarly, the characteristics most admired in staff members include self-awareness, lack of pretense, and compassion.

(2) Intraception is found again in the *social structure* of the hospital. Social structure includes features of organization such as the recruitment of new members, training in specific roles, technology, and sanctions (modes of social control). Intraception plays a part in all of these. Intraceptive qualities are sought for in the recruitment of staff at all levels. The training of resident psychiatrists, nursing students, clinical psychologists, and others gives special emphasis to the development of intraceptive skills. Psychotherapy is the favored technology. Problems of communication are widely recognized and worked on (though rarely solved). An intraceptive stance is taken even toward the structural handling of sanctions: rewards and punishments are defined more in the currency of emotions than in tangible, material terms. At its best, the social structure of the mental hospital fosters a degree of openness, intimacy, non-punitiveness, and responsibility rarely found in other settings. At its worst, it produces an immobilizing self-consciousness, mutual dependency, and indecisiveness.

(3) The relevance of intraception for the various *occupational roles* is implied in the above comments about the hospital culture and social structure. Staff members of every occupation are expected to take a therapeutic stance, rather than a conventionally judgmental one, in their dealings with patients. The more professionalized occupations provide formal teaching, and a broad professional ideology, in which intraceptive values and skills are emphasized; for individual staff members who are committed to this viewpoint, the development of intraception is both a professional goal and a personal aspiration.[15] What is involved, then, is not merely the learning of professional knowledge and techniques, but the development of the *self*. These roles require an unusually high degree of personal commitment. They invoke a heavy burden of self-investment, and at the same time they hold forth the promise of self-fulfillment. In this respect, as in many others, the demands and opportunities of hospital life are similar

for patients and for staff. The patient may be seen also as having an occupational role in the hospital. He, too, is asked to give fully of himself and is promised in return a basic change in the self. His readiness and his capacity to meet this challenge, to engage in the varied kinds of intraceptive work that it requires, play a crucial part in determining the course and outcome of his hospital career.[16]

(4) The above considerations lead directly to a fourth level of analysis—that of the *personality* of the individual hospital member. We have said that anyone entering the modern mental hospital, whether as staff member or as patient, is faced with many intraceptive requirements and opportunities. These stem from the socio-cultural system of the hospital and from role definitions given by his particular occupation. However, intraception is not merely a feature of his environment. It is also present, in greater or lesser degree, in the personality of the newly entering member. It is, in other words, a *role-relevant personality disposition*, one that will strongly influence his evolving role and his further personal and professional development. As noted above, the interpenetration of role and personality is especially great in a setting that seeks to induce great personal commitment from its members. Some members achieve only minimal commitment or, rejecting what is offered, form a kind of negative commitment. More often, new members have the motivation and values needed to sustain them in the work of self-generated change.

Thus, from the viewpoint of the hospital, intraception is a required personality characteristic; it operates in the recruitment, socialization, and performance of members. And, within the individual, the nature and degree of intraceptiveness has major implications: it influences his definition of occupational goals, his selection of a place to work, his development of role commitment, and the uses he makes of the hospital experience.

Toward the Definition and Empirical Study of Intraception

It would take us too far afield here to explore further our work on the interrelations of personality, role, and organizational system. Let us, instead, return to the concept of intraception. We have proposed earlier that intraception be regarded as a relatively unified yet internally complex disposition. What is the nature of this disposition? We shall begin with a one-sentence conceptual definition and then develop a more extensive formulation.[17] *Intraception is the disposition, expressed through various modalities, to emphasize and differentiate psychological aspects of oneself and of the external world.* Let us consider briefly the key terms in this definition. What we have to say here will of necessity be incomplete, because of time limitations and because we are still working on the difficult theoretical issues involved.

(1) The focus of intraception is on *psychological aspects*. This is perhaps the crucial term in our definition. It refers, first of all, to the most personal qualities of human experience—feelings, wishes, the private meanings and fantasies that so often accompany more logical rational thought. The prototypic "psychological aspects" are experiences such as delight, joy, love, awe, tenderness, longing, rage, passion, fear, and guilt—experiences in which clearly or vaguely sensed feelings, desires, and meanings are intertwined. Perhaps the central aim of the intraceptive disposition is to know oneself and others in this elemental sense, and then to build upon the primary knowing in various ways such as writing poems, developing psychological theories, becoming an empathic friend or a shrewd manipulator of others. Whatever its further elaboration and its form of expression, the primary definitive content of intraception involves the raw materials of emotional experience and striving. The non-intraceptive person, on the other hand, is concerned with other, non-psychological aspects of himself and others—for example, with physical appearance, social status, or behavioral characteristics that he does not relate to the more inner-psychological qualities noted above.

(2) Intraception is reflected in both an *emphasis* upon and a

differentiation of psychological qualities. By "emphasis" we mean simply that the intraceptive person attends more strongly, and responds more actively, to the psychological aspects of self and outer world than to other aspects. "Differentiation" is expressed in one's grasp of the subtleties of personal experience; in a sense of the interconnectedness of seemingly disparate wishes and feelings; in the ability to make complex inferences regarding individual character and human relationships. Degree of differentiation clearly carries the implication of ability or skill. Indeed, "intraceptive intelligence" may be a heretofore neglected component of general intelligence; it has special relevance for one's capacity to pursue certain professional and artistic careers.

(3) The definition states that intraception is *expressed through various modalities*. One of these is valuing, that is, giving a high position in one's system of values to intraceptive pleasures and the pursuit of intraceptive goals. The intraceptive disposition is expressed as well through other modalities such as thinking, imagining, wanting, and behavioral striving.

Of particular importance are the *cognitive* modalities, that is, the ways in which one gains intraceptive knowledge (impressions, ideas, and theoretical or esthetic constructions) concerning the psychological aspects of the self and the external world. We are especially interested in two cognitive modes: (a) immediate apperceptive knowing; and (b) abstract intellectual knowing.

Apperceptive knowing is derived quite directly from immediate concrete experience. This might well be called "experiential" intraception. Directed toward oneself, it involves the capacity to experience vividly and richly, to be self-aware, to "know" in a concrete sense the nature of one's inner life and proclivities. The central concept here is "self-insight": openness to inner life; the readiness to acknowledge many aspects of the self, including both one's virtues and aspects that are value-violating and disturbing. Directed toward other persons, apperceptive knowing takes the varied forms of intuitive sensitivity, empathy, and a capacity to grasp the implicit language of emotional communication. The central concept here is empathy or *Einfühlung*, the ability to grasp and to share another's feelings. Apperceptive knowing, as a mode of intraception, is dramatically exemplified by certain clinicians (especially those who communicate well with psychotic patients), by poets such as Dylan Thomas, and by novelists such as Dostoevsky. Directed toward inanimate nature, it is expressed in highly personalized experiences such as those described in the poems and novels of D. H. Lawrence, Hardy, and Pasternak.

What we have called *intellectual knowing*, on the other hand, is a more abstract, conceptual form of intraception, several steps removed from immediate apperceptual experience. It involves the construction of psychological concepts and makes greater use of reasoned inference and abstract thought. This modality produces, as it were, knowledge *about* psychological matters rather than knowledge *of* such matters. It is sometimes found, in relatively pure form, among students in clinical psychology and psychiatry who have strong intraceptive values and theoretical interests but who have not been ready to undergo the pains of more immediate intraceptive experience. The ego-defensive process involved here is "intellectualization of affect."

The distinction between experiential and intellectual modalities is of course an analytic one. Most persons can, to some degree, make use of both. The development of one will in part facilitate the development of the other. In the training of psychotherapists, for example, we draw upon both the experiential and the intellectual modalities and seek to integrate them. The good therapist must be intraceptive both in his immediate grasp of "how it is" with the patient and himself, and in his ability to understand and develop abstract psychological concepts and generalizations. At the same time, we must ask whether the two modalities are, in some ultimate sense, contradictory or mutually inhibiting. The goal of synthesizing the capacity for intense personal experience and the capacity for systematic intellectual work is one of man's noblest visions. As with other such visions, it is worth holding and struggling for even if, in the end, it should prove unattainable.

(4) Finally, we have identified intraception as a *disposition*. As such, it is a relatively unified but internally complex structure,

one that is relatively stable and not easily changed. This formulation, once again, is tentative and in need of empirical validation. We know very little about the internal structure of intraception or about its susceptibility to change. To say that it is relatively stable is not to say that it is absolutely static. Through our experiences as teachers and investigators in a clinical setting we have formed two equally strong impressions: first, that it is extremely difficult to aid a student in becoming more intraceptive, when the initial disposition is of limited strength; and second, that some students, who start with seemingly minimal intraceptive motivation and talent, blossom remarkably in an intensely intraceptive milieu. However, this change goes beyond the simple learning of formal concepts and techniques; it is a true "blossoming," a process of personal-professional growth.

To summarize, let us restate in slightly expanded form the definition given earlier. Intraception is an internally complex, relatively stable personality disposition. The primary aim of this disposition is to emphasize and to differentiate the psychological aspects of persons and events. It may be expressed through various modalities: apperception, intellection, imagination, desires, values, strivings and life goals. It may be directed toward oneself, toward other persons, toward collective human affairs (as in the intraceptive study of history or sociology), toward inanimate nature, or the like.

This is, of course, a conceptual definition, not an "operational" one. We subscribe to the view that it is best to start with a conceptual definition, then to find ways of translating it into terms that facilitate empirical observation and measurement, and then to maintain a continuing dialectic between concept and findings.

It is beyond the scope of this chapter to discuss in detail our empirical measures and data. We shall conclude, however, with a few comments on this aspect of our work. Our methodological approach combines the study of the individual case with the development of multiple measuring devices. Our sources of data include: (1) accounts of the lives of markedly intraceptive men such as Freud, Proust, D. H. Lawrence, and Eugene O'Neill; (2)

ethnographic data on intraceptive cultures; (3) studies of college
students, psychiatrists, and others, including ourselves; and (4)
the measurement of specific variables by means of quantitative
ratings of clinical material as well as newly developed scales and
tests. Theoretically, then, we move back and forth between
concepts and sets of empirical variables. Methodologically, we
move between the intuitive analysis of clinical materials, the
quantitative rating of clinical materials, and the use of structured
tests measuring specific variables.[18]

One of our techniques is a scale that measures Acceptance or
Rejection of Intraceptive Values. Another is the Self-Deception
Scale, which deals with the tendency to deny, or to acknowledge,
value-violating and conflictual aspects of the self. A third device
is the Self-Description Test, in which the person is asked simply
to describe himself in a paragraph or two. The responses are
rated on a 1–7 scale by means of a specially devised scoring
manual. The cues used in assigning a higher (more intraceptive)
score include: vivid, subtle description of inner life; distinction
between public and private, surface and depth aspects of the self;
acknowledgment of inner contradictions, of the coexistence of
valued and disvalued characteristics within oneself; and sense of
curiosity and wonder about the workings of the psyche. Finally,
we have made over-all ratings of intraception based on the
analysis of several-hour interviews with subjects who also took
the above tests.

The intercorrelations among the various measures are of the
order of .3 to .6—evidence suggesting that some unifying factor
is involved, and that diversity is present as well. It is too soon to
conclude that intraception is best conceived of as a single structure with partially independent components, or, alternatively,
that there are several distinct intraceptive modalities, each quite
independent of the others.

Since our several measures were positively correlated, we
combined them into a single composite index of "over-all intraception," in order to explore its antecedents and correlates. Two
findings will be noted for illustrative purposes. First, a high

degree of intraception tends *not* to coexist with a high degree of conscious self-esteem. Intraception involves not only self-awareness but also *self-criticism*. The intraceptive person, more attuned than others to inner contradictions and dilemmas, more ready to confront the disparity between aspiration and reality, bears a greater than average burden of guilt and self-doubt. Though he may make constructive use of this burden, the personal cost is often considerable, particularly among adolescents and young adults.

A second finding concerns the early family experience of intraceptive college students. Through semi-structured interviews we found that intraceptive subjects, significantly more than others, had experienced a certain kind of family constellation. This constellation included a pattern of *alliance-creating confiding* between mother and son. In childhood the overt relationship of these boys with their mothers was emotionally intense and intimate. The mother would confide in the son regarding her most personal feelings, including those toward the father, who was somewhat devalued and excluded from the primary mother-son coalition. This constellation is to be found in the family backgrounds of highly intraceptive writers such as D. H. Lawrence and Eugene O'Neill. It seems to be more common in Jewish culture than in many others. The son's experience of illicit intimacy, in an alliance with mother against father, has far-reaching developmental significance in the formation of an intraceptive orientation. We venture to suggest, and certainly to hope, that this is not a necessary condition for the development of intraception. In any case, much more needs to be known about the social and psychological conditions under which intraception can flourish.

In conclusion, we venture to predict that the concept of intraception, so imaginatively conceived and initially nurtured by Murray, has survived the stresses of infancy and will be fostered by others. The concept has notable relevance for the scientific and cultural world in which we live, and it will become increasingly important as we seek to cope with the hazards of an affluent, and more and more automated, society. As one of man's most distinctive characteristics, an essential part of his "humanness," intraception merits our interest.

NOTES

1. Henry A. Murray, *Explorations in Personality* (New York: Oxford University Press, 1938), p. 148.

2. William James, *Pragmatism* (New York: Longmans, Green, and Company, 1907).

3. Carl Jung, *Analytical Psychology* (London: Balliere, 1922).

4. Murray, *op. cit.*, pp. 210–216.

5. *Ibid.*, pp. 213–214.

6. *Ibid.*, p. 214.

7. *Ibid.*, p. 215.

8. *Ibid.*, pp. 215–216.

9. For example, the work of clinicians such as Fromm, Sullivan, Horney, and Kardiner; also academic personality theorists such as Allport and Lewin. A systematic review is given by C. Hall and G. Lindzey, *Theories of Personality* (New York: John Wiley and Sons, 1957).

10. T. W. Adorno, Else Frenkel-Brunswik, D. J. Levinson, and R. Nevitt Sanford, *The Authoritarian Personality* (New York: Harper and Brothers, 1950).

11. Wilhelm Reich, *The Mass Psychology of Fascism* (New York: Orgone Institute Press, 1946).

12. Erich Fromm, *Escape from Freedom* (New York: Farrar and Rinehart, 1941).

13. Myron R. Sharaf and Daniel J. Levinson, "Patterns of Ideology and Role-Definition Among Psychiatric Residents," in M. Greenblatt, D. J. Levinson, and R. H. Williams (eds.), *The Patient and the Mental Hospital* (Glencoe: The Free Press, 1957), pp. 263–285.

14. See M. Greenblatt, D. J. Levinson, and R. H. Williams (eds.), *The Patient and the Mental Hospital* (Glencoe: The Free Press, 1957), especially Chapters 1, 3, 11, 15, and 20. Also D. C. Gilbert, "Ideologies Concerning Mental Illness: A Socio-Psychological Study of Mental Hospital Personnel" (unpublished doctoral dissertation, Radcliffe College, 1954); Daniel J. Levinson, "Role, Personality, and Social Structure in the Organizational Setting," *Journal of Abnormal and Social Psychology*, LVIII (1959), 170–180; and Myron R. Sharaf and Daniel J. Levinson, "The Quest for Omnipotence in Professional

Training: The Case of the Psychiatric Resident," *Psychiatry*, XXVII (1964), 135–149.

15. For an account of this developmental process in psychiatric residents, see Sharaf and Levinson, "Patterns of Ideology and Role-Definition Among Psychiatric Residents" and "The Quest for Omnipotence in Professional Training." For the case of senior psychiatrists who are hospital administrators and professors, see R. L. Hodgson, D. J. Levinson, and A. Zaleznik, *The Executive Role Constellation* (Cambridge: Division of Research, Harvard Business School, 1965).

16. D. J. Levinson and E. B. Gallagher, *Patienthood in the Mental Hospital* (Boston: Houghton Mifflin Company, 1964).

17. This conceptualization is a direct outgrowth of the one presented by Sharaf in a study of college students. Myron R. Sharaf, "An Approach to the Theory and Measurement of Intraception" (unpublished doctoral dissertation, Widener Library, Harvard University, 1960).

18. For a more extensive discussion of variables and methods, see Sharaf, *ibid*.

Suggested Readings

Adorno, T. W., Frenkel-Brunswik, Else, Levinson, D. J., and Sanford, R. Nevitt. *The Authoritarian Personality*. New York: Harper and Brothers, 1950.

Allport, Gordon W. *Personality: A Psychological Interpretation*. New York: Henry Holt and Company, 1937.

Barron, F. *Creativity and Psychological Health*. Princeton: D. Van Nostrand Company, 1963.

Bronfenbrenner, U., Harding, J., and Gallway, M. "The Measurement of Skill in Social Perception," in D. McClelland, A. Baldwin, U. Bronfenbrenner, and F. Strodbeck, *Talent and Society*. Princeton: D. Van Nostrand Company, 1958.

Dymond, R. "A Scale for the Measurement of Empathic Ability," *Journal of Consulting Psychology* (1949), 13:127–133.

Freud, Sigmund. "Constructions in Analysis," in *Collected Papers*. London: The Hogarth Press, 1950.

Fromm, Erich. *Escape from Freedom*. New York: Farrar and Rinehart, 1941.

Gilbert, Doris C. "Ideologies Concerning Mental Illness: A Socio-Psychological Study of Mental Hospital Personnel," unpublished doctoral dissertation, Radcliffe College, 1954.

Greenblatt, M., Levinson, D. J., and Williams, R. H. (eds.). *The Patient and the Mental Hospital*. Glencoe: The Free Press, 1957.

Hall, C., and Lindzey, G. *Theories of Personality.* New York: John Wiley and Sons, 1957.

Hodgson, Richard L., Levinson, D. J., and Zaleznik, A. *The Executive Role Constellation.* Cambridge: Division of Research, Harvard Business School, 1965.

Holt, Robert R., and Luborsky, Lester. *Personality Patterns of Psychiatrists.* New York: Basic Books, Inc., 1958.

Horney, Karen. *The Neurotic Personality of Our Time.* New York: W. W. Norton and Company, 1937.

James, William. *Pragmatism.* New York: Longmans, Green, and Company, 1907.

Jung, Carl. *Analytical Psychology.* London: Balliere, 1922.

Kardiner, Abram. *The Individual and His Society.* New York: Columbia University Press, 1939.

Katz, R. L. *Empathy: Its Nature and Uses.* Glencoe: The Free Press, 1963.

Kris, E. "On Some Vicissitudes of Insight in Psychoanalysis," *International Journal of Psychoanalysis* (1946), 37:445–455.

Levinson, Daniel J. "Role, Personality, and Social Structure in the Organizational Setting," *Journal of Abnormal and Social Psychology* (1959), 58:170–180.

———, and Gallagher, E. B. *Patienthood in the Mental Hospital.* Boston: Houghton Mifflin Company, 1964.

Lewin, Kurt. *Dynamic Theory of Personality.* New York: McGraw-Hill Book Company, 1935.

McClelland, D., Baldwin, A., Bronfenbrenner, U., and Strodbeck, F. *Talent and Society.* Princeton: D. Van Nostrand Company, 1958.

McDougall, William. *The Energies of Men.* New York: Charles Scribner's Sons, 1933.

Murray, Henry A. *Explorations in Personality.* New York: Oxford University Press, 1938.

Reich, Wilhelm. *The Mass Psychology of Fascism.* New York: Orgone Institute Press, 1946.

Rogers, C. "Towards a Theory of Creativity," in H. Anderson (ed.), *Creativity and Its Cultivation.* New York: Harper and Brothers, 1959.

Schafer, R. "Generative Empathy in the Treatment Situation," *Psychoanalytic Quarterly* (1959), 28:342–373.

Sharaf, Myron R. "An Approach to the Theory and Measurement of Intraception," unpublished doctoral dissertation, Widener Library, Harvard University, 1960.

———, and Levinson, Daniel J. "Patterns of Ideology and Role-

Definition Among Psychiatric Residents," in M. Greenblatt, D. J. Levinson, and R. H. Williams (eds.), *The Patient and the Mental Hospital*. Glencoe: The Free Press, 1957.

—— and ——. "The Quest for Omnipotence in Professional Training: The Case of the Psychiatric Resident," *Psychiatry* (1964), 27:135–149.

Sullivan, Harry Stack. *Collected Works*. 2 vols. New York: W. W. Norton and Company, 1965.

Tolman, Edward C. *Purposive Behavior in Animals and Men*. New York: Appleton-Century-Crofts, 1932. (Reprinted by University of California Press, 1949.)

Witkin, H., Dyk, R., Faterson, H. F., Goodenough, D. R., and Karp, S. A. *Psychological Differentiation, Studies of Development*. New York: John Wiley and Sons, 1962.

CHAPTER **VII**

Concept Formation and Measurement in the Behavioral Sciences: Some Historical Observations

Paul F. Lazarsfeld

Editor's Introduction

Quite fortunately, this next presentation takes up where the last chapter terminated. Once a conception has been formulated, then what does the scientist do with it? More specifically, how can a concept be translated into an empirical measurement? How, for example, would one go about an empirical verification of something such as "intraception"? In this chapter, which discusses the relationship between conceptualization and empirical research, an answer is offered to questions such as these.

Professor Paul F. Lazarsfeld is regarded as one of the outstanding methodological theorists in the field of sociology. Much of his time and interest have been devoted to the construction of quantitative methods for the measurement of social phenomena. Here in an historical context he offers some observations on this aspect of the scientific process. His general concern is to show the relationship between substantive problems and their methodological analysis.

Lazarsfeld's basic thesis is that concept formation and measurement in the behavioral sciences exhibit special difficulties. These can be met by a variety of procedures, but only a careful analysis of the several methods can clarify the problem itself. Essentially, his intention here is to analyze one special method by which it is possible to make what he calls "inferential classifications." The procedure he discusses is called "latent structure analysis." His presentation takes on "the character of a slowly unfolding story." First, he reviews some selected work of scientists who perceived the analytical problem and discussed it from the different points of view of their disciplines; then he examines more recent methods of its application in the behavioral sciences. Using this historical orientation he is able to show the progressive crystallization of his problem area—the nucleus of which refers to "inferential concepts" and the role of probability in concept formation.

The starting point of this presentation is a discussion among psychologists. They were the first of the behavioral scientists to be concerned systematically with the logic of their empirical procedures. Moreover, the psychological situation furnishes a paradigm for the other behavioral disciplines, since the problem of inferential concepts can be demonstrated most clearly in the field of psychology. With particular reference to the work of Titchener, Tolman, and Hull, Lazarsfeld traces the development of the role of "introspection" in psychology; and, in this context, he explores the origin of the idea of "intervening variables" and the major role which this idea plays in psychological research today.

Measurement of intervening variables involves the use of "indicators" that in some way correspond to or express the inferential conception. Now, in cases where there are several corresponding indicators, they have to be reconciled or combined in some manner. This multiplicity of indicators (and variation within any one of them) is the central theme in Lazarsfeld's consideration of psychological "traits." As he did with the intervening variable, he places the concept of trait in its historical perspective, discussing the work of James and Dewey, some of the contemporary work by Allport, and particularly the research of Cattell, who has been concerned with the covariance of indicators. Covariance involves a probabilistic relationship, which, Lazarsfeld argues, is what the inferential concept essentially is.

Lazarsfeld's problem and its analytical technique are not confined only to psychology. He also explores the development and role of "inferential concepts" in the field of sociology, and their application to the analysis of "social facts." His discussion in this respect takes up in particular the work of Durkheim and Weber.

Lazarsfeld next discusses the contribution of the logicians—especially Carnap, Hempel, and Kaplan—to the problem of concept formation and measurement; he is particularly interested in their notion of "disposition concept," which is practically identical to his "inferential concept." Also of great concern in this context is the logician's conception of "property space," which permits more precise formulation of the problem of how to combine a variety of indicators into a single classification. The "objects" of the type of analysis that Lazarsfeld presents have to be located in a "property space." This cannot be done directly, however, since the analysis involves *latent characteristics*—the parameters of which must be derived somehow from *manifest observations* (data that are directly accessible to the investigator). Empirical observations locate the objects under investigation in a manifest property space, but what is really necessary is to know their location in a latent property space. There are a number of reasons for this concern with latent property space. In the first place, its dimensions have a continuity which usually is not found in the data of manifest property space; secondly, the dimensions of latent property space are relatively few in number; and finally, they rule out, or at least minimize, the bias of accidental and idiosyncratic elements, such as specific situational factors. The analytical problem thus is to infer latent property space from the manifest data.

How does one make the transformation from the manifest to the latent property space? Intervening variables, traits, social facts, and disposition concepts are special cases of classificatory characteristics that have one thing in common. They are intended classifications—ways in which the researcher *would like to organize* a set of objects under investigation. Inferential concepts imply an *intended classification* that can be reached by a number of indicators. The process of relating these indicators to the intended classification is called the "diagnostic procedure," which is of the type that focuses upon the covariance of indicators. Actually, the methodological procedure operates backwards. Lazarsfeld describes four steps that comprise the "migration of concepts" through the translation of the intended classification (the inferential concept) into operational measurements for empirical observation. These are as follows: (1) an initial imagery of the concept which results from a creative act on the part of the researcher, (2) the specification of dimensions which divide the conceptual imagery into components, (3) the selection of observable indicators which can be measured empirically, and (4) the combination of selected indicators into indices.

Contrary to the position of Levinson, Sharaf, and Gilbert, as presented in the preceding chapter, Lazarsfeld contends that one cannot begin the research process with clearly defined concepts. Rather, one is forced to begin with only a "conceptual imagery"; hopefully, of course, one ends up with a precise definition once "the migration process" has been completed. Thus, within this schemata, Lazarsfeld would distinguish between an "interpretative concept" (such as "intraception") and a "classificatory concept" (such as "intraceptiveness"). This procedure is intended to describe fundamentally the logic and methodology whereby *ad hoc* instruments are improvised for the kind of behavioral research that involves the utilization of unique and real-life situations rather than constructed, experimental situations.

The critical problem in this four-phase procedure is between steps one and three. It is here that the researcher looks for the "intended classification." This, to repeat, cannot be made directly; rather, it must utilize empirical indicators which have only a probabilistic relationship to the intended classification. This is a crucial point. The procedure outlined here looks very much like operationalism; however, it is not. Here the notion of probability is essential. In the last analysis, Lazarsfeld argues, an inferential, or dispositional, concept is nothing else but an operational measurement that permits a probability inference from indicators to the intended classification. Thus, like Dewey and Weber, Lazarsfeld perceives the existence of certain social phenomena (such as friendship and power) as being constituted only in the probability that these actions will take place.

One might ask why the second of these four steps is necessary. Why does one need to go through the process of specifying dimensions of a concept since they disappear in the research process? That is to say, researchers usually end up with a uni-dimensional scale, so why go through the step of developing dimensions to select the appropriate indicators? Lazarsfeld answers that this is probably the way that the researcher samples his indicators in order to be sure that his selection is appropriate, feasible, and one that will be more productive in terms of interpretation and predictive power.

Ackerman and Parsons stated that no science deals with objects of study in their full concreteness. It selects certain properties—despite the distortion—and attempts to establish relationships among them. Yet, argue Ackerman and Parsons, singling out relevant properties (variables) is of major importance in minimizing this distortion. Lazarsfeld argues, however, that actually it makes very little difference which indicators are selected (unless, of course, this is done in an absurd manner), since the results are much the same regardless of the choice. The reason for this is that the correlation of the indices with the outside variable is always about the same, regardless of the specific "sampling" of the items that go into the indices; one gets only minor variations in the results. Accordingly, the arbitrary choice of an indicator does not make a significant difference, despite the fact that this procedure will not yield a "pure" or "absolute" classification. Discrepancies due to variations in indicator sampling, contends Lazarsfeld, should be no more frightening than the discrepancies in results due to variations in population sampling. Lazarsfeld refers to this phenomenon as the "interchangeability of indices."

The above situation would seem to be a fortunate one for the researcher. There is, on the other hand, a negative and unfortunate aspect. It suggests that the behavioral sciences are still in such an undeveloped state that their measurements are not disturbed by an arbitrary choice of indicators. This clearly points up, in a statistical and mathematical manner, the lack of precision and specification in the behavioral sciences—in other words, the general question to which this Symposium is addressing itself.

The reader who has followed these discussions in the frame of reference that was suggested in Chapter I will be asking himself a question about the validity and the theoretical significance of Lazarsfeld's "inferential concepts." Lazarsfeld's contribution is methodological or analytical, rather than substantive. Methodological analysis is a means to substantive problems, but it does not constitute substantive questions; therefore, it cannot determine their truth or falsity. Even if methodological analysis cannot resolve substantive problems, however, it can serve to clarify their nature. Accordingly, Lazarsfeld is not concerned with a better use of concepts in the interests of refined substantive theory, but merely with an analytical problem that relates to the use of one particular type of concept. Latent structure analysis deals with the intrinsic nature of a concept and not with its relationship to other concepts. Thus, this procedure tells nothing about the validity of a concept, nor anything about its predictive power. Validity and predictability can be determined only by relating one variable to other variables. Nevertheless, the reader is not left completely without an answer. Lazarsfeld's contention is that "inferential concepts" are operational measurements—distinguished, however, by the essential element of a probability weight. Whether, as such, they are nominal or real concepts is a question which is straddled by speaking of the "probable existence" of a given situation or state of affairs. His intention is clearly in the theoretical direction.

Lazarsfeld's presentation is a concise summarization of the relationship between concepts and empirical measurements. His methodological schema locates a number of persistent and polemical problems involving this relationship, and clarifies some of them. It has wide application, since the logic of the translation of concepts into empirical measurements is, as Lazarsfeld has shown, the same—independent of the kind of object involved, be it individual or collective, be it psychological, sociological, or anthropological.

Problems of concept formation, of meaning, and of measurement necessarily fuse into each other.

The present chapter will analyze one special procedure by which it is possible to make what one might call "inferential classifications." Any number of well-known topics are covered by this provisional name tag: a person's attitude as inferred from his behavior; the intention of a document as inferred from certain linguistic characteristics; the morale of a group as inferred from its various performances; and many others. No exhaustive listing nor an explicit definition will be given of the applications that we intend to cover. The basic thesis to be developed is this: measurement, classification, and concept formation in the behavioral sciences exhibit special difficulties; they can be met by a variety of procedures; and only a careful analysis of the procedure and its relation to alternative solutions can clarify the problem itself, which the procedure attempts to solve.

My presentation, then, necessarily will take on the character of a slowly unfolding story. I first shall review some literature selected because the authors saw the problem and discussed it from their different points of view. This will give the reader, I hope, a feeling for the general intellectual intention to which his attention should be directed. Then I shall try to single out more precisely the elements involved in this discussion. Finally, I shall describe briefly the present state of affairs as I see it in its historical light.

My starting point will be certain discussions among professional psychologists. This is not to say that we shall be more interested in psychological concepts than in the notions of sociologists or anthropologists; but psychologists have been the first to be concerned systematically with the logic of their empirical procedures. And in their field, too, the problem of inferential concepts can be demonstrated most clearly. In general, such notions originate if we observe what one might call permanencies under variation. If under similar circumstances one social group survives and another disintegrates, concepts like cohesion develop. If the objects created in two periods of history are markedly different, we introduce notions of style, distinguishing between, say, Gothic and Baroque. But we will be worried always about how to justify the choice of just those concepts. The psychologist seems to have an easier task. He does not only notice that a man behaves more restlessly the nearer he comes to a moment of danger; he himself has experienced anxiety, and furthermore the subject under observation is himself likely to say that he feels anxious. Actually this advantage of psychological concept formation has turned out to be a more tantalizing gift than it would seem to be at first sight. But it is just for this reason that certain methodological discussions among psychologists seem to furnish a paradigm for the other behavioral sciences.

THE INTERVENING VARIABLE

The Shifting Role of Introspection

At the beginning of this century it was generally agreed that psychology was the "study of man's mind." The approved method of study was introspection, either performed by the psychologist himself or by a few students well trained in the art. Complex experience such as thoughts, emotions, and mental attitudes were described, analyzed into their different elements, and compared with each other.

But about this time "animal psychology" began to develop as part of that Darwinian tradition, which stressed the continuity of all biological phenomena. The rise of animal psychology confronted the traditional systematic psychologist with a necessary choice. Was it possible for the introspectionist to accept observations on animals as any part of "psychology" at all? Titchener, the most rigorous of all the introspectionists, considered the matter carefully in his major work, a textbook of psychology completed in 1910. He answered the question in the affirmative: observations on animals could be regarded as "psychology." Here, in selected quotations, is the gist of his argument:

We have agreed that the psychologist is not confined to a knowledge of his own mind . . . he can apply the method [of experimental introspection] indirectly to any number of minds. Psychology is based upon the introspection of a large number of trained observers. . . .

At the same time language is not the only possible means of expression. . . . We can express our ideas by a grimace or a shrug of the shoulders, as well as by spoken words or a written paragraph.

Now the psychologist argues by analogy, that what holds of himself holds also, in principle, of the animal. . . . He argues that the movements of animals . . . record the animals' mental processes. He places the animal in circumstances which permit of the repetition, isolation and variation of certain types of movement or behavior. The animal is thus made, so to say, to observe, to introspect; it attends to certain stimuli, and registers its experience by gestures.[1]

In short, the grand old man of introspective psychology accepted animal psychology as legitimate because *animals were enough like college professors* to make possible valid inferences of their experiences.

But the fledging science, to which Titchener so generously gave the nod, rewarded him with scant gratitude. As animal psychology continued to gain ground, it became more aggressive. By the mid-twenties the behaviorists were denying that introspection had any place in psychology at all. The study of human nature, it was held, could be scientific only to the extent that it emulated the "non-mentalistic" assumptions and methods of animal psychology.

A few more years passed and psychology entered upon a new era. Now another great figure, Tolman, surveyed the scene. In his presidential address to the American Psychological Association (1937), Tolman developed his notion of the role of introspection in systematic psychology. He began by declaring proudly, "I am a behaviorist." How, then, could he go on to say that a rat has "bias," "vigilance," and "demands"? Here is his answer:

> . . . I am at present being openly and consciously anthropomorphic about it as I please. For, to be anthropomorphic is, as I see it, merely to cast one's concepts into a mold such that one can derive useful preliminary hunches from one's own human, everyday experience. These hunches may then, later, be translated into objective terms. But there seems to me every advantage in *beginning* by conceiving the situation loosely and anthropomorphically. . . . I in my future work intend to go ahead imagining how, *if I were a rat*, I would behave as a result of such and such a demand combined with such and such an appetite and such and such a degree of differentiation; and so on. And then, on the basis of such imaginings, I shall try to figure out some sort of rules or equations. And then eventually I shall try to state these latter in some kind of objective and respectable sounding terms such as vectors, valences, barriers, and the like . . .[2]

We see that between the era of Titchener and that of Tolman, psychology had come full circle. Now the behaviorist declared that introspection could have some usefulness. It facilitates the development of animal psychology, says Tolman, because *college professors are enough like animals* so that their experiences can lead to useful categories of behavior analysis.

And yet, in the course of all this, a useful notion had been developed—that of the intervening variable (I.V.). This turned out to be a very stimulating idea. It is true that it never got quite clarified; various authors adapted it differently to their specific kind of work. Nevertheless, the way it "tagged" and focused on a common fund of methodological problems made their discussion fruitful and coherent. It will help us to trace the development of the I.V. idea in more detail.

The Function of Intervening Variables

Everyone wants to know why people behave as they do. In this generality, however, the question cannot be answered; as a matter of fact, it makes no sense. So all the behavioral sciences have to limit it in some way—confining themselves to what differences come about through varying childhood experiences, what through application of drugs, what through propaganda, and so on. One formulation became of special interest to American psychologists: why do people behave differently than they have behaved just before in similar situations? How does repeated experience affect behavior; in other words, how do people (and animals) learn? From one point of view "learning theory" is best described as attending to the following type of problem.

(1) There are subjects (animals and people) characterized by heredity, age, previous experiences, and so on.

(2) They are brought into specific situations under specific conditions: a hungry rat in a maze, a Catholic worker in a radical union; they are supposed to make some kind of decison repeatedly.

(3) Their decisions have certain consequences for the subjects, either in terms of their own satisfactions or in terms of observable changes in the outside world.

Query: What will subjects of type (1) do under conditions (2) as the result of their experiences (3)?

The experimental psychologist thus divides the factors that might account for his subjects' behavior into three groups and handles them differently: the antecedents going back a long time are averaged out; the antecedents just preceding the experiment are systematically varied; and the events during the experiment are watched and explained in the light of the other two groups.

Experiments are applicable both to animals and to people. The rat runs repeatedly through a maze until it knows where to find food; the child hears repeatedly a list of words until it knows them by heart. It also became possible to formulate more clearly what "explaining" meant under the circumstances. Here are subjects exposed to various stimuli ($S_1, S_2 \ldots$), the term "stimuli" combining the experimental conditions (2) and the experiences in the experimental sequences (3) mentioned in our preceding list. The subjects make certain responses (R) to these stimuli. The experimental work shows certain "functional" relations* between S and R, say:

$$R = f(S_1, S_2 \ldots)$$

But the S_i and R are separated in time; the form of the function f varies greatly from one situation to another and seems in all cases quite complicated; additional stimuli might play a role at any time. So the idea is to simplify the approach by interposing between the S_i and R "intervening variables" according to the following scheme. The stimuli S_i are related to the intervening variables, and they in turn are related to the responses:

$$R = f_1(S_i) \text{ becomes}$$
$$R = f_2(I.V.) \text{ and, therefore } (I.V.) = f_3(S_i).$$

The I.V.'s are so chosen that they are less numerous than the S_i, and the functions f_2 and f_3 are supposed to be simpler than f_1. The schematic examples should make the general idea more concrete.

A dog is being trained to give the paw when he is asked to. The trainer says "Give the paw," takes the dog's leg, and gives him a piece of food. After a while he says the word, waits, and then gives the food if the dog happens to extend his paw. In the end the dog will give the paw most of the time when the trainer utters the request. How long will it take for this end to be reached, and how successful (in terms of number of failures) will the training be? The psychologist would still need about a dozen intervening variables to analyze the situation, but we will select just three of them for the sake of illustration. The oftener the dog is rewarded by food, the stronger a habit (H) he develops.

---

* For the time being the mathematically untrained reader may think of a functional relation in terms of simple examples; the longer an egg is boiled, the harder the yoke becomes; the more a bar of iron is heated, the longer it becomes; the more often we read a text, the more of it we remember; and so on. Later we shall give a more precise definition.

So $H = f(N)$ where N is the number of rewarded trials. But the success of his training also depends upon the food used. If the dog has a great desire (D) for the food, the training proceeds more quickly. This is taken account of by introducing the notion of excitatory potential E, which is a measure of readiness in the dog's organism to perform the required task. $E = g(D,H)$ expresses the idea that this readiness depends upon the product of desire D, which is presumed constant for the experiment, and habit strength H, which is built up by repetitive reward during training. Finally, we have the probability p that the dog performs correctly in a given number of exhibitions. So:

$$p = h(E) = h[g(D, H)] = h\{g[D, f(N)]\}.$$

In the end we have a relationship between p and N, both of which can be observed empirically; but this function was derived from the mediating relationships just mentioned. The choice of such intervening variables like habit strength and excitatory potential is the result of elaborate systematic analysis of a great variety of experiments. The claim is implied that these concepts are the ones that are likely to organize existing knowledge in the best way and to lead to new studies with predictable results.[3]

But obviously the choice of the I.V.'s is arbitrary, and, especially in the early stages of a science, a great variety of them can be tried out. Tolman, who introduced the notion of I.V., certainly had different ideas from Hull, who adapted the term to his experimental work. Here is a condensed quotation from one of Tolman's earlier papers, where he still had to argue for the acceptance of I.V.'s as legitimate notions in systematic psychology:

> Suppose a rat be run in a successive discrimination box. Such a box is an apparatus in which the animal has to choose one of two doors at each of four successive choice points. One of the two doors at each such point is lighted and one is dark. The lighted door may be either the one on the left or the one on the right in chance order. Thus at each such point the animal has the possibility of responding either on

the basis of light-darkness or on that of right-leftness. . . . Under these conditions it was found . . . that the rat will pick up one systematic way of behaving after another. In the first two or three days he may pick up, say, the propensity of choosing always the right-hand doors. But then he will shift sooner or later to some new propensity, to that, say, of choosing only the left-hand doors; and then still later to that of choosing alternate right and left doors; . . . we may now define each such intervening condition (or "I") in the organism, behind any one such systematic way of behaving, as a hypothesis.

A hypothesis, behavioristically, in other words, is to be defined as nothing more nor less than a condition in the organism which, while it lasts, produces just such a systematic selectivity in behavior. . . . The rats assert—hypothesize—that it is the right-hand doors, or the left-hand doors, or alternate right and left doors or dark doors, or whatever, which, as such, lead on. And when any one such assertion proves incorrect, an animal sooner or later drops it for a new one.[4]

The rat's hypothesis is an inferential concept of considerable complexity. A situation is observed in which the animal can behave in a variety of ways; it is found that he picks one alternative rather consistently. His choice can be affected by changes in the experimental situation. So the "model" is developed that the rat "wants" the food reward offered to him and forms "ideas" as to how he is likely to get it. The theoretical psychologist infers these wants, ideas, and so on, from observations and introduces them into his system as explanatory I.V.'s.

We do not need to go into further detail. All that was needed here was a general understanding as to the role that I.V.'s play in psychological research. By now a fairly standardized doctrine has developed to which authors adhere when they judge the merit of a specific I.V. It has to be linked to the antecedent stimulus conditions by one set of functions; it has to be linked to subsequent overt responses by another set of relations; and its connection with previously established I.V.'s has to be clarified.[5] But in the two examples we just gave, there is a difference in "intellectual style" which, for our purpose, we should try to make more explicit.

Two Modes of Dealing with Intervening Variables

When we described the training of a dog in simplified Hullian language, all the intervening variables were introduced in terms of equations, relating I.V.'s either to empirical observations or to each other. The functions *f*, *g*, and *h* defined the I.V.'s in principle. In Tolman's example of the rat's hypothesis, such connections were not mentioned explicitly. It is true that Tolman in his general writing stresses their importance. But, as many writers have observed, Tolman—in contrast to Hull—has never proposed any specific equations. He usually refers to a broad class of experimental observations and allocates to them a vivid term taken from general language; the term stimulates the reader to visualize the animal behavior by implicit reference to general experiences with living beings. The preceding story on hypotheses is a typical example. The clue for this procedure might be found in an almost offhand remark that Tolman made in comparing his and Hull's work:

> But what is a theory? According to Professor Hull, a theory is a set of definitions and postulates proposed by the theorist (on the basis presumably of some already found facts) from which other empirically testable facts, or as he calls them, theorems, can be logically deduced. These deduced theorems will be new empirical relationships which the theorist—or more often, his research assistants—can, then and there, be set to look for.
>
> For my own nefarious purposes, however, I wish to phrase this matter of the relationship of a theory to the empirical facts out of which it arises and to which it leads in somewhat other terms. A theory, as I shall conceive it, is a set of "intervening variables."[6]

This paper appeared in 1938 when Tolman was still fully immersed in animal work. For him, even then, the construction of the I.V.'s themselves was important theoretical business, irrespective of the propositions into which they were to be fitted. He seemed to feel that at an early stage of a science the formation of concepts is as important as the establishment of relationships between them. Fifteen years later, when we know in which direction Tolman's interest turned, we understand his emphasis even better. The man who advocated an anthropomorphic approach to rats joined, in 1949, with a group of sociologists to apply his notion of I.V. to a joint "theory of action." His contribution consisted of an eighty-page discussion "which contains, it is believed, all the descriptive and theoretical constructs necessary for explaining and predicting the action or behavior of individual persons."[7] In such a program, obviously, general propositions hardly can play any role because they just do not exist yet in any area where human relations are being studied. Not surprisingly, therefore, this paper simply presents a system of intervening variables which is called a "model," probably because it makes elaborate and skillful use of graphical presentations. The definition of an I.V. is the same as that given by Tolman in his original paper. But obviously the scope of references and examples is now much more vast than when I.V.'s were linked up only to the behavior of animals under experimental conditions. As a result, the sources of suggestions are greatly enlarged. Tolman states the turn of affairs as follows:

> Theories which exhibit the *trend toward a sui generis model* invent a set of explanatory structures and processes (hypothetical constructs) which draw on analogies from whatever other disciplines—mathematics, physics, mechanics, physiology, etc.—as may be deemed useful. Freud's water-reservoir concept of the "libido," Lewin's "topological and vector" psychology, and the theory to be presented in the following pages belong primarily in this third category.
>
> The theory to be presented here will then be quite frankly one which develops (by various analogies drawn

from simple physics and mechanics, from Lewin's "topo-
logical and vector" psychology, and from common experience) *a sui generis* model. This model has its own (tentatively) ascribed intervening constitutive structures and
processes and its own variety of interconnecting causal
functions.[8]

We have now before us such I.V.'s as belief-value matrices and
locomotion in psychological spaces. When complex matters like
identification and repression are discussed, additional I.V.'s are
suggested, or new features are added to ones introduced before.

The merit of such procedures, of course, can be judged only
by reading the original text; it would be out of turn here even to
attempt an evaluation. But it is clear that this development in the
use of I.V.'s is quite different from Hull's use, where all the
emphasis was on just one idea—namely, the systematic organization of experimental results in a limited field of learning with the
help of a minimum number of I.V.'s and their interconnection. In
retrospect, then, the difference between Hull and Tolman becomes much more significant than it was at the time when
contemporary critics thought that both scholars used the notion
of an I.V. in the same way and for the same purpose. We shall
come back to this point once more.

How to "Measure" an Intervening Variable

One element in this difference is especially significant for our
discussion. Hull was never concerned much with problems of
measurement. The dimension of his concepts, like habit strength
or excitatory potential, grew necessarily out of his basic equations. But Tolman, from the beginning, was concerned about
how the intervening variables are arrived at, operationally defined, measured, or whatever other terms he used in pointing to
the problem.

The answer Tolman gave fifteen years ago, when he was
concerned with the behavior of rats at a choice point, is the same
as the one he gave more recently when the whole system was
"elaborated for the specific case of a hungry actor going to a
particular restaurant and ordering and eating a particular food."[9]

In certain carefully chosen, controlled, and "standard" experimental set-ups, one tries to hold all but one, or one small group, of the independent variables constant and studies the functional connection between the variations in this one independent variable, or this one limited group of independent variables on the one hand, and the correlated variations in quantitatable features of the final behavior on the other. For example, one holds all the independent variables but, say P_1 (time since last feeding) constant. And in doing this, one chooses certain "standard" values for all the other independent variables such as P_2, S_1, S_2, et cetera. And then, under these conditions, one observes the correlations between the variations in P_1, on the one hand, and the resulting variations in some aspect of the behavior B, on the other.[10]

By an operational definition of an intervening variable I shall mean, first, a statement about a standard defining experiment in which a certain measurable variation in some feature of the observed behavior will, by definition, be assumed to be a given intervening variable. Second, such a definition will involve an assumption about the linear or nonlinear nature of this mathematical function connecting the measured feature of the dependent behavior to the intervening variable. And, third, the specific constants in this form of mathematical function must also be known, or assumed, before such definitions will be final.[11]

The idea is about as follows. We can find certain indicators for intervening variables. Everything else being constant, the variations in the indicators correspond to the variations in the I.V. We shall meet this general idea repeatedly and will finally examine it in considerable detail. For the moment, we need, rather, a more concrete idea as to how it works in actual research. Let us look at one set of intervening variables—an "actor's" belief-value matrix, which consists of his opinions about various restaurants, his food preferences, and so on. How will we find out about this I.V.? One way is through

. . . mere questionnaires or interviews. Thus, for example, one could ask the subjects: (1) "What are you ready to do when you haven't eaten for a considerable length of time?"

(2) "What kinds of food do you like? Name six varieties of food in order of preference. What do you like about each of these six?" (3) "For each of these six foods what types of restaurants would you go to and in what order? List all the considerations you would take into account in choosing the one kind of restaurant or the other."[12]

The repeated references to questionnaires in this paper make it easy to predict what problems Tolman would face if he really were to develop measurements along his line of argument: the student experienced in social research knows that answers to questionnaires vary considerably, if, for example, wordings are changed slightly or if the interview is done under slightly varying conditions. There just is no way to develop a "standard experimental set-up" or "standard defining experiment." We will have to face the fact *that to an intervening variable there will correspond a variety of indicators and that they will have to be reconciled in some way.* We suspect that the same will be true if one were to examine more carefully laboratory experiments that were proposed to define other I.V.'s like needs or valences. But this goes beyond the scope of the present discussion.

THE TRAIT

In the preceding section we tried to sketch how introspection becomes a source for inferential concepts. For instance, we experience anxiety, and its role in our own course of action (R). We observe how other people act in situations (S) which, we know, would bring on our anxieties; we notice that their reaction R is similar to ours. As a result, we file away in our minds that as a rule such a "stimulus" S is likely to be followed by response R. We "explain" such S–R sequences with the help of an intervening variable—anxiety. The value of this I.V. becomes particularly apparent if many S–R situations are observed where the S and the R vary, but where the same I.V. (anxiety) seems appropriate. We then can organize our observations in a somewhat more economical way: we remember the series of *x* situations which create anxiety and the series of *y* responses by which anxiety is expressed. Instead of registering *x* times *y* relationships of the S-R type, we need only remember $(x + y)$ findings—the *x* prompters to, and the *y* indicators of, anxiety.

In this schema one element is still missing. As we transferred from our own experience to the observation of other people, we undoubtedly noticed something else: in a given situation different people show varying amounts of anxiety. That is, some are prone to lose their heads quickly; others are able to maintain their balance. Individual variations of this kind lead to the notion of "traits."*

If we are willing to accept an over-simplification, we can put the matter as follows. The notion of I.V.'s serves the purpose of making introspective material accessible to scientific treatment; the notion of traits serves the same purpose for our observation that other people vary in their responses to the same situation. In this sense, the "trait" is likely to lead us farther afield. We can organize other people's responses into conceptual clusters even if we can find nothing that corresponds in our own experience.

The Pragmatistic Tradition

Traits became the topic of more systematic reflection in connection with moral problems—at least as far as American psychological literature goes. One starts naturally with William James's *The Principles of Psychology* (1890); there one does not find the term "trait" in the index. In the chapter on habits (Chapter X), however, there is an extensive discussion on how people can acquire desirable habits, like industriousness, or lose undesirable ones, like drunkenness. This intertwining of ethical problems with the question of traits, their acquisition and change, is still equally strong in John Dewey; it is the main theme of his *Human Nature and Conduct* (1922). Dewey also uses "habit" as his

* There is also the experience, of course, that other people, as well as ourselves, vary in their responses under varying circumstances—as they grow older, for example, or move to another part of the country. For the time being, we shall not make a distinction between this and the more strictly inter-individual kind of variations.

central term; he considers it interchangeable, however, with terms like "trait," "characteristic," "attitude," and "tendency."* Dewey's concern with the changing of habits, the examples he chooses, and the advice he gives are often very similar to James's treatment.

The moralist observes differences in his and other people's conduct, tags them as good or bad, and reflects on how valuable traits can be strengthened. The methodologist starts from the same observations but is more interested in defining, classifying, and measuring these traits. The pragmatist was a combination of moralist and logician, and he found a way to fuse his double motivation into a view that combined his activistic philosophy and his operational idea of scientific work. James's main maxim on self-improvement (which he derived from physiological considerations of habit) is: "Seize the very first possible opportunity to act on every resolution you make and on every emotional prompting you may experience in the direction of the habits you aspire to gain."[14] He was convinced that the "expression" of a trait would in turn reinforce its "existence"—for better or for worse. On the negative side, he was of course sure that every drink reinforced the trait of drunkenness. But he thought that "even the excessive indulgence in music *for those who are not performers themselves* has probably a relaxing effect upon the character."[15] In his later career as a philosopher he paralleled this relation between a trait and its expression on a logical plane. He was, as is well known, much concerned with meanings, and it is in his last book, on *The Meaning of Truth*, that we find the following passage:

> Suppose, e.g., that we say a *man is "prudent."* Concretely, *that means that he takes out insurance, hedges in betting, looks before he leaps.* . . . As a constant habit in him, a permanent tone of character, it is convenient to call him prudent in abstraction from any one of his acts. . . . There

---

* He explains at one point why the word "habit" seems to him slightly preferable in view of common language usage (p. 41). But this term clearly covers such things as honesty, peevishness, and courage (p. 16).[13]

are peculiarities in his psycho-physical system that make him act prudently. . . .[16]

We are not surprised to see that James is very explicit about the relation between an inferential concept and the indicators connected with it. He is, after all, the one who coined the phrase "concepts signify consequences." He felt that abstract descriptions are often useful enough, yet they are "sucked up and absorbed without residuum into the concrete ones, and contain nothing of any essentially other or higher nature which the concrete descriptions can be justly accused of leaving behind."[17] Here is picturesque language, the precise meaning of which is not easily checked. But it is safe to assume that James inclined toward identifying the concept and its indicators. Now this leads to obvious difficulties. Do all prudent people always look before they leap? Where do we take account of the amount of insurance taken out? How about people who show some, but not all, of the symptoms mentioned by James? Inversely, should not other indicators have been included?

Dewey was obviously aware of these difficulties. As a moral philosopher he was not less convinced than James of the mutual interaction between "disposition" and "doing"; today's tradition of progressive education is testimony to his point of view. But as a logician, he saw a looser connection between concepts and indicators. He warned that one should *not* "assume that there is or ever can be an exact equation of disposition and outcome."[18] It was characteristic for habits, he said, "that their outworking in any particular case is subject to contingencies, to circumstances which are unforeseeable and which carry an act one side of its usual effect."[19]

At the end of the previous section we noticed the emergence of one idea: to an inferential concept there will correspond a variety of indicators. Now a second idea comes to the fore, although it is rather shadowy at first—the notion of probability. It is easy to see how the progress from James to Dewey can be reformulated. The prudent man is likely to look before he leaps because any specific behavior item is only a probable but not a related trait.

We shall now show how the probability character of indicators was elaborated as traits became part of a more specialized discipline—personality research. In the 1930's the first textbooks on personality began to appear in this country. Two of their authors, Allport and Cattell, are especially significant for our little survey.

Trait and Intervening Variable

In an early systematic discussion Allport tried "with the aid of eight criteria to define trait and to state the logic and some of the evidence for the admission of this concept to good standing in psychology." Two of his criteria, numbers 4 and 7, are pertinent here.

> (4) The existence of a trait may be established empirically and statistically. . . . in order to know that an individual has a trait it is necessary to have evidence of repeated reactions, which, though not necessarily constant in type, seem nonetheless to be consistently *a function of the same underlying determinant.*
>
> (7) Acts and even habits that are inconsistent with a trait are not proof of the non-existence of the trait . . . There are in every personality instances of acts that are *unrelated to existent traits, the product of the stimulus and of the attitude of the moment.* Even the characteristically neat person may become careless in his haste to catch a train.[20]

Here both elements necessary for the diagnosis of an inferential concept are used: multiplicity of criteria, and probability relation between criterion and trait. Allport in 1937 gave a rather complicated definition of trait, the core of which was that it would render "many stimuli functionally equivalent" and would initiate "equivalent forms of adaptive and expressive behavior."[21] At that time, personality theorists were engaged in debates that have no bearing on our topic. But Allport's definition was "translated" by a subsequent writer into a form that is interesting from our point of view. D. C. McClelland, in a 1951 textbook on personality, quotes Allport's definition and adds:

What Allport appears to be saying is that a trait, on the one hand, renders stimuli equivalent and, on the other, initiates equivalent responses. These two functions of a trait can be illustrated by a simple diagram:

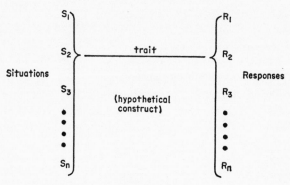

Figure 1.

This figure shows how a trait for Allport is a kind of intervening hypothetical state which serves to unite or knit together what might otherwise be dissimilar stimuli and responses. He apparently feels that a trait is both an inference the observer finds necessary to explain equivalences (on the S or R side) and a living reality or force which acts within the individual to produce the equivalences.[22]

It should be obvious why we find this formulation revealing. In the twenty years since Allport's original formulation, the "intervening variable" had made its victorious appearance on the academic scene. McClelland's scheme is practically identical with the one Tolman used to introduce this concept. Traits, in this analysis, turn out to be a special kind of intervening variable.

The last sentence in McClelland's analysis points to a disturbing intertwining of ideas which we had best unravel at this point. It was remarked before that the pragmatists had a tendency to condense two arguments: that habits are expressed and in turn affected by actual behavior; and that habits, as inferential concepts, have somehow to be defined and "measured" by behavioral items. It seems that this intertwining of ideas remains a tradition in the experimental area of personality research. Even after McClelland has remarked on the double content of Allport's definition, he himself defines trait as a learned tendency of an individual according to how he has reacted successfully in the past in similar situations.

There is nothing basically wrong in stating within one sentence what a trait is supposed to be, what its function is, and how it has developed. But for a general discussion of inferential concepts, it is probably better to isolate the definitional element from all the others. If this is done carefully, then it turns out that one topic is still unsettled. Inferential concepts come into play where we intend to characterize a set of objects in an indirect way. We assume that the intended classification can be reached through a number of indicators. Each of them has only a probabilistic relation to the "underlying characteristic." But by using a number of them we hope that our classification will be "correct"— which at the moment shall mean only that it conforms to whatever theoretical or practical goal the investigator has set himself. Using an obvious analogy from medicine, we will call this relating of indicators to intended classification "the diagnostic procedure." It deserves some preliminary reflections.

The Diagnostic Procedure

We can distinguish at least four ways in which our inferential classification can make use of indicators. It could be that independent laws are known that link the observed properties with those the investigator really wants to know about. A Geiger counter indicating radioactivity, or a bacillus in the sputum indicating tuberculosis, would be examples of this first type of diagnostic procedure. Such cases do not exist yet in the behavioral sciences and therefore do not need further discussion.

In a second type of procedure, while such laws are not known, they are at least temporarily—and often in a vague form— assumed. A psychoanalyst who has an image of unconscious desires and their repressions uses dreams and slips in everyday life for diagnostic purposes. There the methodologist has the task of spelling out the assumptions implicit in the diagnostic procedures. Lindzey's analysis of the use of thematic apperception tests to judge people's anxieties or ambitions is an excellent example of such work.[23] But it, too, is outside the scope of this paper.

For the third type, take as an example an experimenter who wants to know how hungry a given rat is at a certain moment; he uses as a measure the amount of electric shock the rat is willing to endure in its effort to get food. In this type of procedure, obviously, the diagnosis of hunger is based on the kind of intervening variable that was reported above as characteristic of Hull's work. Kenneth Spence has called it the "S–R" kind; for, while it is conjectural, it is derived from previous experiments where stimuli were varied and the consequent variations of responses were observed.[24]

In distinction from the S–R mode, Spence then introduced the "R–R" kind of intervening variable. Here inferences are drawn from the fact that a variety of responses are sometimes likely to vary together. We notice that under certain conditions people have a heightened pulse rate, they bite their nails, they pace up and down; therefrom we derive the notion of anxiety. In this instance, it is the covariance of indicators which is the source for our intervening variable and not the variation of a response subsequent to the variation of a stimulus. This is the fourth type of diagnostic procedure, and, as it will turn out, it is for our purpose the most important one. It is in these terms that we can also relate the trend from Tolman's earlier to his latest writings: they represent an increasing shift from an S–R to an R–R conception of intervening variables.

Spence properly gave as one R–R example the work of factor analysts. Among them Raymond Cattell has provided the most articulate description of their intention, and so a brief reference to his formulations should be helpful.

If a trait is expressed by a variety of indicators, then these indicators are bound to be related to each other in a variety of ways. If upon repeated observation a person is seen to exhibit one indicator frequently, then the other indicators are also likely to be observed frequently; this is what is meant when authors talk about *intra*-individual covariance. But if we have observations on many people at one time we will expect also an *inter*-individual covariance; people exhibiting one indicator also will be more likely to exhibit all the others.

It is such considerations that have made correlation analysis the main tool of modern trait research. The outstanding representative of this approach is Cattell, who has no doubt that " a unity can be detected from the fact that the consistent elements in a trait covary."[25] Cattell has devoted a life's work to the systematic survey of all the correlations that have turned up in empirical studies. From them he has derived a system of basic personality traits. The essence of the idea is the inference from covariation of responses to the "existence" of underlying units. Cattell puts it drastically, as follows:

> . . . what the psychometrist has to deal with is a series of actual behavior manifestations. He is like a plumber who is given no map of the underlying conditions but is asked to deduce, from the rates of flow from many faucets—and their mutual interferences—what conduit system exists. . . ."[26]

Cattell does not use the term "intervening variable" in his extensive writings on the theory of traits. But his "underlying conditions," his image of a "conduit system" controlling observable flows, serve the same conceptual purpose.

It will turn out that the covariance of a set of probabilistic indicators and its relation to inferential concepts are crucial issues for our whole discussion. But I shall interrupt the sequence of our discussion and raise a question that might have come to many a reader's mind. Are the problems discussed so far peculiar to psychologists or do they also arise for sociologists, who are more interested in people collectively than in individual persons? I shall try to make a case for the affirmative side.

THE SOCIAL FACT

The diagnostic procedure of latent structure analysis belongs to the type that focuses on the covariance of indicators. It requires observation of a large number of units and a study of how they change together; from this observation and study, inferences then are made as to the "underlying structure" and the position of a specific unit in it. For a sociologist the appropriate unit would be a collective rather than a person. But for quite a while the objects of sociological interest were either specific communities or society as a whole. Only recently there has emerged a study of small groups, of cities, and of primitive cultures which is logically comparable to the statistical analysis of individual behavior. To what extent this development will in turn affect the general thinking of sociologists is very difficult to predict. In order even to see the situation clearly, it will be advisable to proceed in reverse order for the present section. I shall first discuss some concrete research findings and then try to show what bearing they have on more enduring trends in sociological writings.

The studies I have in mind contain empirical propositions about properties of collectives. Tank platoons composed of friends perform better in maneuvers than platoons composed of soldiers randomly selected. Similarly, teams of workers in a factory produce more if they are composed of friends. In play groups more fights develop among the children if their leader is authoritarian than if he takes a permissive attitude. The larger a discussion group, the more difficult it is to get agreement on issues under debate. Occasionally this kind of proposition is found in studies of larger units. Certain indicators of "goodness of life"—for example, a low crime rate, large per capita contributions to community chests, and use of the public library—are positively correlated in American cities of more than 100,000 population. Primitive tribes, if migratory, are less likely to form political alliances than are tribes who have settled in villages; the settled tribes are also more likely to have a more complicated internal social structure.[27]

All these findings have the same formal character that we are used to from innumerable studies on individuals, interrelating such properties as I.Q., income, and voting. The well-known "scatter diagrams" could be drawn up; only now each point would correspond to a collective like a boy-scout group, or a city, or one of the several hundred tribes included in the Yale cross-cultural survey.

It is therefore not surprising that other elements of quantitative research also have been applied to "populations," the elements of which are themselves collectives. Students have developed dimensions according to which collectives can be classified. This leads naturally to the notion of profiles. For example, a military department and a committee within a large university would be compared. They have about the same degree of "flexibility" and "permeability" but "control" and "stratification" are much greater in the governmental unit, while "hedonic tone" and "stability" are superior in the academic group.[28] Finally, indices have been developed to combine various properties: indices of integration for cities, standard of living indices for countries, and so on.

Yet very rarely does one find any discussion of these empirical data in the terms that are so familiar to psychologists. There is no talk of underlying concepts, no parallel to the notion of intervening variable, no discussion of diagnostic procedures, although there is certainly no lack of the object itself. Sociological theorists deal continuously with the cohesion of groups, the stratification of societies, and the intimacy of interpersonal relations. These are, in formal terms, *traits of collectives*. One would expect, therefore, that they could be subject to the same kind of analysis that has been reported in our preceding sections.

One reason for the lack of interest in this parallel is certainly a confusion of its formal and its substantive elements. A social psychologist, R. B. MacLeod, has made the point, with arguments that come very near to the notion of diagnostic procedures in sociology, that behavioral scientists should be more interested in "phenomenology." A crucial and typical statement of his deserves closer attention.

> Are there characteristics of groups, of a psychological order, which can be studied as such without any necessary reference to the characteristics of any particular member of the group? This, I submit, is a reasonable question for research, and I do not think that the answer is obviously in the negative. In our twentieth-century sophistication we tend to reject the word "mind" because it smacks so much of something that rats do not have and which is therefore not scientific. But we do like the word "attitude"; we feel quite at home with words like "characteristics," "tendencies," "traditions," and "customs," and we grow positively smug when we can work in an expression like "pattern of culture" or "social norm." All these terms can be as readily applied to groups as to individuals, often much more readily. . . . We have, then, identifiable processes and relationships which are properly regarded as group characteristics and which without too much strain on our part can be regarded as mental or psychological.[29]

In the last sentence the intertwining of two separate ideas is especially marked. The main position seems to us correct: individual traits as well as national characteristics are underlying concepts; the one is predicated on an individual, the other on a collective; both have to be inferred from observable data. But why call such properties "mental or psychological"? A more neutral term like "inferential" undoubtedly would make the sociologist more willing to participate in the study of the common problem—the study of diagnostic procedure. For it is not long ago that a major concern of sociologists was to prove that sociology had a subject matter and a method of its own. As a result, what is common to all the social, or behavioral, sciences got rather scant attention. A general scientific policy orientation made some of the classics bypass or blur an important methodological problem. I shall trace this in two cases.

Durkheim and Weber

In 1895 Durkheim tried to write for the new science of sociology a Magna Charta. In his *The Rules of the Sociological Method*, the central and reiterated proposition was that "social facts are to be treated as things." The first of his six chapters is entitled: "What Is a Social Fact?" And when, in the Introduction to the second edition, he wanted to clarify his ideas against his critics, he tried to sharpen his definition. We read there statements like these:

> Things include all objects of knowledge that cannot be conceived by purely mental activity, those that require for their conception data from outside the mind, from observations and experiments, those which are *built up from the more external and immediately accessible characteristics to the less visible and more profound.*[30]

From the many examples Durkheim gives of these social objects, it becomes clear that one of his aims was to establish, on a large scale, propositions of the kind that we reported in preceding pages. He speaks of a "comparative method" when he mentions observations like the following one:

> . . . when one comes in contact with social phenomena, one is . . . surprised by the astonishing regularity with which they occur under the same circumstances. Even the most minute and the most trivial practices recur with the most astonishing uniformity. A certain nuptial ceremony, purely symbolical in appearance, such as the carrying off of the betrothed, is found to be exactly the same wherever a certain family type exists; and again this family type itself is linked to a whole social organization.[31]

These are statistical statements, the units of which are collectives. One might therefore expect that Durkheim would be much concerned with the question of how a variety of indicators have to be combined so that one can really distinguish various family types, social organizations, and so forth. But this problem he nowhere discusses. As a pioneer of a self-sufficient discipline of sociology, his interest concentrated on the mere existence of persistent relations between properties of collectives, for then they deserved a study of their own, different from the psychological study of individuals. At one point Durkheim argues that indicators for such properties are really easier to come by than indicators of an individual's attitude. For the latter, "an effort of abstraction is necessary."

> Social facts, on the contrary, qualify far more naturally and immediately as things. Law is embodied in codes, the currents of daily life are recorded in statistical figures and historical monuments; fashions are preserved in costumes; and taste in works of art. By their very nature they tend toward an independent existence outside the individual consciousnesses, which they dominate.[32]

The last three words are, clearly, gratuitous. The formal nature of such indicators, their "independent existence outside the individual consciousnesses," have nothing to do with the question of whether or not they "dominate" the individual. But Durkheim was so eager to score a policy point that he did not go on to study more carefully how one would go about actually developing what today often are called structural variables. It is worthwhile noticing, incidentally, that when MacLeod, the psychologist, and Durkheim, the sociologist, agree that individuals as well as collectives have properties from which we can infer "underlying characteristics," each cannot help claiming in the same breath the superiority of the material with which he is professionally concerned.

But Durkheim, in addition to this professional bias, seems to have held a logical conviction which practically cut him off from the problem that we are concerned with in this review. One of the "corollaries" to his first rule reads as follows: "The subject matter of every sociological study should comprise a group of phenomena defined in advance by certain common external characteristics, and all phenomena so defined should be included

within this group."[33] From the context in which this is enunci-
ated one can infer Durkheim's imagery. A "social milieu" would
be characterized by certain indicators, and *all* of them seemed to
him necessary to establish its existence. In his time the detailed
comparative work of the Yale cross-cultural survey type was not
yet conceived. As a result Durkheim never faced the problem of
what he would do if *only some* of the required indicators were
present. Working with selected and rather vaguely described
examples, he probably greatly over-rated the likelihood that he
ever would find many cases where all the "common external
characteristics defined in advance" would be present. We found a
similar situation when we discussed the transition from the
pragmatists to the beginnings of detailed personality research.
Once the general program was applied to concrete investigations,
the probability character of indicators came sharply to the fore-
ground. And, indeed, Max Weber, who was much closer to social
research in the modern, or if you please, American sense, had a
clearer sense of the problem of inferential concepts. While he did
not see all its implications, he felt that one had to cope with it
even on the level of broad-scale social theory.

At the time prior to the First World War, there began
discussions on the notion of probability which by now have led
to quite revolutionary developments in the philosophy of all
sciences. Weber followed these developments with great interest
and gave much thought to their bearing upon sociological theory.
Sometimes he used them quite explicitly to clarify methodological problems, like the nature of interpretation in the writings of
historians.[34] At other times they provided him with an opportunity to develop a telling figure of speech; and then he would
use probability notions more or less to indicate a problem,
without following it up in detail. This was what happened in the
context that interests us here—the explication of sociological
concepts. We frequently find in his writings passages like the
following one:

> . . . it is only the existence of the probability that . . . a
> certain type of action will take place, which constitutes the

"existence" of the social relationship. Thus that a "friend-ship" or a "state" *exists* or has existed *means this and only this:* that we, the observers, judge that there is or has been a probability that on the basis of known subjective attitudes of certain individuals there will result in the average sense a certain specific type of action.[35]

Weber specifically stresses that only in such probabilistic terms can the meaning of social relationships be caught. They cease to exist, he says, "whenever there is no longer a probability that certain kinds of meaningful oriented social action will take place."[36] In other contexts[37] he defines "power" and related concepts as the *probability* that a person is "in a position to carry out his own will despite resistance" or that a command will be obeyed "by a given group of people."

Here Weber is well aware that if he deals with intended classifications of interpersonal relations or social structures he has to look for appropriate indicators. And they are linked to the inferential concept, not by rigid functional relations (as Tolman thought), nor by necessary definitions (as Durkheim required), but by probability relations. Their precise nature, however, Weber did not specify. As a result he overlooked a problem whose importance we have intimated before. What if a variety of indicators do not behave in the same way? For instance, mutual support in emergencies might be more "essential" for friendship than similar tastes in food. "Certain command" can apply to a variety of topics: some of them, if not obeyed, might show that "imperative control" is not present; others might be flaunted with various degrees of frequency without undermining the control structure. And what is more serious, if we have data on such a set of indicators, how do we combine them—if combining is desirable—into one index that would permit us to order classes of friendships and to distinguish degrees of authority?

Weber overlooked this problem, probably because he too wanted to stress the peculiar aspect of the behavioral sciences. In his case the notion of the "ideal type" served this purpose and kept him from putting his thinking into the terms of research procedures with which he was well acquainted. This becomes especially evident at a point where he was confronted inevitably with a multiplicity of indicators. He defined a bureaucratic organization by a set of criteria;[38] among them were the requirements of hierarchy, of separation of professional and personal obligation, and of separation of the members from ownership of the tools of work. He defined as "ideal-type" those organizations that satisfied all the criteria. But how about those that satisfied only a proportion of them?

Carl J. Friedrich, in a critique, correctly pointed out that omitting an answer to this question precluded any empirical study of concrete organization.[39] He wanted to compare bureaucracies in various countries. In doing so, he had to use the Weber criteria, or similar ones, as "measuring rods for determining the degree of bureaucratization"; he needed "the judgment of more or less." Because Friedrich compared only five countries, his ranking could still be made in somewhat impressionistic terms. But suppose that he had wanted to study scores of organizations. He would have been in the same position as a psychologist who wants to order people according to their degree of extroversion. And his problem would have been to combine the degree of absence or presence of a set of indicators into one or a few indices of bureaucratization. Thus the closer the social theorist comes to empirical work, the more clearly he is confronted with the research problem that we are unfolding in these pages. It is not surprising, then, that we come nearest to its explicit discussion with authors who actually have focused on the comparative study of communities or on the comparative status of people within a community.

Types of Societies

Most social theorists have been concerned with a distinction for which Tönnies has coined the two terms *Gemeinschaft* and *Gesellschaft*. The next notable application of his ideas were Redfield's studies on the folk society. Redfield's idea was to take a number of Mexican villages and rank them according to the degree of contact they had with modern urban centers. His hypothesis was that the more isolated they were, the more they would have preserved the character of intimate *Gemeinschaft*. He characterized a folk society as follows:

> Such a society is small, isolated, nonliterate, and homogeneous, with a strong sense of group solidarity. The ways of living are conventionalized into that coherent system which we call a "culture." Behavior is traditional, spontaneous, uncritical and personal; there is no legislation or habit of experiment and reflection for intellectual ends. Kinship, its relationships and institutions, are the type categories of experience and the familial group is the unit of action. The sacred prevails over the secular; the economy is one of status rather than of the market.[40]

Here collectives are characterized clearly by a number of properties—traditional behavior, no legislation, prevalence of the sacred, and so on. And the basic hypothesis requires a ranking of communities according to the way these properties have combined into patterns. Thus inevitably the question had to come up: if communities qualify on some of the criteria, but each on different ones, where do they stand on the imputed continuum going from folk to the urban society?

Quite a number of studies out of the Redfield tradition are now available, and recently Horace Miner published a systematic review.[41] The author reports many controversies and notes that the disputants are likely to confuse two problems: whether communities can be ordered along the postulated continuum; and whether this order is related to the degree of contact with the outside world. The latter is a substantive problem, the former a classificatory one. Miner shows that some writers are discussing the merits of the indicators selected for study; others worry more about ways of combining them. He himself feels that "no adequate methodological techniques exist for operationalizing and quantifying the characteristics themselves."[42] In spite of a careful reading of the article we cannot tell whether the author is quite clearly aware of the ordering problem involved. But his discussion certainly comes as near to a fruitful formulation as any sociologist has provided so far.

One other point in Miner's paper deserves notice. As a community moves over time away from the folk-society pattern, it is not to be expected that "the traits change at the same rate or that they are all independent in the same way in all circumstances."[43] This is indeed a serious problem. Whenever we deal with a problem of change over time, the probability relation between the inferred classification and the indicators can itself change. If then a unit under study changes its observable property, this can be due to one or both of the following alternatives: that the unit has changed its position in the "underlying structure"; or that the diagnostic role of some of the indicators has changed.

Cattell introduced the term "syntality" of a collective to indicate his program of developing its "traits." This is meant to show the formal parallel with his work on personality traits, which I have discussed before.

> The term syntality has been used throughout these studies to refer to that in a group which corresponds to personality in the individual. Thus if *personality* is that formula which enables one to predict the behavior of an individual in defined circumstances, so *syntality* is that which enables one to estimate the behavior of the group as a whole in certain defined material and intergroup (international) stimulus situations.[44]

Cattell's procedure consists of collecting large numbers of data on small groups or countries. In the former case his material would come from experiments, where groups are given collective tasks to perform and then are observed in many aspects of their procedure; included are averages of the members' abilities and attitudes. In the case of countries, he would collect all available demographic data, would add information on the intellectual and economic production of the countries and supplement all this by ratings of experts on such cultural matters as the sanctity of the family. He would then submit this data to factor analysis and interpret his findings in terms of such underlying characteristics as "Conservative Patriarchal Solidarity" or "Bourgeois Philistinism." Cattell stresses that some of these characteristics coincide with traditional sociological concepts; others he considers new creations; and still others he himself presents as very tentative. Following his own tradition, he tries to concentrate on factors that have appeared repeatedly in different studies, using different material.

It will have been noted that Cattell's logical position is very similar to that of MacLeod; and therefore it is not surprising to find that Cattell, too, pleads for a reconsideration of McDougall's work in modern revision. Cattell also quotes an early Austrian sociologist, Gumplowicz, as one who "outdistanced most of the psychologists of a generation later by conceiving that laws can be formed about the behavior of groups."[45] But the convergence of thinking in this field is enhanced still further by Cattell's emphasis on different ways in which factor analysis can lead to inferential concepts. In two of his papers he uses data not from different countries, but from the same countries collected at different periods over approximately the last one hundred years. According to his interpretation the same underlying characteristics are applicable. However, this might raise the same problem that confronted the folk-society students. There too, as we mentioned, they noticed the difference between two problems: whether at a given time a number of communities can be ranked on a continuum; and whether with increasing "urbanization" communities develop along the same continuum.

THE LOGICIANS' CONTRIBUTION

I now turn to three topics that have been dealt with not by behavioral scientists but by philosophers of science. The first is most closely related to the main point toward which this whole review has aimed. In very recent writings of a few logicians we find a discussion of "disposition concepts" which is practically identical with my notion of "inferential concepts." The only reason why I prefer the latter term is an editorial one: it focuses

more on the diagnostic procedures, on the way in which inferences are made from actual observation to intended classification.

The Disposition Concept

"Disposition terms" refer not to a directly observable characteristic, but rather to a disposition on the part of some physical
objects to display specific reactions under specifiable circumstances. The definition of such terms seems to create considerable
difficulties. A famous paper by Carnap on "Testability and
Meaning"[46] has convinced most of his fellow philosophers that
for the introduction of such a term a somewhat different kind of
logical operation is needed, which he calls partial definition or
reduction. Following Hempel's simpler presentation, the correct
way to "define" the disposition term "magnetic" would be as
follows:

> If a small iron object is close to X at [time] T, then X is
> magnetic at [time] T if and only if that object moves
> toward X at [time] T.[47]

This definition is partial for one obvious reason. If there is no
way to approach X with small iron objects—if, say, X is at the
bottom of a lake—we could not determine whether it is magnetic
or not.

> The [area of] indeterminacy in the meaning of a term
> introduced by a reduction sentence may be decreased by
> laying down additional reduction sentences for it which
> [concern the same term, but] refer to different test condi-
> tions. Thus, e.g., if the concept of electric current had been
> introduced previously, . . . [the first partial definition]
> might be supplemented by the additional reduction sen-
> tence: If X moves through a closed wire loop at [time] T,
> then: X is magnetic at T if and only if an electric current
> flows in the loop at T.[48]

Continuing this trend of thought, we find to our pleasant
surprise that the modern logician is disclosing a practice of the

natural sciences, which was considered to be an embarrassing practice by many social scientists. That is, they define important concepts as "intervening variables" or underlying constructs which must be inferred from a list of test situations, which may have to be used simultaneously.

An historian of science might one day try to prove that this discovery of the logical nature of disposition concepts results from the growing importance of the behavioral sciences. It is not without interest that the psychological term "disposition" is here introduced into the epistemology of the natural sciences. The connection with the problem of introspection, which was the starting point in our present review, is explicitly referred to in Carnap's paper. In an autobiographical remark on how he developed his notion of reduction he says:

> . . . the members of our [Viennese] Circle did not wish in former times to include into our scientific language a sentence corresponding to the English sentence S: "This stone is not thinking about Vienna." But at present I should prefer to construct the scientific language in such a way that it contains a sentence corresponding to S.[49]

The formal analysis of the procedure is, of course, independent of its history and its terminology. The question is whether it really covers the research procedure with which we are concerned here. To decide this we must add two more elements in Hempel's exposition. First is his distinction between the empirical and the theoretical import of concept formation.

> . . . science needs terms which not only are suited for the description of particular occurrences, but which also permit the formulation of general laws and theories. The first of these two desiderata for scientific terms calls for empirical import; the second requires, in addition, theoretical fruitfulness or theoretical import. . . .
>
> In the theoretically advanced stages of science, these two aspects of scientific concept formation are inseparably connected; for, as we saw, the [assignment of an] interpreta-

tion of a system of [theoretical] constructs presupposes a
[theoretical] network of general statements in which those
constructs occur. *In the initial [pre-theoretical] stages of
research, however, which are characterized by a largely
observational vocabulary and by a low-level generalization,
it is possible to separate the questions of empirical and of
systematic [theoretical] import; and to do so explicitly may
be helpful for a clarification of some rather important
methodological issues.*[50]

This distinction between the theoretical and the empirical
aspects of concept formation has immediate bearing on the
enterprise in which we are engaged here. Indeed I am trying to
clarify how we create "underlying" concepts like traits, attitudes,
and group characteristics from a set of empirical observations.
And no one can seriously deny that most of the social sciences
are in what Hempel refers to here as the "pre-theoretical stage of
research." On this point, then, the Carnap explication of disposition concepts is fully transferable to our problem area.

On another point, however, we must look for an additional
development. Hempel points out what is implied when we use a
variety of reduction sentences. Let us go back to the example of
magnetism, where attracting metal and inducing currents are
used as two test situations.

But, since the two conditions are not [mutually exclusive,
i.e., may be jointly satisfied by a physical body, the two
reduction sentences together entail the assertion that whenever this is the case, the two corresponding reactions will
occur jointly, too; more specifically, (the two definitions)
together imply a statement to the effect that]. . . . Any
physical body which is near some small iron body and
moves through a closed wire loop will generate a current in
the loop if and only if it attracts the iron body. But this
statement surely is not just a stipulation concerning the use
of a new term—in fact, it does not contain the new term,
"magnetic," at all. . . . Hence, while a single reduction
sentence may be viewed simply as laying down a notational

convention for the use of the term it introduces, this is no longer possible for a set of two or more reduction sentences concerning the same term, because such a set implies, as a rule, certain statements which have the character of empirical laws. . . .[51]

The reader who has followed my examples in the previous sections will have noticed that there the reduction sentences are different in one respect. A "magnetic personality" is one that is *likely* to attract other people, that is *likely* to induce in them currents of enthusiasm. As we have pointed out repeatedly, the items of observations are linked to the concepts to be defined by probability relations. One other logician has seen this point very clearly. In a short paper on "Definition and Specification of Meaning," Abraham Kaplan moves on from Carnap's partial definition. He recapitulates the position in the following words:

Whenever a term is introduced into a context of inquiry . . . situations . . . are described in which the term may be applied. Any such description may be called an indicator for the term. But . . . *indicators assign to the application of the term* under the described conditions, *not a logical certainty but only a specified weight*. Thus failure to interbreed is an indicator for distinctness of species; but that two animals do in fact interbreed does not logically entail that they belong to the same species but only adds some weight to the assumption.[52]

Kaplan draws his examples from biology, and occasionally from one of the social sciences. The importance of his analysis lies in his clear recognition that the relation between the "indicators" and the concept to be specified need not have the rigidity that the original Carnap formulation implies. In short, says Kaplan, "What is suggested here is that indicators be formulated in terms of some type of probable implication."[53] He is also aware of an important consequence of this more general approach to our problem. It means that if we have two test situations it is not necessary that their outcome be related by a rigid law. To turn once more to the example of magnetism, it is now sufficient to say that attracting iron objects and inducing electric current are correlated, that they frequently occur together but not necessarily always. This is precisely the notion of covariance, which was previously found to be connected ultimately with another disposition concept, the personality trait. Covariances can be of different degree, and we are free to decide what amount of covariance entitles indicators to be included in the list that serves as the basis for the specification of meaning. And what is more important, the list of specifying items need not be final, but can change as a result of improved inquiries.

While Hempel stressed that such concept formations are characteristic of an early stage of a science, Kaplan stresses the fact that they facilitate flexibility of thinking and therefore leave the road open for new developments. In Kaplan's formulation:

> Thus the specification at any stage is a provisional one. . . .
> We begin with indicators in terms of which the initial application of context can be confirmed. As the context of application grows, the specified meaning grows—and changes—with it. The stipulation of new indicators effects the weight of the old ones, while they in turn limit the range of choice in the stipulation. The adequacy of a particular indicator is not judged by its accordance with a predetermined concept; the new and old indicators are appraised conjointly.[54]

Thus something that had seemed an embarrassing shortcoming of behavioral science concepts (such as I.Q., or introversion, or cohesion) becomes the common property of a large group of concept formations in all sciences. In all such cases we have to decide what items should be included in the base of observations from which intervening variables of any kind are inferred. Kaplan adds the important point that this choice need not be final at any point in time: the progress of theoretical thinking and empirical work might lead to changes and improvements in the selection of indicators, items of observation, basis for reduction, or whatever term is used for this part of the whole scheme.

And yet this explication of the disposition concept is too general for our purpose. Today's behavioral science concepts do not form part of a tight logical system. Their role is to summarize a variety of observations and to store them, one might say, for systematic use in a "theory" which we hope will one day develop. In our case the specification of meaning consists mainly in making explicit what kind of observations are to be combined and for what general purposes the "variables" we form are intended. This more specific operation requires the introduction of an additional notion. My central theme was the characterization of objects—be they people or groups—by a variety of indicators. Now this can be put in a terminology which at the first moment sounds strange but which will turn out to have considerable advantage.

The Property Space

The term "space" has had an interesting biography. Originally it was used to connote the direct experience people had when they located things in their surroundings. Then it was seen that the points in a space could be described in algebraic terms. Now everyone is acquainted with the notion of "coordinates." Starting, say, with the corner of a room, any other location in this room can be indicated by saying how high up it is from the floor and how far it is from the two walls that meet at the original corner. To each point there corresponds a triplet of distances. This leads to the extension of the notion of dimension. While the points in the room require three data for their location, on a blackboard we can work with only two coordinates—which is identical with saying that the face of the blackboard (or any other plane) has two dimensions. Correspondingly, four-dimensional sets become easy to grasp. The best known is the space-time continuum. A bug in a room can be characterized by the point at which it rests and the amount of time it has been there.

An inversion in terminology finally developed around the notion of dimension. Whenever a set of objects is characterized by a multiple of data one would now talk of them in terms of points in a space. This space would have as many dimensions as the data of each of the objects under consideration needed in order for it to be characterized. The advantage of this terminology is that it brings out formal similarities between materials which otherwise would be overlooked because we habitually give them different representation. Take as an example two students who were given three tests—in language (L), social science (S), and natural science (N). Assume that their test profiles look as follows:

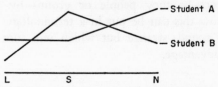

Figure 2. A test profile of two students.

Now the test scores are three groups of data and therefore can be considered coordinates in a three-dimensional space. To each test there corresponds an axis, and the two students now become two points.

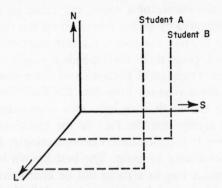

Figure 3. The same tests as above in terms of a test space.

Returning to the two profiles, it is a reasonable question to ask how they can be compared. If a series of such profiles were given, could we order them according to their similarity to each other? "Similarity" is, of course, a vague term and can be "measured" in a variety of ways. But the space representation of Figure 3 suggests that the distance between the two points A and B would be an appropriate index.[55] Suppose, further, that a large number of profiles are studied and that we find that their corresponding "points" in the test space are bunched in several parts of the space while the other parts are fairly "empty." This finding would lead to a definition of "types," which would be applicable to a large variety of materials.[56]

So far all my examples have assumed that the basic data that characterize our objects are in some way quantified. But quantification is not necessary, and with this last step the most general notion of property space is reached. The dimensions, for example, may be rank numbers merely of positions in a pre-established list. All people with Christian, middle, and family names can be put into a three-dimensional "initial space" in which each dimension has twenty-six "classes"—the letters of the alphabet. Therefore, a man with the parameters (4, 1, 3) would have the initials D.A.C., and David Arthur Chester and Donald Avery Casey would belong in the same "point" in this set of objects. In other cases, the properties might well be dichotomies, that is, attributes that take on two values only. Suppose, for example, that people are classified according to whether they are male or female; native or foreign born; above or below thirty-five years of age; residing in a city above or below 100,000 population. This would provide a space of four dimensions, but on each of them objects could have only two distinguishable positions; or to put it still another way, each of the four coordinates could take on two values only. The whole "space" therefore would consist of $2 \times 2 \times 2 \times 2 = 16$ "points." [57]

It is important to acquire a certain facility in adapting a variety of subject matters to a property space representation. Suppose, for example, that the administrator of a housing project is concerned with the "state of occupancy" for the ten buildings of the project. This term might correspond to a one-dimensional space, if the administrator thinks of the total number of apartments rented. It might be ten-dimensional, if the vacancies in each building are to be distinguished; then each building is one dimension, and the number of occupied apartments in each building is one of the ten properties by which the "state of occupancy" is characterized. A manufacturer might wish to compare the state of satisfaction existing in a number of shops through the use of a three-dimensional space: total number of complaints expressed in each shop, number of topics on which complaints are expressed, and proportion of workers in each shop who express complaints. The number of properties and the selection of indicators to represent a vague term like "satisfaction" are substantive problems. The notion of property space, however, applies to whatever decision is made, even when the decision is not explicitly stated.[58]

The Relation of Manifest to Latent Property Space

The explication of disposition concepts and the notion of property space merge into a rather precise formulation of our main problem. To begin with, we have to see the close connection between definition and classification. One should not be deceived by differences in wording. Many of the authors I have reviewed seemed to be asking: "What is friendship, prudence, cohesion, or satisfaction?" Actually these writers visualize themselves as being confronted with concrete cases of "friendship" or "prudence" and want to know how to recognize them, how to relate them to each other, and so on. If we could ask these writers some further questions, they would say something like this: "We want to distinguish 'types of friendship,' or 'degrees of prudence,' " or "We want to distinguish between 'friendship' and 'love,' or between 'prudence' and 'distrust.' " From a research point of view, these are all problems of classification—although classification of a special kind, as will be seen in the progress of our discussion. "Measurement" is also a special case of classification; it is irrelevant at this point to distinguish "measurement" from "ordering" and from other classification devices.

The reader should have no difficulty in referring to the many examples given in the preceding sections, and in verifying that the terms mentioned—such as "traits," "social facts," and "disposition concepts"—are really special cases of classificatory characteristics. They have one thing in common: they are *intended* characteristics, that is, they are ways in which we *want* to organize a set of objects under investigation. This locating of "objects" (individuals, groups, social relationships) cannot be done directly in the cases that we have discussed. We are dealing with *latent characteristics* in the sense that their parameters somehow must be derived from *manifest observations*. The terms "manifest" and "latent" have no other connotation here beyond the distinction between data directly accessible to the investigator (manifest) and parameters (latent) which in some way must be inferred from the manifest data.

The matter can be reformulated in the following way. Empirical observations locate our objects in a manifest property space. But this is not what we really are interested in. We want to know their location in a latent property space. Our problem is to infer this latent space from the manifest data, and this inference is identical with what before was described as the diagnostic procedure. The advantage of this reformulation lies in the fact that now we can raise the following question: why do we give preference to latent property space? There are three reasons for this.

(1) Consider the kind of manifest observations that the behavioral scientist works with. They are qualitative data: answers to questionnaires, existence of certain things (does a city have an opera house? has a person voted or not? and so on). But we would like to work with more continuous variables so that objects can be ordered and differences, if possible, measured. We would like to talk about the cultural level of a city or the degree of political interest in an individual. It will turn out that the dimensions of a latent property space indeed have this character of continuity, which the data of the manifest space usually do not have.

(2) Our manifest observations are likely to have very many dimensions: a questionnaire contains numerous questions; the usual way to assess the purchasing power of an area requires the consideration of numerous data like taxes paid, number of registered cars and telephone, volume of retail trade, and so forth. But

all these data are collected for the final purpose of classifying objects within very few dimensions. Most often we try to achieve one-dimensional schemes, especially in attitude research; or we try to reduce the social and economic world of a person to two dimensions, like power and prestige. Again it will be seen that latent property spaces are likely to have only a few dimensions, as compared to the high dimensionality of manifest observations.

(3) In any empirical classification guided by conceptual considerations, we try to overcome the accidental elements inherent in the use of indicators. Suppose that we want to order people according to how they feel about the role of government in economic affairs. We might ask them a series of questions as to public ownership of railroads, mines, banks, and so on. It is reasonable to assume that the more someone favors laissez-faire, the fewer of these items he will answer in an assertive way (for public ownership). Still we know that many individual idiosyncrasies will creep into the answers. For example, a strong laissez-faire person has just read about a mine accident, and under this impact he gives an assertive answer to the mine item; a strong interventionist happens to know a very fine bank president and therefore excludes the bank item from his list of assertive responses. In the manifest property space we are at the mercy of these vagaries. But in the latent space, as we shall see, we can take them into account and thus achieve a more "purified" classification.

Actually these three points are interrelated. We achieve continuity in the latent space by reducing the number of dimensions from the manifest space. We buy, so to speak, continuity and pay with dimensions. We correct for accidental elements by assigning a mediating role to the latent positions. They are derived from the totality of all manifest data and therefore permit adjustments in any part of the manifest space. But all this can be understood only after we really have studied how the transformation from the manifest to the latent space is carried out and what assumptions are implied in this operation.

THE STRUCTURE TODAY
The Flow from Concepts to Empirical Indices

Today the social research practitioner is likely to follow a process when he establishes "measurements" for complex social objects. This process by which concepts are translated into empirical indices has four steps: (1) an initial imagery of the concept, (2) the specification of dimensions, (3) the selection of observable indicators, and (4) the combination of indicators into indices.

I shall describe briefly these steps, point out how they are related to the historical development just sketched, and show some of the still unresolved problems.

STEP 1. IMAGERY. Out of the analyst's immersion in all the details of a theoretical problem, he creates a rather vague image or construct. The creative act may begin with the perception of many disparate phenomena as having some underlying characteristic in common. Or the investigator may have observed certain regularities and be trying to account for them. In any case, the concept, when first created, is a vaguely conceived entity that makes the observed relations meaningful.

Let us take as an example the concept of "intelligence." By now the development of intelligence tests has become a large-scale industry. But the beginning of the idea of intelligence was that if you look at little boys, some strike you as being alert and interesting and others as dull and uninteresting. This kind of general impression set the wheels rolling for a measurement problem.

I purposely use the word "imagery" in a context where other writers talk of a definition. I do not believe that concepts in the behavioral sciences can ever be defined precisely by words. As we mentioned in the section on the intervening variable, the starting point is always some general observations that require an intended classification. The contemporary literature on "construct validity" seems for the most part to share my position.

STEP 2. CONCEPT SPECIFICATION. The next step is to take this original imagery and divide it into components. The concept is specified by an elaborate discussion of the phenomena out of which it emerged. We develop "aspects," "components," "dimensions," or similar specifications. They sometimes are derived logically from the over-all concept, or one aspect is deduced from another, or empirically observed correlations between them are reported. The concept is shown to consist of a complex combination of phenomena, rather than a simple and directly observable item.

Suppose you want to know whether or not a production team is efficient. You start with a notion of efficiency. Somebody comes and says, "What do you really mean? Who are more efficient—those who work quickly and make a lot of mistakes, so that you have many rejections, or those who work slowly but make very few rejects?" You may answer, depending on the product, "Come to think of it, I really mean those who work slowly and make few mistakes." But do you want them to work so slowly that there are no rejects in ten years? That would not be good either. In the end you divide the notion of efficiency into components such as speed, good product, careful handling of the machines—and suddenly you have what measurement theory calls a set of dimensions. Almost every concept that we use in the behavioral sciences is so complex that breaking it down into dimensions is absolutely essential in order to translate it into any kind of operation or measurement.

These specifications correspond, of course, to setting up the dimensions of an attribute space. At this stage, then, the intended classification is clearly multi-dimensional. Whether it should stay so, or whether the attribute space should be reduced to fewer or even one dimension is a matter of strategy which we cannot take up here. In any case, the specification is of practical importance because it makes our subsequent decisions more explicit.

STEP 3. SELECTION OF INDICATORS. After we have decided on these dimensions, we embark on the third step—finding indicators for the dimensions. Here we run into a number of problems. First of all, how does one "think up" indicators? Take the example of James's prudent man. Indicators might vary considerably, depending on his social setting. Among students in a Protestant denominational college, for instance, we may find little betting and rare occasions for taking out insurance. Still a measure of prudence can be devised that is relevant to the setting. We might use as indicators whether a student always makes a note before he lends a book, whether he never leaves his dormitory room unlocked, and so on.

A second problem arises from the fact that each indicator has not an absolute but only a probabilistic relation to our underlying concept; this requires us to consider a great many possible indicators.

Another difficult problem is to decide when to stop. Which indicators are considered "part of" the concept, and which are considered independent of or external to it? If we start listing indicators of the "integration" of a community, is the crime rate a part of the conception of integration, or is it an external factor which we might try to predict from our measure of integration?

The selection of indicators is the step that is still most controversial from a methodological point of view. Louis Guttman has given the problem a very appealing general formulation. To each concept corresponds a "universe of items" which is, to say the least, very large. A concrete measuring instrument selects a sample from it. But the specific nature of the universe and of the sampling process still is not fully clarified. Fortunately, an empirical rule of thumb, which we shall discuss presently, alleviates many difficulties in practice.

STEP 4. FORMULATION OF INDICES. The fourth step is to put Humpty Dumpty together again. After the efficiency of a team or the intelligence of a boy has been divided into six dimensions, and ten indicators have been selected for each dimension, we have to put them all together, because we cannot operate with all those dimensions and indicators separately.

For some situations we must make one over-all index out of the indicators and dimensions. If I have six students and only one fellowship to give, then I must make an over-all rating of the six. To do this I must in some way combine into an index all the information that I have about each student. At another time we may be more interested in how each of several dimensions is related to outside variables. But even so, we must find a way of combining the indicators, since by their nature the indicators are many, and their relations to outside variables are usually both weaker and more unstable than the underlying characteristics that we would like to measure.

To put it in more formal language, each individual indicator has only a probabilistic relation to what we really want to know. A man might maintain his position in the intended attribute space, but yet he might by chance shift on an individual indicator; or he might change his basic position, but by chance remain stable on a specific indicator. But if we have many such indicators in an index, it is highly unlikely that a large number of them will all change in one direction, if the subject we are studying has in fact not changed his basic position.

In recent years a number of mathematical models have been developed in order to clarify these four steps and to make alternative procedures more comparable. A very suitable review of these models can be found in a monograph sponsored by the Social Science Research Center and written by Warren Torgerson.[59]

Finally, let me come back to the empirical lifesaver to which I referred before. In the formation of indices of broad social and psychological concepts, we typically select a relatively small number of items from a large number of possible ones suggested by the concept and its attendant imagery. It is one of the notable features of such indices that their correlation with outside variables usually will be about the same, regardless of the specific "sampling" of items that goes into them from the broader group associated with the concept. This rather startling phenomenon has been labeled "the interchangeability of indices."

The Interchangeability of Indices

To present an example, we chose an index of "conservatism" used in a recent study[60] of the response of college teachers of social sciences to the difficult years of the "McCarthy period," with its frequent attacks against colleges and professors for "leftist leanings."

One of our problems in this Teacher Apprehension study was to sort out those teachers who, because of their own convictions, could not possibly be the objects of such attacks—the men and women who hereafter, using the favorite term of their own spokesmen, will be called the "conservatives."

From the beginning of our study we sought to find an acceptable way to locate this conservative group correctly. How was that to be done in a relatively short interview in which most of the questions necessarily were concerned with the "non-conservatives," who were the ones mainly involved in the controversies? This is a problem of classification common to all survey research. What indicators were we to select?

In our study we could have asked our respondents whether they approved of certain conservative writings submitted to them; or we could have selected the organizations they belonged to or the magazines they read as indicators. As a result of much previous experience, however, we preferred to choose indicators more closely connected with the rest of the interview. We submitted to each respondent a series of rights and prohibitions, most of them taken from academic life, and asked whether they were for or against them. Out of this material an index of conservatism was formed. Since we were aware that quite different material would have been equally suitable, we tested our index against a series of other possibilities.

Two questions in our series of rights and prohibitions had to do with the respondent's attitude towards student activities: "If there are students who want to join it, do you think that a Young Socialist League ought to be allowed on this campus, or not?" The attitude toward socialists seemed a good indicator because whether or not the socialists should be classified with communists is an issue on which educated conservatives and their opponents are likely to disagree. Fourteen per cent, or 355 professors, reported that they would be definitely against such a policy. Characteristically enough, the second question, also pertaining to student activities, yielded almost the same number of conservative replies. We asked our respondents to suppose that they were faculty advisers to a student organization on the campus that "proposed inviting Owen Lattimore, Far Eastern expert (now under indictment in Washington) to speak at a public meeting here." Again, about 14 per cent of the sample, in this case 342 professors, put themselves on record that this "ought to be allowed."

To both questions we get practically the same number of conservative answers—355 and 342, respectively. One might expect that practically the same professors furnish these replies in both instances. This, however, is not completely the case. Table 1 shows how the answers are related.

TABLE 1

A Cross-Tabulation of Answers to the Two Questions on What Students Should Be Permitted to Do

FORM A
SOCIALIST
CLUB   INVITE LATTIMORE

	Approved	Undecided	Disapproved	Total
Approved	1686	95	124	1905
Undecided	118	27	46	191
Disapproved	152	31	172	355
Total	1956	153	342	2451

We see that the great statistical similarity of replies to each question is really the result of a considerable amount of "turn-over." Of the people who approved of a Socialist Club, 124 would be against an invitation to Lattimore; conversely, 152 people who approved this invitation would not want students to form a Young Socialist League. This is neither surprising nor disturbing. Any single indicator has a specific element and can never be taken as fully representative for the classification that we are striving to achieve—in this case, the classification of conservative respondents. Many of the interviewees made qualitative comments on their answers, and they did it most often when they saw that on a specific point their response was somewhat out of line with their whole attitude pattern. We know fairly well, therefore, what explains the position of the people in the upper-right and lower-left corners of Table 1. Some of the respondents who were against inviting Lattimore disliked him personally. Others felt that a legal matter was at issue—a man who is under indictment should not be permitted to talk on a college campus. Inversely, the professors who would let Lattimore talk but who were against a Young Socialist League sometimes commented that on their campus there was a general policy against political student organizations or that they felt that a socialist organization could be especially open to subversive infiltration.

Suppose we decided to use one of the items in Table 1 as a crude index to conservatism. A serious discussion could start over which of the two questionnaire items is a better "measure" of conservatism. The Lattimore question is tinged with personal idiosyncrasies and legal implications. The Socialist League item has an element of ambiguity: do those who would forbid such an organization express their own opinion or the policy of their college? Neither of the two items is a very pure "measure," and therefore arguments could continue for and against each of them. Actually, however, it would make very little difference which one is used. And this is a point that needs to be driven home. Classifications in social research mainly are used to establish relations among a number of variables. The crucial question, therefore, is whether these relations, the empirical findings we are looking for, are affected much if we interchange one reasonable index with another.

To exemplify the matter we needed an "outside variable." For it we chose the answer to an item that forced the respondent to make a hypothetical choice between the rights of the individual and the claims of the institution:

If you had to make a choice, in a case in which a member of the faculty is accused of being subversive or of engaging in un-American activities, which do you think is more important for the college (university) administration to protect— the reputation of the college (university) or the rights of the faculty members?

What was the relation of conservatism to the concern for individual rights? This concern was the outside variable that we wanted to relate to conservatism. For the latter we had two measures available. Each of them could be tabulated against the choice between the protection of individual rights or the reputation of the college. What difference was there in the choice between the two indicators, namely the Lattimore or the Socialist League item?

The essential fact is that we got practically the same result, irrespective of which of the two indicators we used to separate the conservative respondents from the others (Table 2).

TABLE 2

Proportion Giving Priority to Faculty Rights Related to Two Measures of "Conservatism"

Attitude on Lattimore Speech	% Giving Priority to Faculty Rights	Attitude on Socialist League	% Giving Priority to Faculty Rights
Conservative	46	Conservative	43
Neutral	50	Neutral	51
Permissive	70	Permissive	70

Among the "conservatives" to be found in the first line of either column, less than half would feel that the faculty rights were paramount. Among the "permissives" in the bottom line more than two thirds would feel this way. The whole numerical trend in the two columns is about the same, irrespective of which indicator had been used for classificatory purposes.

In actual research practice, a larger number of items, rather than one item alone, are used for the purpose of classification. This is done for a variety of reasons. For example, indices based on more items permit finer distinctions, and they tend to cancel out the peculiarities of any single item. These are details that need not be elaborated upon here. Even if we use several items for classificatory purposes, we always have a selection out of a much larger pool of reasonable possibilities.

This, then, is the general rule based on very diversified research practice: If we are dealing with a rather broad concept like conservatism, and if we want to "translate" it into an empirical research instrument, a large number of indicators will always be eligible to form an index for classificatory purposes; however, only a relatively small number of such items are practically manageable in most field research situations. If we choose two sets of such reasonable items to form two alternative indices, the following two facts usually will be found.

(1) The two indices will be related, but they will not classify all the people in a study in precisely the same way; Table 1 exemplifies this.

(2) The two indices usually will lead to very similar empirical results if they are cross-tabulated against a third outside variable; Table 2 exemplifies this.

One pays a serious but unavoidable price for the practical advantages of the interchangeability of indices. We can never reach "pure" classifications. Whatever index we use, the items will have "peculiarities" which will result in some cases being misclassified, and therefore the empirical relationships that we find will be lower than they would be if we had more precise measures of the variables with which the study is concerned.

The tentative character of the rule should be stressed, however. There are some variables that are of great and general significance, and therefore over the years ever better instruments have been developed. Intelligence tests, for example, use a very large number of carefully selected items. If we were to use two such tests to classify the same group of people, the number of contradictions would be much smaller than that found in our Table 1. If a long series of studies were to be carried out over many years in order to see whether the number of conservatives in the population increases, or how conservatism is related to a great many other variables, then it would be worthwhile to develop a very refined classification device. But in a study like that of Teacher Apprehension, where a large number of variables have to be introduced for the first time, the only practical course for the researcher is to use fairly simple indices, and to make sure that he does not deceive himself or his readers about the remaining uncertainties.

CONCLUSION

My intention in these pages has been to delineate, by means of some selected literature from the behavioral disciplines, the problem of inferential classifications, and to single out some of the central elements which are involved in this issue. Finally, I have described briefly the present state of affairs as I see it in the light of this historical perspective. The schema that I have employed was intended to locate a number of much-discussed problems and to clarify some of them. Of course, as always, it leaves very much more for future considerations. Yet, hopefully, this may be regarded as the beginning of a coherent summarization of the relationship between concept formation and measurement.

NOTES

1. The entire first chapter of Titchener's book deals with this kind of argument. My quotations are taken from pp. 30–31 of a 1921 reprinted edition. Similar ones can be found on pp. 26–28 and 32–34. E. B. Titchener, *A Textbook on Psychology* (New York: The Macmillan Company, 1910).

2. Edward C. Tolman, "The Determiners of Behavior at a Choice Point," *Psychological Review*, XLV (1938), 24. Italics from Tolman.

3. The main papers on intervening variables are reprinted in Melvin H. Marx (ed.), *Theories in Contemporary Psychology* (New York: The Macmillan Company, 1963).

4. Edward C. Tolman, "Psychology Versus Immediate Experience," in *Collected Papers in Psychology* (Berkeley: University of California Press, 1951), pp. 109–110. Italics mine.

5. A systematic and instructive job was done on the concept of frustration as an I.V. It will be found in J. S. Brown and I. E. Farber,

"Emotions Conceptualized as Intervening Variables—With Suggestions Toward a Theory of Frustration," *Psychological Bulletin*, XLVIII (1951), 465–495.

6. Tolman, "The Determiners of Behavior at a Choice Point," p. 9.

7. Edward C. Tolman, "A Psychological Model," in Talcott Parsons and Edward A. Shils (eds.), *Toward a General Theory of Action* (Cambridge: Harvard University Press, 1951), pp. 279–361.

8. *Ibid.*, p. 283.

9. *Ibid.*, p. 288.

10. Edward C. Tolman, "Operational Behaviorism and Current Trends in Psychology," in *Collected Papers in Psychology* (Berkeley: University of California Press, 1951), p. 122.

11. Tolman, "A Psychological Model," p. 333.

12. *Ibid.*, p. 295.

13. John Dewey, *Human Nature and Conduct* (New York: Henry Holt and Company, 1922; New York: Random House, Inc., 1957).

14. William James, *The Principles of Psychology* (New York: Henry Holt and Company, 1890), p. 147.

15. *Ibid.*, p. 148.

16. William James, *The Meaning of Truth* (New York: Longmans, Green, and Company, 1909), pp. 149–150. Italics mine.

17. *Ibid.*, p. 149.

18. Dewey, *op. cit.*, p. 48.

19. *Ibid.*, p. 49.

20. Gordon W. Allport, "What Is a Trait of Personality?" *Journal of Abnormal and Social Psychology*, XXV (1931), 368–372. Italics mine.

21. Gordon W. Allport, *Personality: A Psychological Interpretation* (New York: Henry Holt and Company, 1937), p. 295.

22. David C. McClelland, *Personality*. Copyright (c) 1951 by David C. McClelland. Used by permission of Holt, Rinehart and Winston, Inc., publishers, p. 202.

23. Gardner Lindzey, "Thematic Apperception Test: Interpretive Assumptions and Related Empirical Evidence," *Psychological Bulletin*, XLIX (1952), No. 1, 1–25.

24. Kenneth W. Spence, "Types of Constructs in Psychology," in Melvin H. Marx (ed.), *Theories in Contemporary Psychology* (New York: The Macmillan Company, 1963).

25. Raymond B. Cattell, *Description and Measurement of Personality* (New York: World Book Company, 1946), p. 12.

26. *Ibid.*, p. 110.

27. For a review and discussion of these and other studies, see Daniel M. Goodacre, III, George P. Murdock, and Alex Bavelas, "Interrelationship of Group Properties," in Paul F. Lazarsfeld and Morris Rosenberg (eds.), *The Language of Social Research* (Glencoe: The Free Press, 1955), Section IV B.

28. John K. Hemphill and Charles M. Westie, "The Measurement of Group Dimensions," *Journal of Psychology*, XXIX (1950), 325–341.

29. R. B. MacLeod, "The Place of Phenomenological Analysis in Social Psychological Theory," in John H. Rohrer and Muzafer Sherif (eds.), *Social Psychology at the Crossroads* (New York: Harper and Brothers, 1951), p. 217.

30. Émile Durkheim, *The Rules of the Sociological Method* (Chicago: University of Chicago Press, 1938), p. xliii.

31. *Ibid.*, p. 94.

32. *Ibid.*, p. 30.

33. *Ibid.*, p. 35.

34. Max Weber, *The Methodology of the Social Sciences* (Glencoe: The Free Press, 1949), pp. 180–188.

35. Max Weber, *The Theory of Social and Economic Organization* (New York: Oxford University Press, 1947), p. 119. Italics mine.

36. *Ibid.*, p. 118.

37. *Ibid.*, p. 152.

38. Max Weber, "The Essentials of Bureaucratic Organization: An Ideal-Type Construction," in Robert K. Merton (ed.), *Reader in Bureaucracy* (Glencoe: The Free Press, 1952).

39. Carl J. Friedrich, "Some Observations on Weber's Analysis of Bureaucracy," in Robert K. Merton, *ibid.*, p. 27.

40. Robert Redfield, "The Folk Society," *American Journal of Sociology*, LII (1947), 293.

41. Horace Miner, "The Folk-Urban Continuum," *American Sociological Review*, XVII (1952), 529–537.

42. *Ibid.*, p. 531.

43. *Ibid.*, p. 533.

44. Raymond B. Cattell and Marvin Adelson, "The Dimensions of Social Change in the U.S.A. as Determined by the P-Technique," *Social Forces*, XXX (1951), No. 2, 191.

45. Raymond B. Cattell, "Concepts and Methods in the Measurement of Group Syntality," *Psychological Review*, LV (1948), 54.

46. Rudolf Carnap, "Testability and Meaning," *Philosophy of Science*, III (1936), 419–471, and IV (1937), 2–40.

47. Carl G. Hempel, "Fundamentals of Concept Formation in Empirical Science," *International Encyclopedia of Unified Science* (Chicago: University of Chicago Press, 1952), Vol. II, No. 7, 26.

48. *Ibid.,* p. 27.

49. Carnap, *op. cit.,* p. 5.

50. Hempel, *op. cit.,* pp. 45–46. Italics mine.

51. *Ibid.,* pp. 27–28.

52. Abraham Kaplan, "Definition and Specification of Meaning," *Journal of Philosophy,* XLIII (1946), No. 11, 283.

53. *Ibid.,* p. 283.

54. *Ibid.,* pp. 286–287.

55. This has been explored in detail by Lee J. Cronbach and G. C. Gleser, "Assessing Similarity Between Profiles," *Psychological Bulletin,* L (1953), 456–473.

56. See Carl G. Hempel and Paul Oppenheim, *Der Typusbegriff im Lichte der neuen Logik* (Leiden: A. W. Siythoff Publishers, 1936).

57. Paul F. Lazarsfeld, "The Algebra of Dichotomous Systems," in Herbert Solomon (ed.), *Studies in Item Analysis and Prediction* (Stanford: Stanford University Press, 1961).

58. For further examples of such property space and their applications to social research problems, see Allen H. Barton, "The Concept of Property Space in Social Research," in Paul F. Lazarsfeld and Morris Rosenberg (eds.), *The Language of Social Research* (Glencoe: The Free Press, 1955).

59. Warren Torgerson, *Theories and Methods of Scaling* (New York: John Wiley and Sons, 1958).

60. Paul F. Lazarsfeld and Wagner Thielens, *The Academic Mind* (Glencoe: The Free Press, 1958).

Suggested Readings

Allport, Gordon W. "What Is a Trait of Personality?" *Journal of Abnormal and Social Psychology* (1931), 25:368–372.

———. *Personality: A Psychological Interpretation.* New York: Henry Holt and Company, 1937.

Barton, Allen H. "The Concept of Property Space in Social Research," in Paul F. Lazarsfeld and Morris Rosenberg (eds.), *The Language of Social Research.* Glencoe: The Free Press, 1955.

Brown, J. S., and Farber, I. E. "Emotions Conceptualized as Intervening Variables—With Suggestions Toward a Theory of Frustration," *Psychological Bulletin* (1951), 48:465–495.

Carnap, Rudolf. "Testability and Meaning," *Philosophy of Science* (1936–37), 3:419–471, and 4:2–40.

Cattell, Raymond B. *Description and Measurement of Personality.* New York: World Book Company, 1946.

——. "Concepts and Methods in the Measurement of Group Syntality," *Psychological Review* (1948), 55:48–63.

——, and Adelson, Marvin. "The Dimensions of Social Change in the U.S.A. as Determined by the P-Technique," *Social Forces* (1951), Vol. 30, No. 2, 190–201.

Cronbach, Lee J., and Gleser, G. C. "Assessing Similarity Between Profiles," *Psychological Bulletin* (1953), 50:456–473.

Dewey, John. *Human Nature and Conduct.* New York: Henry Holt and Company, 1922; New York: Random House, 1957.

Durkheim, Émile. *The Rules of the Sociological Method.* Chicago: University of Chicago Press, 1938.

Friedrich, Carl J. "Some Observations on Weber's Analysis of Bureaucracy," in Robert K. Merton (ed.), *Reader in Bureaucracy.* Glencoe: The Free Press, 1952.

Hempel, Carl G. "Fundamentals of Concept Formation in Empirical Science," *International Encyclopedia of Unified Science.* Chicago: University of Chicago Press, 1952, Vol. 2, No. 7.

——, and Oppenheim, Paul. *Der Typusbegriff im Lichte der neuen Logik.* Leiden: A. W. Siythoff Publishers, 1936.

Hemphill, John K., and Westie, Charles M. "The Measurement of Group Dimensions," *Journal of Psychology* (1950), 29:325–341.

James, William. *The Principles of Psychology.* New York: Henry Holt and Company, 1890.

——. *The Meaning of Truth.* New York: Longmans, Green, and Company, 1909.

Kaplan, Abraham. "Definition and Specification of Meaning," *Journal of Philosophy* (1946), Vol. 43, No. 11, 281–288.

Lazarsfeld, Paul F. "A Conceptual Introduction to Latent Structure Analysis," in Paul F. Lazarsfeld (ed.), *Mathematical Thinking in the Social Sciences.* Glencoe: The Free Press, 1954.

—— (ed.). *Mathematical Thinking in the Social Sciences.* Glencoe: The Free Press, 1954.

——. "Evidence and Inference in Social Research," *Daedalus* (1958), 87:99–130.

——. "The Algebra of Dichotomous Systems," in Herbert Solomon (ed.), *Studies in Item Analysis and Prediction.* Stanford: Stanford University Press, 1961.

———, and Rosenberg, Morris (eds.). *The Language of Social Research*. Glencoe: The Free Press, 1955.

———, and Thielens, Wagner. *The Academic Mind*. Glencoe: The Free Press, 1958.

———, and Oberschall, Anthony R. "Max Weber and Empirical Social Research," *American Sociological Review* (1965), 30:185–192.

Lindzey, Gardner. "Thematic Apperception Test: Interpretive Assumptions and Related Empirical Evidence," *Psychological Bulletin* (1952), Vol. 49, No. 1, 1–25.

MacLeod, R. B. "The Place of Phenomenological Analysis in Social Psychological Theory," in John H. Rohrer and Muzafer Sherif (eds.), *Social Psychology at the Crossroads*. New York: Harper and Brothers, 1951.

Marx, Melvin H. *Theories in Contemporary Psychology*. New York: The Macmillan Company, 1963.

McClelland, David C. *Personality*. New York: Holt, Rinehart and Winston, Inc., 1951.

Merton, Robert K. (ed.). *Reader in Bureaucracy*. Glencoe: The Free Press, 1952.

Miner, Horace. "The Folk-Urban Continuum," *American Sociological Review* (1952), 17:529–537.

Parsons, Talcott, and Shils, Edward A. (eds.). *Toward a General Theory of Action*. Cambridge: Harvard University Press, 1951.

Redfield, Robert. "The Folk Society," *American Journal of Sociology* (1947), 52:293–308.

Rohrer, John H., and Sherif, Muzafer (eds.). *Social Psychology at the Crossroads*. New York: Harper and Brothers, 1951.

Solomon, Herbert (ed.). *Studies in Item Analysis and Prediction*. Stanford: Stanford University Press, 1961.

Spence, Kenneth W. "Types of Constructs in Psychology," in Melvin H. Marx (ed.), *Theories in Contemporary Psychology*. New York: The Macmillan Company, 1963.

Titchener, E. B. *A Textbook on Psychology*. New York: The Macmillan Company, 1911.

Tönnies, Ferdinand. *Community and Society*. East Lansing: Michigan State University Press, 1957; New York: Harper and Row, 1963.

Tolman, Edward C. "The Determiners of Behavior at a Choice Point," *Psychological Review* (1938), 45:1–41.

———. "A Psychological Model," in Talcott Parsons and Edward A. Shils (eds.), *Toward a General Theory of Action*. Cambridge: Harvard University Press, 1951.

————. *Collected Papers in Psychology*. Berkeley: University of California Press, 1951.

Torgerson, Warren. *Theories and Methods of Scaling*. New York: John Wiley and Sons, 1958.

Weber, Max. *The Theory of Social and Economic Organization*. New York: Oxford University Press, 1947.

————. *The Methodology of the Social Sciences*. Glencoe: The Free Press, 1949.

————. "The Essentials of Bureaucratic Organization: An Ideal-Type Construction," in Robert K. Merton (ed.), *Reader in Bureaucracy*. Glencoe: The Free Press, 1952.

CHAPTER **VIII**

A Discussion of
the Issues

Editor's Introduction

Bringing together several scientists, especially from specialized disciplines, is bound to give rise to differences of opinion. More often than not, this type of a situation, when explored, produces beneficial consequences for the scientific objective.

The purpose of this chapter is to provide the proceedings of a discussion among the symposiasts concerning their respective contributions to the theme of this Symposium. Their commentary incorporates answers to written questions that were posed by the audience. Those papers that have joint authorship are represented in this discussion, as they were at the Symposium, by the senior author. Professor Gordon J. DiRenzo conducted the discussion. No attempt was made at the outset to delimit or to evaluate the major themes or issues of the several presentations. This will be done by the editor in the concluding chapter.

Professor DiRenzo:

We have had an excellent presentation of papers. There was much similarity of theme in all of them, however diverse they were in specific content. In keeping with my own specialized interest in this Symposium, I have paid particular attention, of course, to the question of conceptual definition. An array of concepts was offered and delineated in the several presentations. It is gratifying that much concern has been devoted to some of the issues that I tried to present in my paper—concern not only for the fundamental question of determining the validity of scientific concepts and the significance of validity for scientific explanation, but also for the problem of establishing empirical verification and for the process of translating concepts into empirical measurements for theoretical analysis.

No doubt each of you has comments that you would like to make about other presentations. May I suggest that for an initial procedure each of the symposiasts, following the order in which the papers were presented, take a few minutes to make an extension of his remarks or any other type of observation. Specific questions, then, may be addressed to any of the speakers.

PROFESSOR ACKERMAN:

We have been—if you will forgive my mysticism—haunted throughout these presentations by the number "four." Professor Sherif has found in his small-group research the four structural components of the human group—roles, norms, values, and what may be termed "collectivity." Professor Anderson gives us a black box, two input factors (problem and program), and one output (solution). Professor Lazarsfeld speaks also of "four"— indicators, image, breaking the image into internal components, and recombination. It seems to me that the fact of all these fours is provocative; and I would like to give some sort of organization to my comments by noting Professor Anderson's reference to birds and airplanes and the question, "Is there a general model of which they both—birds and airplanes—are empirical specifications?" Is there a general model of which all these "fours" are empirical specifications?

It seems to me that we have now in our disciplines such a general model. It is the one devised primarily by the man whom I represent today—the AGIL paradigm of Talcott Parsons' "action theory." Most briefly, that model—the AGIL paradigm—emphasizes four functions (adaptation, goal-attainment, integration, and latent pattern-maintenance); and we who are guided in our thinking by action-theoretic concepts "theorize" that within a complex system there are structural components "differentiated" with respect to these four functions.

I doubt that Sherif, Anderson, and Lazarsfeld have been guided in their analyses by action theory; but they have arrived at conclusions (independent of such theory) which are consistent, I think, with action theory. It seems to me that the empirical phenomena they refer to are specifications to their different systems of the AGIL paradigm. Sherif's "role" accomplishes the articulation with the environment that we refer to as the adaptive sector and, I believe it can be argued, so do Anderson's "problem" and Lazarsfeld's "indicators." To the goal-attainment function or sector I would refer Sherif's "collectivity" (he does not, of course, use the term—it is an action-theoretic one—but the phenomenon is in his formulations), Anderson's "solution," and Lazarsfeld's "recombination" into representativeness. Sherif's "value," Anderson's "program," and Lazarsfeld's "image" all seem specifications of pattern-maintenance, the highest informational component of a system. Integration seems to be accomplished by Sherif's "norms," Anderson's "black box" (a set of internal processes articulating aspects of problem-solving), and, of course, Lazarsfeld's analogous process of breaking the image into internal aspects and specifying it.

If it is *general* theory that we are after, and if, following Sherif, we feel that theory should take into account empirical data, is it not of some importance that three such widely divergent systems and processes as those discussed by Sherif, Anderson, and Lazarsfeld may be discussed in terms of a single model?

I have only two further comments, both concerning *interpenetration*. Professor Levinson's concept "intraception" is a fascinating one—most particularly, from my point of view, because of its *locus* in systemic analysis. He seems to me to be referring to a "bridging flow" between systems. The "energy" that is delivered up to and deposited in role-occupancy by the personality is already partially structured—by, of course, the Superego. What Levinson seems to be suggesting is a kind of structuring that takes place before role-occupancy, constraining the choice of role and the degree and kind of role-cathexis. The *locus* of this seems fairly firmly to imply interpenetration.

Another aspect of interpenetration—at an entirely different system level—is presented by Professor White, whose "symbolates" interpenetrate the social system at the value level, rather than at the role level. An action theorist must, however, be somewhat uneasy with some aspects of Professor White's emphases; we would probably prefer to place a greater emphasis on the "pure information" aspect of the symbolate, guided to do so by our hierarchical considerations. Certainly, we would not fear that such emphasis in any way might constitute denying "existence" or "reality" to the phenomena.

PROFESSOR SHERIF:

I would like to make an over-all remark about the general methodological problems of which we should always be mindful in defining research topics. In my opinion, this consideration should be at the core of this Symposium.

Our problems in social science today are not new problems. They are as old as human beings themselves. For example, such topics as the structure of a human relationship, leader-follower relations, intergroup relations, interpersonal attitudes, communication, and so on, are as old as human history. Moreover, people did not wait for social science to be concerned about these problems before they theorized about them and discussed them. By their very nature, these are vital problems to human beings.

There have been solutions offered for them on a religious basis. In fact, all religions have their own systems which define what human relations are and what they should be. Philosophers from at least the time of Plato to the great systematizers of today have offered answers for these same problems. The distinctive claim of the social sciences is that systematization should rest on available empirical findings and should be capable of predicting new findings. As a result, some policy-makers have turned their attention to the social sciences in the hope that they may be helpful.

For example, in this shrinking world today, the over-riding problem is intergroup relations. Problems of war and peace, which directly or indirectly include most of the problems of social science, have led some policy-makers to support social science research in the hope that we operate like engineers. If a bridge is ordered, engineers are supposed to design and build it on the basis of established laws in the physical sciences. Nowadays the social sciences are expected to perform in a similar manner. However, the policy-makers and the foundations that support social science research as if it were engineering do not know that, as yet, we have very few established principles on which to base predictions. Even the basic definitional problems have not gone beyond the stage of controversy between more or less closed intellectual schools. If we are clever, let us keep that fact to ourselves; but let us not delude ourselves in the process.

Every social science discipline has found out by now that it is not a law unto itself. No one of these sciences is sufficient for the huge task of dealing with human problems single-handedly. Interdisciplinary research is needed as well as interdisciplinary theory. But what kind of interdisciplinary research and theory?

One interdisciplinary orientation centers under the banner of "behavioral science," a term used very loosely and meaning all things to all people. This orientation frequently over-stresses behavior as the datum of social science. The logical outcome of this emphasis, of course, would be to make psychologists of everybody. And, in fact, it is not difficult to find, for example, social scientists studying a hospital ward who have become so over-awed by psychology and psychiatry that they adopt the jargon of those disciplines. If these social scientists would stick to their problems at the social science *level,* they could make a greater contribution to interdisciplinary study, and, let me add, they would be in a much stronger position in the establishments where they work. For an interdisciplinary approach to become effective, it is much better to develop first-rate social scientists instead of turning them into second- or third-rate psychiatric workers or psychologists.

Some other interdisciplinary efforts seem to proceed from the assumption that just because a number of specialists from different disciplines talk about the same problems the result will be interdisciplinary. As my illustration, I shall take—with respect—one of the more ambitious theoretical undertakings of our time, Parsons and Shils' *Toward a General Theory of Action.* Before commenting on this work, let me hasten to say that there should be more and renewed attempts such as this on a grand scope. Hence, my evaluation does not concern the desirability of the attempt as such, but the particular contents between its two covers.

More properly, I believe, this book might have been called something like *Views on Social Science and Related Topics by Some Eminent Scholars.* Parsons and Shils have written not a theory, but a categorical scheme. One can search far and wide within their book for "action" and one finds not "a theory" but several very different theories by some of the most distinguished psychologists and sociologists of our day. For example, one of the authors, Sheldon, dissents from the very basic proposition that culture "as a system is on a different plane from personalities and social systems."[1] Another author, the anthropologist, Kluckhohn, disagrees with the separation of social structure and systems, on the one hand, and culture, on the other.[2] The distinguished psychologist Tolman focuses on learning in a way that may be congenial to other authors but has very little to do with what they write.[3] An equally eminent psychologist, Gordon Allport (by the way, a teacher of mine), treats prejudice but specifically denies the applicability of a general theory to the phenomenon "for the time being."[4] Robert Sears, cautions that "an appallingly small number of the relationships that have been discovered in social psychology can be generalized. . . . With respect to attitude measurement, for example, one might well ask whether *any* general principles of an antecedent-consequent nature have been found."[5] And, finally, Stouffer, an empiricist who developed outside the grandiose theorizing, warns against "an excess of optimism about the necessary usefulness of any new system of highly general orienting ideas."[6]

What is wrong here? Two things, I think. One is that talking about the same or related problems does not necessarily build a coherent interdisciplinary theory. The other is that general theory presumes the incorporation of findings from all social science disciplines into an integrated system. We preach and preach about empirical research, with the aim of attaining reliable and valid indicators as the end product of conceptual definitions and research operations—just as Professor Lazarsfeld has been insisting. Yet some systematists take too little stock of empirical results being accumulated in different social sciences on the same problems. Theorizing is necessary. But, as I tried to stress in my paper for this Symposium, theorizing must be checked through the evidence that is accumulating at the time.

Let me illustrate one of the things that needs to be done. One of the principles that everybody preaches—in different schools of psychology, sociology, and anthropology—is that a system affects the properties of its parts. Psychologically, this has been established time and again—by Gestalt psychologists, by Bartlett, and by many other investigators. But when we engage in interdisciplinary study, we act as though this principle were unimportant. We compartmentalize our tasks and our findings and say, "Oh, I'm a psychologist. The sociology part is being done in New York or Buffalo or somewhere else. When we are through, we will put the studies side by side." The researcher cannot operate this way. The theorist cannot operate this way. If the aspects being studied are parts of the same system, there has to be coordination from the very beginning, so that the different parts will fit together as they do in the system.

If the system affects the properties of its parts, the systematizer cannot give mere lip service to this principle; he must translate it into logical operations in terms of concepts, procedures, and measures. For example, when we study the roles of individuals in a group, we first have to place the group in its cultural setting. Then, in a definite sequence, we are prepared to study the group as a system, and only then to understand the roles of particular individuals. The point that I am trying to make here has been made for many years by many social scientists, at least in words. But when we get down to the real brass tacks of research, its implications are either forgotten or muffled somewhere. For example, in theorizing about youthful sub-cultures and misbehaviors, there has been a pronounced tendency to use the concept of "reaction-formation," which is borrowed from a highly individualistic psychological system, instead of bringing the behavior into the context constituted by the gamut of influences from the general social system and noting the similarities as well as differences among youth in different socio-cultural settings within the system.

PROFESSOR ANDERSON:

I was very much impressed with how much *traditional* philosophy was involved in the presentations, and not philosophy of science in the way in which it is known contemporarily to philosophers. That is, with the exception of Professor Lazarsfeld's presentation, there was no mention of Carnap or Pap or Popper or—and then one could read off a large list of people who are considered to be at the forefront of this topic. None of them came up, but we heard a great deal about Plato and several metaphysical speculators.

I would like to address one remark to Professor White. It seems to me that there is a perfectly good, technical term that dates from Greek times for the "symbolates" of which you speak. It seems to me that symbolates are simply the "forms" of Plato. They are not endowed with the sort of magical properties that Plato gave them presumably, but they are certainly abstract entities—that is to say, languages in abstraction from the speakers, or the time and places of speech, and so on. I just wondered if you are considering that as a possibility.

PROFESSOR WHITE:

I would like to say that I listened to all the papers with a great deal of interest. I am not sure that I understand everything in each paper, but that is simply my shortcoming and my misfortune.

I think I might make this point, though, about my own paper. With the possible exception of Professor Anderson, I think I was the only one on the panel who is not interested in the behavior of people, as such. I think Professor Anderson divides his interests between people and computers. All the other members are interested in who voted for Stevenson or something in the behavior of people. I have been devoting a great deal of my energy, and time, and ambition in recent years to developing the science of culture, to which I have given the name "culturology." Incidentally, I hope you will not think that I am excessively immodest if I call your attention to the fact that "culturology" has found its way into at least four dictionaries of specialized terms and now into the third edition of *Webster's International Dictionary of the English Language*. Apparently, it is here to stay.

One of the premises of the science of culture is this. The behavior of peoples—plural, not individuals—is a function not of their genetic composition or their biological make-up, but of an external extra-somatic tradition that we call "culture." Variations in this tradition that we call "culture" are not to be explained psychologically or biologically, but culturologically. So the culturologist studies and interprets variations in this cultural tradition as if the human race did not exist. He recognizes full well, of course, that human beings are necessary for the existence of culture; but they are not necessary for a scientific explanation of variations of culture. I thought I might, since I had a chance, point this out. Most of the other panel members are taking cultures as a constant and seeing human beings as variables. The culturologist takes the human species as a constant and is concerned with variables of culture. I think that perhaps this is about all I have to say.

PROFESSOR ANDERSON:

Just one short comment, namely, that I am in complete agreement with Professor White. That is, I want you to count me on your side. I am not interested in machinery. Indeed, that was the point of our paper.

PROFESSOR LEVINSON:

I think that I shall begin with an "intraceptive" comment and say that I have enjoyed this Symposium very much. And I wish that we had more time for more informal interchange.

Let me make just a few comments on the talks of the others. At the risk of being deviant or maybe with the anticipation of it, I will say that I am probably more in agreement with Dr. Ackerman's point of view than most of the others here may be. I have a great fondness for Parsonian theory. Like many other people, I have never been sure that I understood it fully, but I have been able to take things from it and with benefit, I believe. I would also count Parsons among the intraceptive sociologists. Someone asked in a written question how I distinguished psychology, sociology, and anthropology from the point of view of intraception. I think that within each, one can find intraceptive, extraceptive, and anti-intraceptive variants. In sociology, intraception traditionally has been a rather problematic issue. Social psychology has always been a major field in sociology. It is the largest section of the American Sociological Association. At the same time there is also a very strong tradition in sociology, going back at least to Durkheim, according to which human behavior should be explained by means of "sociological" laws rather than "psychological" laws. The relevance of personality is an issue that many individual sociologists have to come to terms with. I believe that Parsons has helped to clarify some of the issues involved and has shown a way in which personality theory can be relevant without the risk that sociology will be overwhelmed entirely by personality theory. And I would say that Dr. Ackerman's presentation contained a psychological sensitivity that I personally admire a great deal.

I have one specific point on the question of order. Dr. Ackerman has said that the ultimate problem of systemic theory, and a basic problem in sociology generally, is the problem of order, but that order is not stasis and that one can be concerned with order without being static. That is, one can conceive of a changing order. I think that there is a dilemma here for Parsonian theory. Changes in the order of the system have been given less consideration than stability. There is some tendency to take the order as given, and then to see it as causing particular events within a system. But there has been less interest in the factors that produce change in systems. I would like to see these considered more. For example, the introduction of new personalities into a system is one of the possible sources of change, although by no means the only one.

I also have many common interests with Dr. Sherif. We also seem, from time to time, to get into apparent differences about the relevance of personality in social psychology. I got an impression from his public comments that he was minimizing the relevance of personality in social psychological research, but afterwards he informed me that he does not want to minimize it. What he wanted to say, rather, was that one ought to begin studying human phenomena by starting with the social situation in which the individuals exist; after understanding it as a system, one then would get to its meaning for the individuals, and to the relevance of their personalities for the ways in which they adapt to the social situation. With this approach I would agree completely. I think it is useful to start with the social context in which individuals live and then move from the outside in—into the individual and from the surface of personality to the depths— and then move back. I am glad we agree on that.

I cannot offer any new perspective on Dr. Anderson's paper, but I do want to say how helpful it was to me. You see, computers and mechanical simulation and so on are problematic for intraceptive persons. We do not want to believe them. After all, machines cannot feel; and if they cannot feel, then clearly they are not human, and we get uneasy when it turns out that they have quasi-human qualities and when, in fact, they can do some things a good deal better than persons can. Therefore it was reassuring to me to hear Dr. Anderson's formulations; they allow me to find value in the work that people are doing in this field, and which I have made use of through employing computers in my research, without my feeling at the same time threatened by the anti-human implications. I am very thankful to him. I hope his view prevails.

Dr. White, sitting next to me, has been a great boon to me in a personal sense. Whenever I got a little steam up about something someone was saying, I could comment on it to him and feel much better. At the same time I may be the one who disagrees with him most strongly on the basic issues of his talk. This again would be something to explore further. My own view is that "culturology" is an appropriate term and that it is a discipline of value in itself and of great importance. As I indicated at the beginning of my talk, I also have a strong interest in the field of personality and culture. I get a little uneasy at some of Dr. White's comments because he seems to be saying that he is interested in the culture and not in the person, and that the kinds of persons in a culture have nothing to do with the way it works. My own preference is to believe that the kinds of personalities that are represented in a culture do, in fact, influence its character and its direction of change just as they are influenced by the nature of that culture. There is, in Dr. Ackerman's words, an "interpenetration," and that is something that I would like to study. I would not want to feel that I am being illegitimate, from Dr. White's point of view, in working at that boundary. That would be the area he and I would discuss further if there were time.

I find myself very responsive to Dr. Lazarsfeld's ideas, but I am not quite sure how in fact to use them. At this time there are far more sophisticated techniques of scaling than there were in 1944 when we first developed the F-Scale. The big controversy in scaling then was whether you used a Thurstone Scale or a Likert Scale, and from the present point of view neither one of them is very sophisticated. Looking back on it, I do not know that the Likert Scale is particularly less sophisticated than the Thurstone. I hold no great brief for the F-Scale. In fact, it is actually a source of some embarrassment to me. There has been a great preoccupation with the technical aspects of the F-Scale—is it unidimensional or not, and does response-set operate, and if so how can we deal with it, and what other scaling devices might be used to improve it? There has been so much preoccupation with these technological issues that by and large people have lost sight of what to us was most important—which was the concept of authoritarianism. Our commitment was primarily to other, non-scale ways of getting at it. We were much more interested in less structured approaches, in a more clinical way of thinking about it and measuring it. That aspect of our approach—which I think was distinctive about our book and made it more than a collection of measures—has been lost sight of to a large extent. So my answer to Dr. Lazarsfeld is: if you can show a better way to measure authoritarianism by means of a scale, I would be delighted to see it. So far I have not seen it. And Dr. Lazarsfeld's notions of imagery and concepts are very intraceptive. I agree with him that we often use a fancy conceptual language to talk about rather vaguely formulated and understood matters. But I must say that what I found missing from the examples that he himself gave of his work on the academic mind were concepts. It is of importance to develop adequate ways of measuring the degree of apprehension one may feel in a given situation or the degree of prominence of the scientist. But from the point of view of psychological theory, we want to talk about dispositions in a person—dispositions of some wider relevance—and I do not see evidence of a concern with those. I wish that Dr. Lazarsfeld would use his great methodological sophistication in the service of measuring concepts that have a broader significance.

PROFESSOR LAZARSFELD:

I would like to ask Professor White and Dr. Levinson each one question.

I happen to be, if I understand him correctly, very much in agreement with Professor White. However, I would formulate the problem somewhat differently. My habit is to formulate your position, not substantively in terms of what exists or does not exist, but in terms of the structure of propositions and the variables that enter into them. One can classify individuals, one can classify organizations, one can classify cultures—each in their own right—and then one can relate these by operating on a much lower level than the cultural.

I shall offer a deliberately very trivial example so that I might get your reaction—a study of about 180 hospitals. The hospitals first are classified essentially into three groups, but we need only two. In the table of organization of a particular hospital, we find that interns have a lower social status than the residents. Some hospitals have a rectangular table of organization wherein interns and residents have approximately the same status. There are, let us say, one hundred interns and one hundred residents. This is a bit exaggerated since the table of organization provides many more interns than residents. Now this is characterizing the hospitals, a mixed group, by a completely external characteristic: just look at how many posts there are and divide them neatly. Then you conduct an attitude survey among the interns. A part of this includes the administration of a scale of competitiveness. You would have questions such as the following: "Do you share your observations here?" "Is there a lot of competition?" It is a typical attitude study of how interns feel about each other and about their collaboration. Let us say that the figure that is found for competitiveness is ten for one category and five for the other. That is an expected result. Of course, if everyone were to have a chance to be promoted to resident, the competitiveness would be less than if only one out of four had a chance to be promoted.

The formal nature of this result, however, is interesting because it relates completely objective, pre-personal variables to the average of the completely personal. I have no objection to saying that it is culture, or in this case the organization of the hospital, which determines the attitude. I think that many of those nominalistic-realistic discussions—such as the priority of the collectivity or the unit—really boil down to the fact that there exist a great many propositions in which objective characteristics of the cultures and organizations are related to attitudes of the individuals who enter the organization. That seems to me to catch the essence of the argument. I think that this can be extended to many other problems because there are certain propositions in which only culture or only collective characteristics are related to each other, and still other propositions where individual characteristics are related. When you offer this more—if you please—philosophical way to formulate your problem abstractly, it seems rather grave to me.

The question that Dr. Levinson raises seems to be the following one, and I think that Dr. Sherif is likely to have opinions on this which may be clearer than what I might say. There is a strange "migration," so to speak, of concepts. They begin as broad interpretative concepts. Take the concept of "reference group," which appeared in, among other places, Newcomb's Bennington study. The behavior of college girls was explained by the fact that they had different reference groups. Only fifteen years later the idea came up: Taking girl A and girl B, can we find out which reference groups they have? For more than ten years, the concept of reference group was used as a notion to explain measured interrelations, but was never measured itself. So one day I began to wonder whether policemen compare themselves more with firemen or with soldiers, and whether or not the particular comparison they draw would explain their wage negotiations. Take "relative deprivation" as another example. Stouffer[7] found that men in the Air Force objectively had a greater chance to be promoted than the military policemen. But the military policemen were more satisfied with their lot because they expected less. The Air Force man who was not promoted was especially unhappy because he saw so many promotions around him. There are very many concepts which begin as a kind of generating formula and slowly get into the classificatory realm.

It was quite interesting that in your terminology you used the word "intraception." That "ion" and the fact that you spent 90 per cent of your time on it indicate that you feel that you are still very much in the realm of the interpretative use of this concept. That is to say, it is an important idea; a lot of phenomena can be explained by it. However, when it becomes a classificatory concept, then first it usually changes its name. It becomes "intraceptiveness." And, secondly then, all those trivial problems of measurement which I tried to describe enter into the picture. I find this migration of the ideas from broad imageries to concrete classificatory devices very interesting. And I think your concern over why we do not measure important concepts might arise from a misunderstanding. What you consider an important concept—in this case, intraception—is something that is still in the phase of generating ideas, and in this phase it cannot be measured. This can only be done when it becomes a classificatory device. So, in a way, we will always come in at the time when you already are bored. For example, I think you are bored with the F-Scale because now it is a classificatory device. It used to be a generating idea, and that is a distinction on which I am not very clear, but which can be traced. Those are the two questions that were asked.

PROFESSOR DiRENZO:

That finishes the democratic round. We now shall entertain any random comments or questions of relevance to the issues under discussion.

PROFESSOR ACKERMAN:

What I want to emphasize is Professor Lazarsfeld's comment that in a sense it does not really make any difference which indicators one chooses so long as they are not utterly absurd. Let me repeat the analogy of my paper. Consider an intercorrelation matrix, prepared for factor analysis. We intend to take from the matrix, regions of dense intercorrelations. We do not have to call it a factor; and I might want to call it a system momentarily. We grant that the boundaries of these "systems" are empirically fuzzy; they are so because of interpenetration. But, I would suggest, *it does matter* what indicators or variables one is using; it does, at least, if one thinks in this way. It does so because "Indicator" A *belongs in* "Factor" or "System" X, and is only a weak indicator of a process in another system. It matters very much analytically where and what we bind together, what we place in *this* system and what in *that*. There *are* areas of density and sparsity of intercorrelation; and a variable *belongs* somewhere, not just anywhere, and it belongs within the analytically bounded "factor" or "system." Could you comment on this, Professor Lazarsfeld?

PROFESSOR LAZARSFELD:

Yes. You leave out one little detail. That is the third variable. If I take a factor matrix, to come back to my example of the indicators of the eminence of professors which was taken from our study in *The Academic Mind*, I do find those clusters that give me the intrinsic dimension and analysis of the notion of prominence or eminence. I completely agree. But, then, I wanted to know whether prominent professors were conservative or non-conservative; I was interested in their politics. You could be interested in something entirely different—whether prominent professors are nicer to their students, for example—but in any case you are going to have an outside variable. Your matrix only analyzes intrinsically the interrelation between the indicators. When it then comes to relating your concept to any outside variable, it will turn out that it makes no difference which indicator you have chosen. It might violate systemic things; I do not know. But empirically, at the present state of knowledge, the predicted value of whatever index you come up with is really about the same, wherever in this system of clusters you sample a few indicators at random.

PROFESSOR SHERIF:

I would like to stick to the basic orientation of this Symposium, namely, definitions and theoretical orientations, rather than going to procedural matters, which are relatively easy. We are interested in sociology and we are interested in psychology. We are interested both in personality and in group and in culture. But on so many topics, our interests are dichotomized and elaborated as distinct and almost insulated "approaches." So we have personality-oriented approaches, group-oriented approaches, or culture-oriented approaches.

It seems to me that there is a place for both a group-oriented and a personality-oriented approach, and both are needed. But this is not an endorsement of eclecticism. I am following Durkheim who stated, in *The Rules of the Sociological Method* and in *The Elementary Forms of Religious Life* for example, that social life is not a continuation of natural life, but an emergent level. This is where he ties in the criteria of exteriority and constraint. With this orientation, we can attack the problem of integrating the group or cultural level and the individual level, including individual personality.

Take social and cultural phenomena as things *out there* and analyze them at a sociological level of analysis, with proper units for that level, such as group organization and institutional structure, customary procedures, routines, and social norms. When we deal with individual behavior, on the other hand, we are working at a different level of analysis, a psychological level; we have to deal in terms of psychological units of analysis. However, the two levels of analysis—the sociological and the psychological—should not be contradictory, if they are valid. On the contrary, they must supplement one another.

Let me illustrate with the case of color blindness. If the

physiologist is studying color blindness, his units of analysis are the receptors, the optic nerve, cerebral functioning, and so on. But, if we are psychologists, we have to use units of analysis appropriate to the psychological level. Here we deal with the individual's perception and behavior in response to selected stimuli, such as the color plates or skeins of yarn in a color vision test. We ask what the person sees on a figure; for example, does he or does he not see the numeral seven? This is a psychological question. There is still the possibility that on casual inspection a person may not respond as expected because the colors in question are not discriminated in the lexicon of colors in his culture. Now, the physiological level of analysis, the psychological level of analysis, and the cultural or sociological level of analysis should supplement one another in elucidating why an individual responds in a particular fashion. It is absurd to struggle with the question of whose prerogative it is to do what. If their findings are correct, the analysis of physiologists, psychologists, and social scientists supplement one another, as indicated in the case of color blindness. The issue is the same in the question of studying personality and group or culture.

The point can be illustrated through our research, begun in 1958, in which we have been studying small groups of boys for a period of from six months to a year. These groups are composed of boys who come together of their own choice and who do not know that they are being studied, the observer appearing to them in the guise of a somewhat older friend. Without exception, the interaction in such clusters produces some kind of pattern. In the most important dimension of power, we have found in every case a hierarchical arrangement (that is, a status hierarchy). Some pattern is an invariant product if a number of individuals interact with one another over a given time span. Now we are involved in determining cutting points to differentiate the various divisions of the status hierarchy in different organizations of this kind. These are not new notions, but we are taking steps toward operationalizing them in terms of specific *indicators* of power.

Now these patterns of relationships in small groups are not ahistorical phenomena. As Rome was not built in a day, so groups are not built in one or a few days. That is why the concept and the analysis of a group differ completely from the ahistoricalism that characterized the earlier period of the movement called Group Dynamics, which was based upon physical analogies. Sociologically, in the study of groups we have no choice but to proceed longitudinally or historically.

The data in this regard warrant a generalization on a sociological level. When a number of individuals with a common interest interact with one another repeatedly over a period of time, they form some kind of pattern or structure. This pattern or organization is obviously a phenomenon at the sociological level of analysis. But, let us turn now to personality. Who occupies what position in the structure and why? Of course, who occupies what position is a function of the unique characteristics of particular individuals constituting the pattern in relation to the activities they engage in most frequently. Only when we can put the individuals in their proper context—namely, into the pattern of relationships in the group—can we come to see the personality characteristics of the individual members in a meaningful way. And even then we will find that the achievement of particular status and roles in a group is not explained by personality characteristics in the abstract. Personality characteristics become relevant in particular situations. Of course this is not a new finding. Thrasher's study *The Gang* includes reports of the variations in the personal characteristics that are the most prized by different groups. In one gang, where toughness was important, the leader would be a tough guy. In another, the leader was a hunchback, who could not actually carry out plans himself, but who became the leader because shrewdness in the ability to steal was at a premium.

In short, psychology and sociology need not wrangle over prerogatives. They should supplement each other, and if each will use the proper level of analysis with its appropriate units, they can validate each other's findings.

PROFESSOR ANDERSON:

I would like to raise this question. In the case Professor Lazarsfeld discussed at length in his original talk, or in similar cases, what have these considerations to do with whether or not one conceives of correlations as *explanations?* Let me put the matter this way. The situation looks to me somewhat like Keplerian astronomy: we know as a matter of fact that the planets move in certain elliptical orbits, but it is not until we get a general theory of the Newtonian sort, from which one can deduce the fact that they ought to move in elliptical orbits, that one feels that one has an explanation of why they do it. I am not absolutely sure why it is that we have this feeling, but it certainly is true that one thinks that Newtonian mechanics *explain* the observations that Kepler made about the positions of the planets. I am just asking this as a question: in what sense do the correlations themselves count as explanations? It always seems to me that there are some additional facts that need to be explained.

In just the same way, for example, one might associate hair color with body type. (This is, of course, not a good illustration.) But, let us suppose that various body types always produce constant hair color. It would seem to me that this is a bit of information—something to be explained—but that the fact itself does not serve as an explanation of anything at all.

PROFESSOR SHERIF:

If you will permit me, I would like to address this problem by discussing the concept of "reference group." Suppose that I am a small businessman assessing how prosperous I am. If I take the "upper class" as my reference point, my judgment of my prosperity would shift downward. But if I take the salaries of teachers, my judgment of my prosperity would shift upward. Here is a bit of information which, as Professor Anderson notes, a correlation does not explain. From the reference group concept, we can predict such systematic variations because it, in turn, was based on the experimental psychology of judgment—that is, of the categorization of objects and events.

Judgments are never absolute. Judgment always involves a process of comparison. One has to have at least two things to compare in order to make a judgment. Now, judgment of particular things varies systematically depending upon the series or context of which they are parts and upon the standard or anchor used as the primary basis for comparison. Judgments vary systematically in direction according to the relationships among the particular objects judged and the stimulus value of the standard or anchor. The relationships governing shifts in judgment have been explored extensively in the psychological laboratory, and the principles discovered are readily generalized to the case in point.

The person uses the position of the group or set of people with whom he identifies as the major anchor or standard for assessing the positions of other groups on the social scale. With reference to upper-class income, the small businessman in our case exaggerates the difference between his own and theirs. This is a *contrast effect*, which occurs when the objective discrepancy between one's standard and the particular item judged is large. It follows that the businessman regards himself as less prosperous when comparing himself to the upper class than when comparing himself with teachers, whose incomes are also discrepant, but lower. On the other hand, if he were to assess the income of, say, academic administrators, the small difference between his own income and theirs would lead him to regard his prosperity as being on a par with university presidents. This is an *assimilation effect*, also well known in the psychology of judgment, which occurs when there are small differences between the standard for judgment and the item judged.

In other words, whether it is the question of judging physical objects or of judging social phenomena, you can predict systematic displacements in judgment provided that you know the anchor value and the values of the items being compared with it. The phenomena are not merely described, but are governed by lawful relationships among standards and comparison stimuli, as you may see in our books on the topic—*Social Judgment* and *Attitude and Attitude Change*.

PROFESSOR ANDERSON:

Let us grant the fact—which would seem to be true—that every judgment we make is made relative to some standard or some, let us say, anchor point. Granting this, one might then be moved to ask "Why?" Why do we do it that way? Why do we not do it some other way?

PROFESSOR SHERIF:

Psychologically, the "why" is specified in terms of relationships between anchors (either the person's psychological anchor or an objective stimulus standard) and the objects of judgment. If you want a further answer to "why," you would have to work on a different level of analysis, namely the physiological or biochemical, in terms of units applicable to the central nervous system. Many principles of judgment are equally applicable to a variety of sensory and perceptual phenomena, indicating that they are not dependent solely upon the operation of the receptor organs. It turns out that they are also applicable to the ways an individual appraises himself relative to others, provided that you know his reference groups.

PROFESSOR ANDERSON:

But, in Newtonian physics, one does not do that. What one does is to derive Kepler's laws from the more general principles.

PROFESSOR SHERIF:

Let me be clear that I am not stating a logical premise, but an empirical generalization. It is an explanation in the sense that you can derive other things from it. But we do not have our Newton yet in psychology or in social science. When we do, no doubt there will be a body of more general principles and their specific corollaries. If so, my guess is that they will include social, psychological, and physiological variables. As far as I am concerned I will be more than satisfied if we advance in social science from our primitive state in the twentieth century to the level that Kepler achieved in the first half of the seventeenth century.

PROFESSOR ACKERMAN:

I am quite in agreement with Professor Anderson that the correlation is a fact to be explained. What constitutes "explanation"? So far as I am concerned, the set of general statements from which one could generate the correlation constitutes the explanation. With reference to all the fours that have appeared in these discussions, I would submit (1) that we could generate these by the AGIL paradigm and that (2) *therefore*—until phenomena come along that we cannot subsume—action theory constitutes an explanation of them.

PROFESSOR DiRENZO:

Thank you, gentlemen, for these comments. Your discussion has clarified some of the issues that we have been talking about today. Unfortunately, limited time inevitably results in having to leave behind many unanswered questions. We certainly did not intend to resolve the problems involved in the many issues that were discussed. Let us hope, nonetheless, that our deliberations may provide a significant contribution in that direction.

NOTES

1. Richard C. Sheldon, in Talcott Parsons, *et al.*, "Some Fundamental Categories of the Theory of Action: A General Statement," in Talcott Parsons and Edward A. Shils (eds.), *Toward a General Theory of Action* (Cambridge: Harvard University Press, 1951), p. 7, n. 9.

2. Clyde Kluckhohn, in *ibid.*, pp. 26–27, n. 31.

3. Edward C. Tolman, "A Psychological Model," in Parsons and Shils, *ibid.*, pp. 277–361.

4. Gordon Allport, "Prejudice: A Problem in Psychological and Social Causation," in *ibid.*, p. 384.

5. Robert R. Sears, "Social Behavior and Personality Development," in *ibid.*, p. 466.

6. Samuel A. Stouffer, "An Empirical Study of Technical Problems in Analysis of Role Obligation," in *ibid.*, p. 480.

7. Samuel A. Stouffer, *et al.*, *The American Soldier* (Princeton: Princeton University Press, 1949).

Suggested Readings

Durkheim, Émile. *The Rules of the Sociological Method.* Glencoe: The Free Press, 1938.

———. *The Elementary Forms of Religious Life.* New York: Collier Books, 1961.

Lazarsfeld, Paul F., and Thielens, Wagner. *The Academic Mind.* Glencoe: The Free Press, 1958.

Newcomb, Theodore M. *Personality and Social Change.* New York: The Dryden Press, 1943.

Parsons, Talcott, and Shils, Edward A. (eds.). *Toward a General Theory of Action.* Cambridge: Harvard University Press, 1951.

Sherif, Carolyn W., Sherif, Muzafer, and Nebergall, R. E. *Attitude and Attitude Change: The Social Judgment–Involvement Approach.* Philadelphia: W. B. Saunders Company, 1965.

Sherif, Muzafer, and Hovland, Carl I. *Social Judgment.* New Haven: Yale University Press, 1961.

Stouffer, Samuel A., *et al. The American Soldier.* Princeton: Princeton University Press, 1949.

Thrasher, Frederic M. *The Gang.* Chicago: University of Chicago Press, 1927.

CHAPTER IX

Toward Explanation in the Behavioral Sciences

Gordon J. DiRenzo

Editor's Introduction

Some of the major differences among the various disciplines of science are those which are important in the conduct of scientific inquiry. Our specific concerns in this Symposium have been primarily methodological ones. The principal intent of these proceedings has been to put into sharper focus the relationship of methodological analysis to substantive problems of theoretical explanation in the behavioral sciences. In this concluding chapter, the editor delineates some of the more central issues which have been the focus of the several contributions to this Symposium, and provides his own critical assessment of them.

The major topics that have been selected for discussion are: scientific epistemology, scientific explanation, analytical loci and boundaries, concepts, empirical measurement and verification, and the scientific convergence of interdisciplinary activity. These selected methodological issues are ones which, according to Professor DiRenzo's assessment of the preceding chapters, need to be confronted with serious determination before significant progress toward explanation in the behavioral sciences can be expected. His procedure attempts to show the unity among these major topics as progressive steps in the logical sequence of the scientific process.

Basic to theoretical explanation in any discipline is the question of scientific epistemology—the study of the sources and methods whereby science comes to know the phenomena of reality. DiRenzo suggests that there is a rather extensive neglect of epistemological considerations on the part of the behavioral scientists. These concerns, he argues, have been left by and large to the philosophers of science. Since all scientific activity, however, is necessarily and inescapably accompanied by some kind of epistemological system, and since a slight modification in epistemological perspectives may imply a major change in theoretical conclusions, the scientist needs to become cognizant of epistemological elements, their implications, and their consequences. DiRenzo does not suggest a wholesale invasion by philosophy into the empirical realms of scientific investigation; rather, he pleads for the utilization of only the *appropriate* contributions of the philosophy of science, especially epistemology and logic, to the theoretical activity of the empirical scientists.

DiRenzo argues that epistemological considerations are methodological considerations, and as such comprise a very vital segment of the research process which cannot be neglected. To make these epistemological considerations explicit—to know their nature and their implications—is to make a major advance toward the fruitful construction of scientific theory. He reaffirms his position that behavioral scientists should assume a particular epistemological orientation—an empirical epistemology, or an epistemic empiricism. Yet, this very epistemology, he contends, by no means has been exhausted analytically. There are a number of methodological questions involved in such an epistemology that the behavioral sciences have yet to scrutinize thoroughly.

Next, the editor inquires into the nature of scientific explanation. Showing that there are different types of explanation, DiRenzo raises the more specific question of when scientific explanation is achieved satisfactorily. What is an adequate and complete answer? Explanation often is said to be complete when it has arrived at theory, but "theory" has been given various meanings and applied to a host of different things, many of which are not explanations at all. In this context, the editor discusses in particular the role of models, which have been the subject of much concern in the preceding chapters.

What is the nature of explanation in the behavioral sciences? Which type of explanation do we need? Which type of explanation can we get? DiRenzo distinguishes two fundamental species of explanation: *description* (which simply explains *what* happens, and is concerned with the definition and classification of phenomena); and *interpretation* (which offers explanations of *why* given phenomena occur and which determines the nature of relationships among these phenomena). To provide a complete explanation, he argues, is to say not only *what* happens, but also *why* it happens. DiRenzo contends that one of the major drawbacks of explanation in the behavioral sciences is that there has been too much mere description and not enough interpretation. The consequences of this situation are incomplete—and, therefore, not only limited, but often distorted—explanations.

The question of the nature of explanation begs consideration of the nature of the phenomenon to be explained. Science seeks to explain reality—but what is the nature of the reality of the phenomena with which the behavioral sciences concern themselves? What is the nature of the existence of such things as "personality," "society," and "culture"? How real are statistical correlations and mathematical probabilities? These questions become more meaningful when the behavioral scientist realizes how different his data are from much of those in the physical sciences. Such questions as what constitutes an adequate and complete explanation become much more significant when the behavioral scientist realizes that explanation cannot be confined to the data of the manifest property space; rather, it must, of necessity, be concerned with the latent property space. It is the structure and dynamics of latent property space which constitute the fundamental reality to be explained.

DiRenzo attempts to dispel the particularly confusing error that reality consists exclusively in physical existence. Behavioral phenomena, argues DiRenzo, are just as ontologically real as physical phenomena. It is important, he argues further, to distinguish between subjective and objective reality, and to recognize the consequences that such a distinction has for the explanatory process. Both types are just as real in their consequences, as they are theoretically in a causal and inferential sense. But, logical reality does not imply metaphysical reality. DiRenzo takes to task in particular the "as if" postulation and that of "scientific mythologization." How much pretension is legitimate, and how much mythologization can be tolerated, he asks, without frustrating the fundamental objective of achieving an affinity between conceptual/theoretical formulations and metaphysical reality, by precipitating distortion in scientific explanation? "As if" realities, argues DiRenzo, are hypothetical and speculative—and as such constitute a fictitious premise. Accordingly, whatever theory is constructed on such assumptions has no exact counterpart in reality, and thus would be false. DiRenzo contends that we cannot be so self-defeating as simply to resign ourselves to the inevitable position that, because they involve some degree of distortion, all scientific facts are "myths." However true, what we must do is to minimize scientific mythologization while making every attempt—regardless how apparently futile—to eradicate it entirely.

One particular problem which DiRenzo alleges to be at the base of this difficulty is that many scientists shy away from so-called "ultimate

reality," which he contends is nothing more than ontological reality.
Such evasive action is paradoxical on the part of the scientist. Since
science seeks to explain reality, it seeks to confront ontological
reality—that is to say, "ultimate reality." This aim implies fundamentally an affinity between scientific explanations and metaphysical
reality. To achieve such an affinity it is necessary to know the nature
of both. The "levels" of reality, which often are used to delimit the
scope of several disciplines, are man-made and fictitious, and thus
misleading. Accordingly, the behavioral scientist cannot arbitrarily
delineate the scope of his investigations without a concern for probable distortion and for the consequences that these delimitations may
have for the adequacy and the completeness of his explanations.
Rather, the scientist should respect the fundamental position of
science that all reality is a unity. DiRenzo suggests that what is needed
is the development of metascientific interests in the behavioral sciences, and he offers these as a legitimate dimension and an integral
part of science. He argues that science should strive to exhaust the
intelligibility of reality. To do so, it is necessary to act *as if* reality can
be mastered by the genius of man. This position, maintains DiRenzo,
needs to be nothing more than a fundamental postulate of science,
which as such is perfectly consistent with scientific epistemology.
After all, human knowledge remains probable, since the search for
truth is a seemingly endless task.

After one has gone about deciding what constitutes explanation, and
how best to achieve it, then the next logical problem that remains to
be settled is the question of what it is that is to be explained—the
"locus" problem. Decisions must be made concerning which aspects
(loci) of the analytical problems are the most productive in terms of
yielding explanations that are most comprehensive, as well as most
free of distortion and error of any kind—or, at least, free of the
potentialities for producing such defects.

This question of determining what is to be studied also involves
ascertaining the priorities in these investigations. DiRenzo suggests
that we need to give some thought to specifying the "logical" and
"realistic" approaches to our phenomena. Consideration of the phenomena under investigation in all sciences as a fundamental unity
implies, he argues, that there is a necessary primacy of elements—both
in time and in place—which, if replicated logically in the theoretical
process, should produce not only valid theory, but more particularly a

more thorough and productive explanation. This is a matter of perspective which in no way diminishes the focus of concern for the individual scientist. It simply puts his specific focus in a proper analytical locus—one which is realistically sound.

Related to this issue of analytical locus is that of analytical boundaries. Where these are staked affects the quality—and hence, the validity and the adequacy—of theoretical explanation. Analytical boundaries in a more general sense relate to the scope of individual disciplines. DiRenzo argues that the arbitrary limits of disciplinary boundaries must be transgressed whenever they tend to distort or to prevent theoretical explanation. He suggests that a comprehensive interdisciplinary perspective is a proper means both for effecting and for respecting a meaningful concern with analytical boundaries, since it keeps the researcher mindful of the interpenetration which is realistically descriptive of the phenomena constituting his data.

The focus of this Symposium has been on the formation and the definition of scientific concepts, and their significance as the fundamental and pivotal elements of theoretical explanation. These proceedings have exposed the reader to many concepts, as well as to several types of concepts. The editor reviews, somewhat extensively, this central topic. Current concepts in all the behavioral sciences have a certain vagueness which is a basic, and major, obstacle to the successful construction of theory. One principal cause of this unfortunate conceptual confusion, and the erroneous thinking which results from it, is the traditional and extensive use of common, everyday vocabulary which, because of its historical connotations and multiple epistemological meanings, is very semantically ambiguous. DiRenzo suggests that, if they are to achieve conceptual precision, the behavioral sciences are in need of thorough reconceptualization and respecification for all of their existing conceptual apparatus—including particularly those pivotal concepts which have constituted the "primary abstractions."

DiRenzo further exhorts for a respectful acknowledgment of the distinction between the legitimate utility of a concept and its claims to truth. He suggests that a similar distinction be made for types of concepts. All types of concepts must lead, eventually and ultimately, to real concepts as the indispensable elements of substantive theory. If they are to do this, contends DiRenzo, we must get beyond the use of relative (methodological and nominal) concepts, which have no

implicit claims to truth, to those of an absolute nature (substantive
and real concepts). His major argument is directed against those
scientists who wish to confine theoretical analysis to the utilization of
nominal concepts (such as those exemplified by operational definitions). This approach, he asserts, emphasizes functionality at the
expense of validity. DiRenzo's fundamental plea is that scientific
concepts have to be more than sets of operations, or of mathematical
formulas, or of logical realities, or of sheer descriptions—if we are
looking for laws of human behavior. They need to have empirical
implications of an absolute character. Scientific explanation cannot
terminate at the descriptive level of nominal concepts. Concepts need
to have not only descriptive, but also interpretative, power. Only a
conceptual scheme constituted of real concepts can produce substantive theory—the ultimate goal of all scientific inquiry.

Problems of conceptual definition and formation are necessarily
related to problems of measurement and empirical verification. (In the
behavioral sciences, due to the particular nature of their phenomena,
measurement and verification present special problems.) Unfortunately, however, the consideration of empirical verification is often
avoided or its significance is not fully appreciated. Much of this is due
to an unrealistic dichotomy of interests between the staunch theorists
and the die-hard methodologists, who fail to perceive and to respect
the fundamental unity of theoretical explanation. What is needed is a
balance of interest and a respectful concern for the reciprocal and
complementary role which these two phases of scientific research
constitute for theoretical explanation. DiRenzo calls for "intradisciplinary" collaboration to resolve this problem. As the methodologist
needs to become theory-conscious, so too must the theorist become
empirical-minded with regard to verification. Measurement is indispensable for empirical verification, which is, in turn, the *sine qua
non* for scientific validity.

Verification requires the achievement of empirical correspondence.
Successful prediction on the basis of a theoretical system and its
conceptual apparatus, DiRenzo suggests, is sufficient evidence of an
empirical confirmation, and therefore of its validity. More thought
needs to be given, he argues, to the way in which the procedures of
measurement and experimentation may introduce distortion into the
formulation of theoretical explanations. Here is a special application
of the role of interference in the theoretical process on the part of the

scientist. One has to question the influence of the modes of research on the research process itself. A slight modification in this respect may result in significantly different conceptual and theoretical consequences. The validity of the methodological procedures and techniques that are used for the formation of concepts and theory is a greatly neglected problem.

The final topic which the editor discusses is that of scientific convergence. Synthesis and specialization traditionally have rivaled each other for influence in directing the course of scientific activity. DiRenzo maintains that the latter orientation usually dominates; provincialism is found extensively in many quarters of science. As scientific specialization becomes more and more inevitable and extensive, as a consequence of the never-ending growth of knowledge, the problems implicit in specialization are becoming increasingly acute.

All knowledge is one, DiRenzo contends, and we must fix our attention upon the fundamental principle of the systemic nature of reality—and, hence, of knowledge and truth as its reflections. He argues that the single discipline in isolation is as artificial as the single fact in isolation, since the division of the behavioral sciences into separate disciplines is arbitrary. He endorses both the denunciations of reductionism made in the preceding chapters, and the exhortations that the individual disciplines need to complement and to supplement one another. One reason for the lack of logically closed systems or of adequate closure in theoretical explanation for the behavioral sciences, he argues, may be the lack of a unifying perspective—the lack of synthetic orientations. Human behavior cannot be studied in a series of vacuums. Its components interpenetrate too intimately for that; for an adequate and a complete explanation, they must be synthesized on the theoretical level.

DiRenzo states that the fundamental obstacle to multi-disciplinary activity seems to be an "identity anxiety" on the part of the behavioral scientist. He argues that this need not be the case because interdisciplinary activity does not imply that the entirety of one discipline must be related to or converged with the totality of another, since many phases of any discipline always will remain outside the boundaries of any interdisciplinary enterprise; nor does interdisciplinary activity require physical collaboration or collective action on the empirical level. The editor's appeal is for the serious, and a more widespread, assumption of an interdisciplinary *orientation*, particularly at the theoretical level. He offers some suggestions that would be helpful in this direction. The first is the development of an awareness of what is going on in neighboring and related disciplines—with particular attention to the relevance of this activity for one's own theoretical interests.

The second proposal is to develop a sensitivity to convergence—to recognize, and to strive to recognize, where the several disciplines do, and must, come together theoretically, and to facilitate such a union. DiRenzo contends that we need to focus more closely on the arbitrariness of disciplinary boundaries and to give more attention to their interpenetration. This involves a removal of the ambiguity which inevitably characterizes these conventional lines of analytical demarcation. These problems, he argues, constitute analytical loci of the most urgent priority for all of the behavioral sciences.

The third specific suggestion is the standardization of scientific concepts and the development of a common scientific language for the behavioral sciences and, wherever possible (such as in methodology), for all scientific disciplines. It is most difficult, maintains DiRenzo, to make scientific progress with the persistent use of common, everyday language whose ambiguous vocabulary with its multiple connotations presents a major impediment. Conceptual consensus is obviously a necessary step for scientific convergence; yet, as the editor pointed out in Chapter I, this needs to be developed first of all within the single disciplines of behavioral science.

The state and quality of substantive analysis is reflected directly in the state and quality of methodology. The editor, in conclusion, asserts that theoretical progress in scientific explanation for the behavioral sciences rests in great part on the resolution of these methodological questions, since they are fundamental considerations which show a logical priority in the scientific process. Contending that such progress is impeded by the failure to appreciate the position that the knowledge produced by the behavioral disciplines should belong epistemologically among the sciences and not among the humanities, DiRenzo urges, finally, that the researchers in these disciplines must assume a scientific mentality and orientation in order to achieve the goal of theoretical explanation for human behavior and our world of social and cultural reality.

Our intent in these pages has been to put into sharper focus the relationship of methodological analysis to substantive problems of theoretical explanation in the behavioral sciences. Specific concerns for the most part have been methodological ones, although there has been considerable preoccupation with several substantive issues that relate to theoretical explanation for human behavior and our world of socio-cultural reality.

The working theme of this Symposium was "Conceptual Definition in the Behavioral Sciences." It is interesting to note the variety of ways in which our symposiasts perceive the problem—depending on what they choose to discuss and how they do discuss it. They have exposed us to several issues, and to many divergent points of view, that relate to the fundamental question of theoretical explanation in the behavioral sciences. We have not been so presumptuous as to expect to discuss all the problems which are attendant to theoretical explanation in the behavioral sciences; nor do we pretend to invade all the aspects of the problems that are presented. There remains a host of issues in our theme that have not been given consideration—which is by no means meant to deny their validity nor to minimize their necessity in scientific explanation. What we have done, hopefully, is to select some of the more critical issues.

It is now our task in this concluding chapter to delineate the principal issues of the preceding chapters. Our considerations shall not be confined strictly to the issues that have been presented explicitly in the foregoing pages; they shall include as well certain others which have been suggested implicitly and which, in our opinion, need to be brought to the fore. Again, in this summary chapter, our exclusive concern will be methodological questions rather than substantive ones. We do not intend so much to make a critical assessment of what has been presented in the preceding chapters, as to delineate the more crucial issues. Our focus will be on the continuity, rather than the divergences, of the several contributions. Scientific methodology is concerned with the study of the total procedures of scientific explanation.

Our approach in this chapter is intended to describe in a general outline the major steps that are involved in the scientific process, and to suggest some directions in which these steps should be taken.

Scientific Epistemology

Basic to theoretical explanation in any discipline is the consideration of scientific epistemology—the study of the sources and methods whereby science comes to know the phenomena of reality. This is one of the fundamental problems of scientific methodology. Scientific epistemology is that debatable territory between science and philosophy which treats of the nature of knowledge. Once we assume that knowledge of human behavior and of our world of social and cultural reality can be had, then we must, first of all, assess the implications of the process by which we propose to derive this knowledge.

There seems to be a rather extensive neglect of epistemological considerations—such as the logic of procedure in the theoretical process—on the part of the behavioral scientist. Such questions are usually considered out-of-bounds for the scientist, and by and large they have been left to the philosophers of science. Yet, and not by design. there has been a philosophical tone to much of our proceedings. Moreover, as Anderson has remarked, much traditional philosophy—not strictly the philosophy of science—has been involved in these discussions. Ackerman and Parsons, in fact, apologize for fear that their chapter might sound "too philosophical" to some readers. Nonetheless, their attempt to delimit the "boundaries" as well as the "connectedness" between methodology and philosophy in the theoretical process is a legitimate concern which all too often is not acknowledged in science.

Pure or objective science is non-existent. Even though the scientist (and, unfortunately, more often the student) may have no clear recognition of the fact, all scientific activity is accompanied by some kind of an epistemological system. For example, those who contend that behavioral phenomena cannot be studied scientifically, as can physical phenomena, are holding the implicit metaphysical position—which many of them do not recognize, and would not want to acknowledge if they did—that these two kinds of phenomena represent completely diverse kinds of reality rather than a unified reality of which the different types of phenomena are dimensions. That man is part of the natural world is a fundamental postulate of science.

Scientific pursuits of whatever type necessarily and inescapably involve an epistemological context. Another simple illustration can be had in the contrast between "scientific" and "humanistic" approaches to the study of human behavior. The nature and the scope of each of these approaches is quite diverse. What is the epistemological significance of the differential operations of each of these orientations? To what extent are they reconcilable? The significance of this issue becomes more apparent when one considers the various schools of thought within the individual behavioral disciplines—and within these two major approaches—and the variations in their modes of operations: pragmatism, empiricism, historicism, behaviorism, positivism, determinism—to mention only a few of the more dominant orientations. Yet, if we are differentially receptive and have a differential intentionality toward all things to which we propose a cognitive orientation, then we must know the nature of, and the consequences of, following this differential receptivity and intentionality. As is true with general methodology, a slight modification in epistemology may result in a major change in theoretical conclusions. This resulting situation, of course, presents the inevitable question of validity.

As with theorizing, the very process of formulating and operationalizing research necessarily involves epistemological elements. There are a number of inevitable processes that, by their very nature, are selective on the part of the researcher. They include such steps as the definition of the universe of discourse, boundary establishment, assumptions regarding the nature of the problem, theoretical approach, methodology, and techniques. Each of these inevitably contains epistemological implications. The scientist not only has to become conscious of these elements; but, more particularly, he must become cognizant of their implications and consequences. Research is always guided by such considerations. As Ackerman and Parsons state, ". . . we always have [cognitive] maps before we encounter the 'facts.' Our maps tell us what are the 'facts.'" They plead—and we here concur in their plea—for a conscious recognition of the role of "cognitive maps" —the analyst's "input"—in the analytical and theoretical process. We must not simply admit the existence of these cognitive maps, nor pass them off with a mere acknowledgment and description. Rather, we must know their epistemological nature and their methodological limits, as well as their explanatory powers and their theoretical consequences. What are the theoretical implications, for example, in the epistemological position taken by Ackerman and Parsons that all analytical thought is mythologization—that facts are not encountered but, rather, are created as a consequence of analytical procedures?

Another major question that has relevance in this area, one to which Sherif particularly addressed himself, is that of isomorphism. What are the implications, against which he cautions, of the uncritical extrapolation of models from the mathematical and physical sciences, without assessing the nature and the consequences of their postulations, and the transference into the behavioral sciences of attempts at formalization which have been used—however successfully—in other disciplines? What, as Levinson alludes to, is the nature of the socio-cultural influences on the direction and mode of theoretical explanation—the intellectual climate of the times, current theoretical orientations, methodological fads, and so on? All of these considerations—including the values, motivations, and implicit assumptions of the theorist— form part of his "input" and as such constitute part of the epistemology of any theoretical formulation. We must, in Levinson's words, become "intraceptive" about our approach, and about what we are doing in the scientific process—and its dynamics whereby theoretical formulations are developed. Epistemology is too often divorced from methodology. Many fail to recognize its essential inseparability not only from methodology, but also, as such, from the entire scientific process. As Einstein states:

The reciprocal relationship of epistemology and science is of noteworthy kind. They are dependent upon each other. Epistemology without contact with science becomes an empty scheme. Science without epistemology is—insofar as it is thinkable at all—primitive and muddled.[1]

Several of the papers in these proceedings show a keen concern for epistemological considerations. Anderson and Moore's contribution on the epistemology of mechanical models and computer simulation provides an excellent illustration of the significance of this entire issue which we are discussing. Logically consistent explanations are easy to come by; but, somewhere along the line, the scientist has to ascertain that these explanations are more than merely consistent logic. The fundamental question is whether or not they constitute valid explanations. A recognition of the epistemological and philosophical implications of one's methodology is crucial. Lazarsfeld has shown an extensive concern for the role of logic and epistemology in his work, and more specifically a concern and appreciation for the role that philosophical contributions have played in the formulation of methodological procedures for theoretical explanation in the behavioral sciences. Ackerman and Parsons, of course, have already been acknowledged for their fine contribution in this area. More of the type of concern that has been shown in these proceedings should occupy the interest of the behavioral scientists today.

This is not a plea for the invasion of philosophy (the purely speculative) into the empirical realms of scientific investigation. It is a plea to the empirical scientist to appreciate and to utilize only the *appropriate* contributions and the fundamental tools of the philosophy of science—especially epistemology (the rules and principles of knowing) and logic (the rules and principles of reasoning)—as they apply to scientific procedures. Behavioral science—alas, perhaps all science—needs to face up to such things. Einstein's theory of relativity propounded a new epistemology. Some physicists rejected it as metaphysics, but others claimed that the new epistemological outlook was the very heart of the theory, supplanting a fallacious system of thought that was barring progress.[2] The confrontation of metaphysics does not mean—and should not mean—entanglement. So long as the scientist, in Eddington's view,[3] confines his philosophical concerns to scientific epistemology, he is not outside the bounds of his own subject. That is to say, he would not be concerned, for example, with the relevance of general philosophical systems (such as evolutionism or Thomism or phenomenology) on scientific questions. Not all of philosophy should be his concern, but only the philosophy of science.

To an unfortunate degree the special sciences neglect the necessity of appreciating the relationship which exists between themselves and these handmaid disciplines. We need to subject ourselves to such critical analysis. All science needs the accompaniment of some kind of a critique of its methodology. We need to be more aware of contributions from the philosophy of science and more concerned about its significance for our work in the behavioral sciences. The language of the behavioral disciplines and the number of specialized methods of their investigations are rapidly accruing. Many matters need to be subjected to reinterpretation in the light of advances which have been made not only in the areas of the philosophy and the epistemology of science, but in each of the respective disciplines of behavioral science as well. Theoretical development in these disciplines has been handicapped in part by such problems that have yet to be resolved—or, at least, clarified sufficiently. Criticism is one of the most important forms of scientific cooperation. It should be seen as fundamentally constructive. Invalidation is as helpful as verification. Those who find these concerns to be too speculative may find some consolation in the perspective taken by Ackerman and Parsons. For them, it is merely a matter of labeling whether a consideration of ground and approach (and their consequences) is methodological or philosophical. They contend, as we are affirming here, that it is methodological; and moreover, that the boundary between methodology and philosophy is permeable and shifting. The fundamental fact is that epistemological considerations are methodological considerations, and in that respect comprise a very vital segment of the research process. To make these epistemological considerations explicit—to know their nature and implications—is to make a major advance toward the fruitful construction of scientific theory.

We have suggested in Chapter I—and it certainly shall be most implicit in the following pages—that the behavioral sciences should assume a particular epistemological orientation—an empirical epistemology, or epistemic empiricism. This epistemology does not constitute a philosophy. Rather, it is a cognitive orientation to data. Given the nature of the behavioral sciences as empirical disciplines, this orientation is not only justified but also inevitable. Yet, this very epistemology has by no means been exhausted analytically. It is not sufficient for us merely to adopt it as a fundamental position; we must know its nature—its assumptions and its implications—and work within whatever limitations may be imposed thereby. There are a number of methodological questions involved in such an epistemology that deserve further assessment on the part of the behavioral scientist. Many of the subsequent considerations are some examples of more specific questions that comprise this general epistemological and methodological approach.

Scientific Explanation

It is commonly said that the fundamental goal of science is explanation, but what constitutes *scientific explanation?* To say that the formulation of explanations for the occurrence and the behavior of empirical phenomena is the ultimate goal of science, and to let it go at that, is not sufficient. Nor is it sufficient to say simply that explanation means to bring empirical phenomena together in some meaningful way, to bring order and meaning to facts of reality.

To understand the structure of, and the requirements for, scientific explanation is to understand the basic nature of the scientific enterprise. Explanation—in a very general sense—consists in describing the nature and the functioning mode of the phenomena under investigation. Yet, precisely how and in what manner is this accomplished? When does one have *the* answer? It is imperative to know precisely what it is that one can—and must —do in the process of explanation. Anderson, for example, has asked whether or not statistical correlations can constitute, in any sense, an explanation—that is to say, more precisely, a sufficient explanation. Although there seems to be strong agreement that correlations themselves are facts that need to be explained, the answer as to what correlations themselves explain, if anything, is one of considerable polemics. If one were to submit that a state of affairs is a reality, then the description of the nature and the dynamics of such a real state—in terms of demonstrable correlations—would seem to constitute a valid explanation. But, is this an *adequate* explanation? The researcher is pressed to consider more specifically the question of when scientific explanation is achieved satisfactorily. At, or on, which level of abstraction must it be derived to be complete as well as adequate? When does one have the "ultimate" answer? Perhaps it is not possible to know when, and if, we arrive at an ultimate explanation—that is, an account of the greatest number of phenomena with the fewest possible assumptions—but we can recognize those explanations that make such an approximation, and we can recognize the procedures and the methodology that lead to an ultimate explanation.

Explanation is taken to be tentatively complete when it has become, or it has taken on the nature of, a theory. One is pressed to ask, however, what is theory? Various meanings have been given to "theory," and the term has been applied to a host of diversified, even though related, elements. It has been taken to imply a definition, a speculation, a postulate, a correlation, a deduction, an assumption, a general orientation, an ordered taxonomy, an empirical generalization, a conceptual scheme, a set of logically interrelated concepts, a set of propositions linked into a logical framework, a mathematical formula, an hypothesis, a model, a law, and so on. One may find, furthermore, references to different species of theory. All of these variations have been seen in sufficient degree here and elsewhere, and the implicit problem is reflected amply in the preceding contributions. Ackerman and Parsons, for example, speak of their general "theory" of action as a conceptual model; as such it is not really an explanation of anything, but merely a device to generate an explanation of particular phenomena. Then, too, Sherif seems to define theory as "conceptual orientation"—which, again, as such does not explain anything, but rather offers only an approach to the development of a theoretical explanation. This, of course, is consistent with Sherif's view that the theoretical process operates in reverse for the behavioral sciences; that is to say, the scientific direction in these disciplines is from "theory" to fact. Rather than observing and then attempting to formulate an explanation, one first theorizes and then relates the "theory" to the phenomena that are to be explained. Yet, if each of these elements and procedures is theory, then is that to say that each constitutes explanation? Certainly each does not do so in the same sense or to the same degree as any of the others. What, then, is the difference, and the significance of that difference, in these various "types"?

Each of these types of "theory" is necessary. Each makes its contribution to the explanatory process. There are, however, two fundamental problems that often seem to be overlooked. One is to recognize that there is a difference in the utility of these various types of "theory." Each has different limits to its "explanatory" powers—and it is questionable, as we have shown, whether some of them in fact do explain anything. The other problem involves a decision regarding the kind of explanation that is sought—such as a general or specific theory. This is not a simple question to answer since it depends upon the nature of the phenomena under analysis and the explanatory circumstances under which these phenomena are being investigated.

The distinction between theories and generators or interpretations of theory must be sharply drawn. One of the scientific vogues that has gained considerable attention in the behavioral sciences recently is that of models. Today, as Kaplan has remarked, "model building is science *à la mode*."[4] We find ourselves confronted with all kinds of models—organic, mathematical, conceptual, mechanical, and now the cybernetic (as the chapter by Ackerman and Parsons exemplifies). Models basically are representations. These may be classified into three types: *iconic models,* which in some way look like the represented phenomena; *analogue models,* which represent the original phenomena in another form; and *symbolic models,* which represent phenomena figuratively.

The crucial question for our interests relates, of course, to the significance and utility of these models for scientific explanation. In their chapter Anderson and Moore have provided an excellent summary of the fundamental problem involved in using models. Models, from a theoretical perspective, are simply reproductions of given phenomena in some form other than the original. Models are analogues or metaphors—but not theories—and therefore not explanations. Their explanatory value, however great, is totally heuristic.

One of the major problems which is overlooked in the use of models centers upon one of the principal issues which Sherif discussed—namely, that of the isomorphic problem which exists between the model that is proposed and the facts of the universe of discourse. Indeed, this was the point of Anderson and Moore's chapter in which they showed that it is not possible to extrapolate from the similarity of behavior (or function) to the similarity of structure, or, in their example, from the behavior of programmed computers to the behavior of human beings. The utility of models must not be confused with their claims to truth. Models do not constitute theory. They can make no assertions, and thus have no claims to truth. Models are devices for generating ideas and explanations.

All of these statements apply to mathematical as well as to every other kind of model. It is important for us to take heed of this in the light of the rampant expansion of mathematical thinking in the behavioral sciences during the recent years. Much of this type of thinking involves mathematical models, or the use of mathematical programs as foundations for mechanical models. Mathematics is a language of explanation. It is, as such, a tool for science—not science itself. This distinction is all too often neither grasped nor appreciated. Mathematical behavioral science, which appears to be making extensive progress—and who knows, may provide many constructive elements for successful theoretical explanation—should be behavioral science first and mathematics only secondarily.

Models of whatever type—but perhaps more especially the mechanical and mathematical ones of late—often become so fascinating in themselves that the original explanatory intent becomes converted into one of mechanical and mathematical manipulation. Electronic simulation per se of human behavior, for example, becomes the final goal. There is no doubt that mechanical models, particularly those produced by electronic computers, have pushed back the frontiers of the behavioral sciences enormously and have made possible the uncovering of data heretofore inaccessible; but, as with similar methodological devices, all too often the researchers who employ them become so raptured with the technique that they lose sight of the theoretical goal for which the model was meant to be but a vehicle. There is a sheer fixation on computers, and this intrinsic interest in computers causes behavioral scientists to get bogged down with techniques at the expense of explanation. We forget that techniques are tools and see them as goals in themselves. This unfortunate situation is likely to get worse with the increased development of computer technology and mathematical thinking in the behavioral sciences. Accordingly, our attention in this respect is all the more imperative.

Models really offer only "what" explanations. They are, as such, only descriptions—reproductive descriptions—that do not in fact explain. The theoretical function of models, therefore, is basically methodological and descriptive. Models, to repeat, do not constitute theory. Even so-called "interpretative models" provide interpretations only *for* a formal theory. Models are devices for generating ideas—for guiding conceptualization—and, therefore, for generating explanations. Ackerman and Parsons, for example, offer their systemic formulation of action theory as a conceptual model to direct the attention of the analyst to the loci of relevant problems. As such, this contribution—as its formulators concede—does not constitute a verified system of substantive theory. On the other hand, a conceptual model, such as that offered by Ackerman and Parsons, may generate a host of theories. And, conversely, a theory may be so powerful as to become, in effect, a general model.

Science seeks to achieve not only a *description*, but more particularly an *interpretation*, of the phenomena it investigates. Description, which involves the definition and classification of phenomena, makes a statement of the empirical relationships associated with phenomena, and simply tells *what* happens. Interpretation, which determines the nature of the relationships among observed phenomena (such as whether these are causative, purposive, structural, and so forth), provides *"why"* explanations. Interpretation involves the reduction of explanation to the smallest possible number of general laws that would account for all of the various specific facts described.[5] Accordingly, a complete explanation says not only *what* happens, but also *why* it happens.

What is the nature of explanation in the behavioral sciences? At what level are the behavioral sciences ready to explain? Which type of explanation do we need? Which type of explanation can we get? Are we looking for statistical and probabilistic explanations or "causal" and "deterministic" laws? It has been said that much modern theory in the behavioral sciences has all the virtues of scientific explanation except that of explaining anything. One of the major drawbacks of explanation in the behavioral sciences is that there has been too much mere description and not enough interpretation.

Many researchers confine themselves to, and content themselves with, the lower echelons of theoretical explanation. In fact, many become so absorbed with the empirical operations of the scientific process that they completely fail to theorize—that is, to advance the research process into the abstract and conceptual levels. This happens because they neither recognize what it is that constitutes theory, nor do they appreciate the unity of the explanatory process which requires one to view the various "types" of theory as actually successive steps in the complete process of theory construction. Their failure in these two respects results in incomplete, and, unfortunately, often distorted explanations. Many who operate in this manner seem to be possessed by a fear of theorizing. Yet, as Sherif has told us, theorizing on conceptual levels is not beyond the scope of the experimenter—despite the lengths to which he may go to maintain "objective" research. Like isolated facts, empirical generalizations do not speak for themselves. Empirical generalizations are but one type of descriptive explanation, which as such constitutes neither an adequate nor a complete explanation. They need interpretation and, as such, crave explanation. The very process of formulating and operationalizing research involves conceptual and theoretical considerations. And, as Sherif also points out, the more explicit these are made, the more meaningful, the more coherent, and the more significant is the consequent research and its results. Theory does and should play the focal and guiding role in all research activity.

A scientific explanation which is complete is one that has assumed the invariable status of a law—a statement of an order or relationship between phenomena which, insofar as can be determined, is invariable under given conditions. Obviously, a law involves confirmation. An adequate and complete explanation in the behavioral sciences must in some manner be one of an empirical nature, one whose validity and precision may be established through empirical verification. The validity and the adequacy of an explanation can be demonstrated by its predictive power. Theories that generate invariably successful predictions assume the status of law. Some behavioral scientists maintain that—given the complexity of the phenomena and their causal factors in their field, what with the variety of subjective elements involved—theory in the behavioral sciences may have to become content with something less certain than laws, which are the culmination of explanatory discovery in the other fields of science. That is to say, the behavioral sciences may have to be satisfied with the prediction of probabilities and not the formulation of laws. On this matter we have had some antithetical views among our symposiasts. Sherif has made some reference to the existence of "psychological laws." On the other hand, Lazarsfeld perceives the existence of certain social phenomena in only the *probability* of their occurrence.

The question of the nature of explanation begs some consideration of the nature of the phenomenon to be explained by the
behavioral sciences. Science, as we all know, seeks to explain
reality. But, what reality? What is the reality of the phenomena
with which the behavioral sciences concern themselves? And
how much of this reality is determined conventionally? Nobody
has ever seen, for example, "personality," "society," or "culture"
per se. What, then, is the nature of their existence—if, indeed,
they do exist? What, for example, is the nature of "intraception"? Levinson tells us that it is a disposition which he defines as
a "generalized and enduring tendency that is reflected in the
various modes of psychological functioning." Can such "things"
as "tendencies" have existence? Can they be real? Likewise, what
is the reality, sociologically and psychologically, of a "group"? Is
it an entity, a state, a process, or something else entirely? And,
then, for example, how real is a "process"? Similarly, one could
inquire about the reality of "culture." Is it a process or is it an
entity? How real are White's "symbolates"? Anderson has
equated them to the "forms" of Plato, thus making abstractions
of them. White insists that they are real—as real as the concrete
artifacts that express them. Is a "statistical correlation" a real
thing—and, if so, in what sense? Lazarsfeld perceives, as did
Dewey and Weber, that the existence of certain social phenomena is constituted only in the probability that these events will
take place. But is a "probability" a real thing?

Whether these phenomena are real or not, and in what sense
they are real, is a crucial question to be resolved. One would not
want to—indeed, could not—explain real phenomena by unreal
elements. Explanation has made one significant advance when it
has determined the ontological nature of the phenomena to be
explained. To establish simply a difference between things as
entities (substantive existence) or as *processes* (formal existence)
—for example, water and wave, respectively—is a significant
accomplishment that places the scientist on the correct path for
his explanation. We confuse these two "types" of reality—substantive and formal. The causal power of the two examples is
"different" structurally, but the same substantively.

All of this becomes more meaningful when the behavioral scientist realizes how different his data are from much of those in the physical sciences. They lack the concreteness which often is so typical of the data for other disciplines. The behavioral scientist fundamentally is pursuing an analysis of the latent property space to which Lazarsfeld made frequent reference in his paper. All of these questions as to what constitutes an adequate and complete explanation become so much more significant when attempting this type of an analysis. The crux of the issue is that one cannot confine explanation to manifest data and to manifest observations. The behavioral scientist necessarily concerns himself, as Lazarsfeld has shown, with the latent property space. It is its structure and dynamics which the behavioral scientist ultimately must attempt to explain. And this brings into focus all the questions that were raised above regarding the level of abstraction at which an adequate and complete explanation can be derived fruitfully.

Reality does not imply a physical existence—although this often seems to be the limit of scientific metaphysics. Processes, such as "interpenetration," and states, such as "intraception," may be—and are—real. That is to say, such processes and states do exist; they *are* "out there." It is sufficient for science that they *are* there. Under such circumstances, they demand an explanation not only for *how* they are there and the consequences of their being there, but, more particularly, for *why* they are there. How are things real? Hallucinations, for example, are real, yet they do not have physical existence. We respond to these things; it is not possible to respond to nothing. Situations are real to people in them; and their responses to these situations are equally real. It is important, then, to distinguish *subjective* reality and *objective* reality. Both of these types constitute concrete reality. Intraception, like an hallucination, is a subjective reality. On the other hand, personality and culture, while requiring people for existence, are not real in the subjective sense. They have objective, even though not physical, existence. We can leave a finite distinction to others, particularly to the philosophers, but it is important for the scientist that he realize that this distinction exists and appreciate the consequences that it has for him vis-à-vis the process of explanation. The distinction, however, between subjective/objective reality and theoretical/ontological reality is crucial. Both are just as real in their consequences as they are real theoretically in a causal and inferential sense.

Nor is reality found in a logically closed system of concepts. Logical reality does not imply ontological reality and, similarly, explanations that have logical validity do not necessarily have empirical validity. Science must discover reality—not create it. We must, in short, move beyond the level of mere constructs of noumenal reality—the creation of the human intellect—in order to confront metaphysical reality. Our concern here can be illustrated, for example, with the approach White advocates for the study of culture, an approach that is quite typical of science— namely, that of considering phenomena *as if* they were real, or at least real in certain respects. His argument is that culture may be treated *as if* it had a life of its own, quite apart from human organisms, just as the physicist may treat a falling body *as if* there were no atmospheric pressure. This, White declares, is an application of the traditional technique of science to culture. Yet, an "as if" reality is not a true reality. It is hypothetical and speculative, and therefore based upon a fictitious assumption. Whatever theory is constructed on these premises would have no exact counterpart in reality, and accordingly would be false.

This is neither a criticism nor a rejection of White's position that culture is real and has a life of its own. Our concern here is only with his method of treating culture as an object of data. It may be legitimate to utilize the "as if" perspective within certain limits and for certain purposes. Our objection is directed only to those who look upon such an orientation as an absolute, exclusive, and often the only legitimate, scientific approach. In some areas of psychology, for example, human beings and their behavior are analyzed as though there were no social or cultural context for this activity. It is not so much the study of phenomena in the "as if" orientation that is problematic as it is the failure to appreciate the significance of the relationship of these phenomena to other phenomena. Such an approach is valid up to a certain point; but, it soon becomes distorting and flagrant with error. We may for limited purposes treat phenomena *as if* they did not have "connectedness," but eventually the analytical boundaries of all these separate analyses must be fitted together. And, if in our analysis we have precipitated distortion, this fit will be hard to come by; until the problem is resolved, the composite explanation will never be attained. So long as we assume that certain knowledge of human behavior can be had, then we must raise the question of how we know, and when do we know, that we are dealing with metaphysical or ontological reality—and not simply a noumenal or logical reality in one form or another. White shows how this issue of reality is central to valid theory. In discussing the reality of culture, he states that an evolution (cultural evolution) is not possible without real things; to explain real processes, and to establish real laws of nature, we require real phenomena.

Science fundamentally strives to achieve an affinity between its conceptual/theoretical formulations and metaphysical reality. Yet, science, as Ackerman and Parsons point out so emphatically, inevitably involves a certain distortion of reality when for analytical purposes the "facts" of investigation are removed necessarily from the "concrete connectedness" of their context. All analytical thought, they argue, involves mythologization. Accordingly, all scientific concepts are only more or less representative of reality, since the approach to ontological reality is through this analytical fiction. We act *as if* things were really this way or that way, but how much pretension can science tolerate? How much pretension is legitimate without frustrating the fundamental objective of achieving the theoretical/ontological affinity?

Ackerman and Parsons contend that this scientific distortion of reality is inescapable: *Ich kann nicht anders.* The selective, and therefore distorting, nature of science is an essential aspect of the very process of human thought. However true this may be, the scientist cannot be so presumptuous, and therefore so self-defeating, as to resign himself to the position that all scientific "facts" are "myths" because they involve some degree of distortion. That truth can be achieved—that the real world can be explained—is a fundamental axiom of science. Even if it can never be entirely eliminated, scientific mythologization must be minimized and every effort must be made to eradicate it. Ackerman and Parsons have made a step in this direction, despite their contention to the contrary. They have striven to construct theory with the aim of minimizing this acknowledged distortion—as is exemplified in their provision of "corrective mechanisms." We applaud this conscientious type of theory construction.

One particular problem seems to be at the base of much of this situation. Many scientists prefer to shy away from so-called "ultimate reality." This term is, perhaps, an unfortunate one because it carries a certain philosophical connotation, which empirical scientists find disturbing—or contrary to their entire epistemological premises. Nevertheless, in common usage, "ultimate reality" refers simply to ontological reality—the real world in the abstract and metaphysical sense. Thus, what this objection means is that these scientists do not want to concern themselves with whether or not the data of their investigations are in fact real and, if real, in which sense. This is not the place to inquire into the nature of ontological reality. Suffice it to say that its confrontation is the goal of scientific endeavor.

We are not calling here for a consideration within the behavioral sciences of "ultimate reality." The commonly accepted epistemology of science is not concerned with the discovery of "absolute truth" about the external world. It does seem paradoxical, nevertheless, for the scientist categorically to evade "ultimate reality." The very purpose of science is to explain reality. If, as is commonly held, this means to find, to describe, and to interpret the laws of nature, then science by definition must be concerned with "ultimate reality."

One distinction, however, which often eludes the scientist is that between epistemic levels of abstraction and metaphysical types of reality. These epistemic levels of abstraction must be recognized as a consequence of the finiteness of the human mind. Traditionally, and to a great extent, they have been used to delimit the scope of several disciplines.

In science, as Sherif points out, major breakthroughs are a result of formulating pertinent and significant problems on the basis of *actualities* of the universe with which we deal. Beyond the observations we have already made, this is not the place to inquire into levels of abstraction or kinds of existence, however legitimate these questions may be. Nevertheless, the answer to this problem would seem to be found in the fact that science seeks to explain *all* of that which is encountered. And, "levels" of reality, however man-made or fictitious, are encountered and demand an explanation, since to draw an arbitrary and unrealistic boundary for the scope of one's explanation may be to invite premature closure, the inevitable consequence of which is theoretical distortion and therefore scientific error. The unity of reality is a fundamental assumption of science. Accordingly, the behavioral scientist cannot arbitrarily delineate the scope of his investigations without a full awareness of the risk of distorting or limiting the adequacy and completeness of his explanation. For the scientist to attempt to escape this question of "ultimate reality" is to contradict one aspect of his fundamental epistemological frame of reference—namely, the assumption of science that there is a reality to be explained. Accordingly, the question, in this respect, is confronted necessarily; what it needs is an adequate and complete answer. Since science does seek to explain reality, it therefore seeks to confront ontological reality. Ultimately, it is this reality—ontological reality—that science seeks to explain.

Fundamentally, what is sought in the effort of science to explain ontological reality is an affinity between scientific explanation and metaphysical explanation. To achieve such an affinity, it is necessary to know the nature, the limits, and the implications of both. What is needed is the development of metascientific interests in the behavioral sciences. Throughout the history of science, there has been considerable question about the legitimate place of such elements. Are they pre- or post-science? Our own view is that they are concurrent with science. Such concerns are legitimate dimensions and integral parts of all science, neglected much too long. We need to know the relationship of the behavioral disciplines—their theoretical and methodological contributions—to persistent metaphysical questions.

What, then, is scientific truth? The search for truth is a seemingly endless task. We would be rash to accept current scientific explanations as immutable truths. Too many of our "truths" have been modified, and even rejected in some cases. The frontiers of knowledge are being rolled back constantly. As the physical sciences have shown, it is possible now to push beyond existing frontiers toward the infinitely small; we have gone from atoms, to molecules, to nuclei. But knowledge remains probable. We must not sit back and shout "Eureka!" because of a seemingly satisfactory (truthful) answer. It may not be true tomorrow, despite empirical verification today. Verification is in part a consequence of theory, method, and the current fund of knowledge from which the explanation is derived. Science must always assume a certain cynicism regarding the reliability of its answers. The search for truth is, from this mortal view, an endless one. We should pursue it avidly—and with enjoyment.

Many distinguished scientists have contended that man cannot hope to uncover the innermost essence of nature. Perhaps the human mind can never achieve, either by empirical or non-empirical methods, the desired goal of full explanation or of complete certainty about our world of reality. Nonetheless, the scientist cannot contradictorily resign himself to such an assumption. It is self-defeating at the very beginning of his endeavor. Here it is necessary to act *as if* such a state of precision, certitude, and truth can be mastered. In doing so we should simply be following a fundamental postulate of science, which would be completely consistent with fundamental scientific epistemology—namely, that all science is based upon certain unverified (and, in some cases, seemingly unverifiable) assumptions. The effort toward certainty—however futile it may seem and however fruitless it may be—must be made. As P. W. Bridgman has remarked, "the scientist has no other method than doing his damnedest."[6] Some contend that one has to place a faith in science. Perhaps, somewhere along the line, this may be true. Yet, faith and science *as modes of knowing* are contradictory. The one should not occupy the domain of the other. And science, rather than faith, as the creative expression of the human intellect, should strive to exhaust the intelligibility of reality.

One of the fundamental questions of scientific explanation concerns the object of inquiry and the selection of the phenomena to be explained. This is our next consideration.

Analytical Locus and Boundaries

After one has gone about deciding what constitutes explanation, and how best to achieve it, then the next logical problem that remains to be settled is the question of what it is that is to be explained. Abraham Edel[7] has called this problem of selecting the basic unit or the ultimate subject matter of and for a scientific inquiry the "locus problem." Ackerman and Parsons perceive the significance of this problem and have addressed themselves to it directly. Their assessment of systemic theory is intended to serve as a conceptual model to direct the attention of the analyst to the *loci* of relevant problems. It is necessary, however, to settle not only the question of what is to be studied, but also to ascertain the priorities of these investigations. Decisions must be made concerning which aspects (loci) of the analytical problems are likely to be the most productive in terms of yielding explanations that are most free of distortion and error of any kind—or, of the potentialities for producing such defects. This involves a consideration of such things as micro- and macro-theoretical perspectives, specific or general theory. Decisions upon loci are difficult, particularly for the behavioral disciplines. Again, the reason for this is that we are working analytically and theoretically in latent property space, but are confined methodologically and procedurally to manifest property space. It is the continuity of the latent property space which is the crux of the problem.

Our proceedings show considerable concern for whether one studies action, behavior, people, personality, social systems, society, culture, or what not. And, in a more inclusive, even interdisciplinary, perspective, the same controversy focuses upon the locus of the initial investigation. Where does one start the

analytical process in the behavioral sciences? Does one commence
with personality, group, society, culture, or simply aspects
thereof? The question is decidedly a controversial one. White, in
specifying the aim of culturology, has shown that one crucial
distinction in the analytical process is whether culture is taken as
constant or as variable, and accordingly for human beings. He
takes the position that, as a culturologist, he is not interested in
the behavior of people as such, and thus he treats people as
constants and cultures as variables. Several of the other symposiasts are of contrary persuasion. They prefer to treat human
beings as variables while holding culture constant. The dominant
position of the symposiasts is that if one is to explain human
behavior (which White admittedly is not attempting to do—although, in some views, culture is included under human behavior),
then one starts from outside the individual and moves inwardly.
That is to say, more specifically, one moves from culture through
society and its sub-divisional groups to personality. Agreement
on this procedure exists between our two psychologists at least;
Sherif and Levinson both advocate this approach of starting with
the socio-cultural context and moving inwardly toward personality. Ackerman and Parsons prefer to approach this problem
by focusing their analytical locus on "action" which involves a
simultaneously multi-dimensional type of analysis.

Where should the analytical focus be made in the behavioral
sciences? Obviously, the answer to this question is contingent
upon the particular problem that confronts the scientist. Nevertheless, given the continuity of reality—and especially the continuity of the analytical domain of the behavioral scientist in
latent property space—the question has to be confronted in a
somewhat more general perspective. Provincialism, of course, is
still characteristic of all scientific disciplines. Yet, even though
each researcher may, and to a certain extent must, operate within
the confines of his own discipline and with its specific orientations, he can to a degree resolve the problem of focus by
specifying some "logical" and "realistic" approaches to his phenomenon. He can decide whether, for example, within the behavioral sciences, as a family of disciplines, one moves more realisti-

cally and more effectively from culture through society to personality, or from personality through society to culture.

Much of this question of analytical focus, of course, involves simply a selection of formal and material objects of analysis. Within each of the several disciplines, this may be an arbitrary selection. When, however, the perspective becomes interdisciplinary—subsequently we shall suggest that it must be—then the approach is no longer arbitrary. Considering the phenomena under investigation in all sciences as a fundamental unity implies that there is a necessary primacy of elements, both in time and in space, which, if replicated logically in the theoretical process, should produce not only more valid theory, but more particularly, a more thorough and productive explanation. From the point of view of fruitful explanation, it makes a most significant difference which approach is selected. This orientation is a matter of general perspective which in no way diminishes the focus of concern for the individual scientist. It simply puts his specific focus in a proper analytical locus—one which is realistically sound, and which should therefore lead more effectively to a valid explanation of the respective phenomena. A properly chosen approach will lead to an analytical and theoretical consistency by merging, with minimal fear of distortion, the separate contributions of the individual behavioral disciplines into a more comprehensive explanation.

This consideration of the analytical locus leads logically to a related issue—that of analytical boundaries. It is as important to know the dimensions of the analytical process and of its locus as it is to know its nature. Several of our symposiasts agree that where analytical boundaries are delimited affects the quality—and hence, the adequacy and the validity—of theoretical explanation. Ackerman and Parsons, in particular, offer the view that whatever boundaries are established, and whatever limits are ascribed, inevitably involve an arbitrariness that makes for a certain artificiality. This difficulty, too, is not an easy one to resolve. It arises, again, largely from the fact that the analytical domain for the behavioral scientist in the microscopic world of latent property space has a continuity which is not present in the manifest property space in which the analyst works methodologically.

Where the analytical boundaries are staked is important in minimizing the mythologization of scientific analysis. Slice up reality one way, and one derives *this* explanation. Slice it up another way, and one derives *that* explanation. This scientific interference and its consequent distortion move us to consider how much of our analytical activity is discovery, and how much is creativity. As it has been suggested, many "facts" of reality are the consequential myths of the way we perceive and respond to reality.[8] Concepts have been the focus of these proceedings—as indeed they are the basis of theoretical explanation. The fecundity, or the sterility, of concepts is, in this perspective, a partial consequence of their inclusive and exclusive limits—that is to say, of their analytical boundaries. Particularly important in this respect, as Ackerman and Parsons point out, are the primary abstractions, because the productivity and the precision of theory, and therefore the domain of its analytical operation, depend upon the primary abstractions. Their scope is crucial. This applies particularly to the inclusive boundaries, since too wide a scope can be as distorting and as detrimental in generating a theory as too narrow a scope. An example of this situation, which also shows the relationship of analytical boundaries to the locus problem, is the following set of concepts. Whether the concept of "culture" or that of "social system" is used to refer to what is commonly called "social organization" raises many serious questions of boundaries which from an analytical perspective involves a critical distinction for explanation and theoretical development. The same problem obtains between "society" and "social system," and between the concepts of "action" and "behavior," particularly as primary abstractions. This starting point—the primary abstraction—is crucial in generating and directing valid and fruitful explanation.

Obviously, the artificiality and the distortion presented by the selection of an analytical locus and the delimitation of analytical boundaries have to be alleviated as much as possible. One such attempt involved in making a crucial discriminant between productive and non-productive conceptual elements, as Ackerman and Parsons point out, depends upon whether or not the theoretical systems which they comprise incorporate "corrective mechanisms." Action theory demonstrates the utility and the effectiveness of these devices for maintaining analytical boundaries that have correspondence in reality, and thus for minimizing theoretical distortion.

Analytical boundaries in a more general sense may be related to the scope of the individual disciplines. The phenomena to be analyzed often depend upon the definition and the scope that one gives to a particular field. White shows clearly the consequences of the delimitation of boundaries for specific disciplines by his reference to the historical situation in which non-biological anthropology found itself defined out of existence by virtue of having no real subject matter, no share in the latent property space to call its own. Every scientist must know, and respect, the conventional boundaries of each discipline, however arbitrary and tentative they may be. Moreover, one must respect the convenient differences that justify the individual disciplines, and one must not transgress their arbitrary boundaries without proper caution. All too often the overly enthusiastic researcher is unwittingly engaged in pursuing his specialized investigations in the domain of another, even though perhaps related, discipline; and, as Sherif points out, he takes on its language (conceptual apparatus) and its methodology which, alas, he may not be able to use with sophistication. Paradoxically, an unfortunate consequence of this improper transgression is a further setback from the intended goal of producing comprehensive knowledge. Frequently, even the several sub-divisions of a particular field arbitrarily are given varying definitions and scope. The end result of this, unfortunately, is a chaotic situation which shows little correspondence to reality.

Appropriate boundaries in part would seem to be dictated by the nature of the subject matter and the extent of its functional autonomy. For example, the function of any one behavioral system (social, cultural, or personality) is not independent of the other two. Consequently, the structural-functional analysis of one system is not independent of the others. Several of our symposiasts have recognized this principle. Levinson and Sherif argue against a sharp demarcation of disciplinary boundaries on the grounds that this would not reflect the empirical situation to be explained. Moreover, our symposiasts recognize that there are different dimensions to human behavior. For example, White, in his own view of cultural analysis, maintains that both culturological and psychological explanations are essential to a comprehensive interpretation of human behavior. He recognizes that it is necessary, in order to avoid theoretical confusion, to know and to respect the proper boundaries of each. We say that it is necessary not so much to avoid confusion as to prevent the distortions and erroneous explanations that result when a particular theoretical perspective is applied in an inappropriate locus. Subsequently, we shall argue for a comprehensive interdisciplinary approach as a proper means of both effecting and respecting a meaningful concern with analytical boundaries. This can be effected genuinely only when recognition is made of the conceptual, theoretical, and explanatory boundaries not only beyond which each discipline *cannot* go, but also of the inclusive boundaries (limits) to which each discipline *must* go for the more complete and accurate analysis in its own dimension—the full consequence of which is the perfection of a synthetic and a more comprehensive explanation. An interdisciplinary perspective is itself a general corrective mechanism against "premature closure" by keeping the researcher ever-mindful of the "interpenetration" (of elements) which is realistically descriptive of the latent property space for which he is attempting to derive a theoretical explanation.

The selection of an analytical locus and the ascription of analytical boundaries find their basic application reflected in conceptual and definitional elements. These are our next concern.

Concepts: The Focus of Explanation

Concepts comprise the indispensable vehicles of thought and the irreducible elements in the process of scientific explanation. The focus of our considerations in this Symposium has been on the formation and definition of scientific concepts, and their significance as the fundamental and pivotal elements of theoretical explanations. Conceptual definition is crucial for scientific explanation; and, in the behavioral sciences, as Lazarsfeld has contended in his basic thesis, concept formation exhibits special difficulties. Particular aspects of this problem, as we have pointed out above, refer to the nature and to the locus of the phenomena subjected to analysis.

We have been exposed to several concepts, as well as to many types of concepts, in these proceedings. That there is a variety of types of conceptual definition for science to employ is a welcomed state of affairs. The critical issue for scientific explanation, however, concerns the validity, and hence the limits of the functional value, of these different modes of definition. Each of these types has advantages and disadvantages as well as limits— both in terms of their utility for methodology and their utility for theory. It is imperative to recognize the diverse functions of these types of conceptual definition and to respect their limitations. Our concern now is to consider which types are legitimate, and which seem to be best suited for the various functions of the scientific process, including particularly, of course, that of theoretical explanation. We shall concentrate on how concepts are introduced and how they function in the scientific process.

Concepts are the tools and the vehicles of all thought, scientific or not. Faulty concepts comprise one of the major causes of erroneous thinking and constitute a prime weakness in our attempts to develop scientific theory. Current concepts in all the behavioral sciences have a certain vagueness. Surely, there was some evidence of this in these proceedings. Many concepts lack precise definition. Often we use a unitary conception for a given phenomenon that is manifested concretely in a host of diversified ways. For example, as we exemplified in Chapter I, the concept of "role" is used descriptively, evaluatively, prescriptively, and even fusionistically. The referents for these different denotations are significantly dissimilar. A fusionistic conception, furthermore, is not only confusing but also unrealistic and distorting, and as such is theoretically unsound. Lazarsfeld argues that the "fuzziness" is in the very nature of some concepts—especially his "inferential concept." This inherent "fuzziness" is the crux of our problem. Already it has led to the creation of all kinds of conceptual labels—models, operational definitions, logical constructs, syndromes, genotypes, ideal-types, and so forth. This conceptual progeny is in many respects a positive accomplishment. On the other hand, the vagueness of conceptual definition has a negative effect in that it continues to stimulate production without end, and the upshot is a population problem of concepts—all of which, fit or not, are striving for survival. The theorist, again as we indicated in Chapter I, frequently fails to tell us what we can do with his concepts, other than to use them as labels to replace the ones already borne by whatever the phenomenon in question.

One of the particularly complicating situations for the behavioral sciences is the traditional, and unfortunate, use of ordinary vocabulary which is semantically ambiguous. Nearly all of these words have several different meanings. The physical and biological sciences have been able to avoid much of the vagueness which is precipitated by the multiple connotations of everyday language, partly because at the time of their development no generally acceptable terminology existed for their phenomena. Then, too, their phenomena are not as immediately accessible to the layman as the phenomena of the behavioral sciences. But behavioral scientists, for many unknown reasons, persist in thinking in the non-scientific vocabulary of everyday usage. Neologisms, however rampant, are confined by and large to supplemental meanings for the standardized vocabulary of common usage. We must face up to the fact that as we in the behavioral sciences discover "new" reality—more and more of it—we, too, need new words to name new concepts as referents for this reality. Precision in conceptual labeling requires a vocabulary that is purely denotative in character—one which is free of all connotative and multiple meanings.

Science cannot content itself with, or by striving for, only a minimal degree of ambiguity in its conceptual apparatus; it must completely remove ambiguity. A primary characteristic of science is accuracy. This demands clarity and precision in concepts. The lack of conceptual precision results in a lack of theoretical precision, which in turn results in predictive powers that share the same shortcoming. All of this is completely contrary to the very nature and orientation of science. This is one of our emphatic points. Science cannot settle for anything less than the most finite precision. We are in many respects a long way from this goal. The behavioral sciences, in order to achieve greater precision for their concepts, need an extensive and thorough reconceptualization and respecification of all of their existing conceptual apparatus, including particularly the more traditional and pivotal concepts which have constituted their "primary abstractions." Some of our current concepts may fall by the wayside as a consequence of this overhauling. Others will stand up under the ultimate criterion of contributing to the formation of a system of theories and laws that in fact do explain reality accurately and precisely, or, at least, offer that hope. It may be that we cannot emulate the "exact" definitions of the physical and biological sciences. Lazarsfeld, for example, contends that concepts in the behavioral sciences can never be defined precisely by words. Such a view from a mathematically oriented method-ologist should not be too disturbing. Nevertheless, perhaps a specification in terms of mathematics or another symbolic language would be quite an instrumental step toward realizing the goal of conceptual precision. Hopefully, a contribution to this reconceptualization and respecification has been offered by this Symposium.

There are, as White points out, two different types of fundamental tasks involved in the problem of conceptual definition, both of which often either are overlooked or are confused. One is to determine the nature of a thing. The other is to determine its composition and which class of phenomena is subsumed within the concept. For example, one first must determine the precise nature of "culture": Is it real or not? Is it entity or process? Next, one must determine the composition of culture, in order to ascertain which "things" (such as symbolates) are or are not comprised by "culture." Yet, there is here an arbitrary and relative element which cannot be admitted in the conceptualization of concepts—not of real concepts, at least. Lazarsfeld similarly considers the role of concepts to be one of summarization. He suggests that we see the connection between definitions and classifications. Thus, concepts for him, as for White, are classificatory devices. But, conceptualization is not simply a matter of conventional classification. And, similarly, concepts and definitions in science are not merely a matter of usefulness for classification. Rather, they involve a question of absolute truth. Words and categories may be determined arbitrarily. Their conceptual referents, however, may not be defined so conventionally. Concepts, or the metaphysical referents for words and classifications, are either given or not given in reality, and thus they are either true or false. This arbitrariness is one of the most besetting sins of the behavioral sciences, and its unfortunate consequences for the construction of valid theory are obvious. The fact is that conceptual definition and theory go hand in hand; the validity and the precision of theory is dependent upon and reflects the validity and the precision of conceptual definition.

Much of the present arbitrariness and consequent ambiguity in conceptual definition is brought about by failing to make a distinction between nominal and real concepts. Concepts and definitions often are used, and rightly so at times, more or less interchangeably. There is a distinction, however, which must not be overlooked. The fact is that they may or may not be synonymous. A *real* concept is necessarily true; it refers to ontological reality. As Bierstedt states, "Its definitions are convertible *simpliciter*."[9] A *nominal* concept, on the other hand, is neither true nor false necessarily. It is a purely synthetic formulation. Real definitions imply and refer to denotata—that is, to actuality; whereas nominal definitions refer to designata, which as such are only symbolic or representative. Thus, there is logically only one real definition—one real concept—for a given phenomenon; but there may be several nominal definitions, and reciprocal conceptions, for the same referent. If a definition is true, it corresponds to its concept, and is convertible simpliciter; the two are synonymous. Accordingly, real definitions and real concepts are synonymous; nominal definitions, not being necessarily true, are not synonymous with their conceptual referent.

It is imperative to distinguish between the legitimate utility of a concept and its claims to truth; and the same distinction must be made for types of concepts. To make these distinctions we must first distinguish between *substantive* concepts—those which deal theoretically with the phenomena under investigation—and *methodological* concepts—those which relate to the process of investigation. As we stated in Chapter I, both types of concepts are necessary in the scientific process. Yet, their diverse functions must be respected; the penalty is simply self-defeat. Nominal concepts as a generic type have a clear edge in science. Most of the concepts that have been presented in the preceding pages are nominal or methodological ones. The question is whether there is any substantive reality that corresponds to them. Real concepts deal with ontological reality. Real concepts are "found" or "discovered," whereas nominal concepts are "created" or "invented." Nominal concepts do not necessarily have any exact counterpart in reality. They are, of course, quite legitimate as methodological concepts. When employed as substantive concepts in a theoretical context, however, their legitimacy becomes questionable; they are used beyond their explanatory limits. Substantive concepts serve no theoretical purpose unless they relate to reality. That is to say, they must involve a direct connection with empirical phenomena. Concepts with no empirical meaning can have no theoretical function. This is not to say that only one type of concept is legitimate—or even satisfactory —for scientific explanation. All types of concepts may be necessary in the scientific process, especially since each does not have precisely the same set of functions. Some concepts, as Lazarsfeld reminds us, just generate ideas—one function, we submit, of nominal concepts. Nevertheless, all types of concepts must lead eventually and ultimately to real concepts/definitions as the indispensable elements of substantive theory. To do this, science must get beyond the use of relative concepts, such as nominal and methodological ones, to those of an absolute nature—to theoretical ones, and therefore to real and substantive ones.

Concepts must be productive of substantive theory. Otherwise, they are sterile. Science cannot stop at, nor become content with, those concepts that hold no claims to truth. Our major argument here is directed against those who wish to confine theoretical analysis to the utilization of nominal concepts, such as (and more particularly) those exemplified by operational definitions. The operational approach, which emphasizes functionality at the expense of validity, has been very influential in many quarters of the behavioral sciences. F. S. C. Northrop, for example, in discussing methodological procedures in anthropological research, claims that the syntactically and semantically sophisticated stage of deductively formulated theory is correlated with operational definitions.[10] Yet, the difficulty here is that operational definitions do not exhaust the scientific—and therefore, true—meaning of a concept. Operational definitions are but means to the real definition of a phenomenon, and as such do not comprise the final step in the process of conceptualization. In an operational definition, the concept is synonymous with the corresponding set of operations employed. Such a definition thus necessitates only the specification of the operations that determine its application. In practice, however, where the operationalist discusses a new phenomenon, he devises a measurement and then defines the phenomenon as what is measured by his measurement.[11] The operationalist, therefore, defines concepts in terms of the measuring operations by which he arrives at the explicandum. But, is it possible to measure that which has not yet been defined or described? An operational definition simply implies that the set of operations *is* the concept. It defines in terms of measurement—that is, in terms of methodology and not ontology. It is not possible, however, to measure that which has not yet been defined or described.

Many researchers confine themselves to operationalism as the only valid method for science. One of the principal arguments in favor of operational definitions is that they allegedly escape metaphysical controversy over "real essences." Yet, as we indicated above, this is not a valid position for science to assume. Somewhere along the line, the scientist must confront the question of reality—that is, of real essences. Is he, or is he not, dealing with phenomena existing in the world of reality—the object of his intended explanation? Scientists cannot legitimately avoid confronting the question of "real essences" in their research for the very reason that it is such things that science seeks to explain. Operationalists shy away from questions of "truth" and "falsity" because they cannot define such questions operationally and therefore do not feel capable of answering them.[12] Some operational definitions, in fact, are thought to be fictitious. For example, *force*, in Newton's famous Law of Motion, is defined as $F = m \times a$ (mass of body times acceleration).[13] But scientists, like metaphysicians, must argue over "truth" and "falsity." Such questions are the very domain of scientific activity. Certainly, the scientist is very much concerned with what *is*—with explaining reality—and, therefore, with metaphysical reality. Unless the scientist operates with this orientation and this intention, he is wasting his time, or at least misdirecting his efforts. One would never know whether his explanations have achieved objective truth or simply a consistent, but factually false, logic.

Another argument advanced in favor of operational definitions is that they avoid subjectivity. This, of course, is a welcomed advantage, consistent with the scientific orientation. Operationalists speak of "the" operations that pertain to a given concept—as indeed they must, if these are not to be purely arbitrary and relative elements that have no bearing on non-arbitrary and non-relative reality. Yet, each scientist—and often even the same one—performs different operations in different situations when allegedly measuring the same phenomenon. This, contrary to the arguments of the operationalists, presents not only the obvious problems of comparability, but more especially, those of validity. On the other hand, science must allow for the possibility of the same phenomenon being measured on the basis of totally different operations. Subtle but significant variations in seemingly the same phenomenon, perhaps as a consequence of context, are crucial in a theoretical perspective. This fact is difficult to reconcile with the assumptions and claims of operationalism. It is not consistent with the operationalist's principle that different operations define different phenomena. Real definitions, and not operational ones, are truly objective and therefore absolute and timeless.

In addition to the fact that the same phenomena may be

measurable by totally different operations is the fact that many phenomena are not amenable to operational definition or measurement at all. Concepts such as "social system" and "culture," for example, do not lend themselves to this kind of definition—at least, not so readily as do concepts that have a more tangible referent. If, then, there exist phenomena that are beyond definition in this manner, how can they be explained? Certainly they cannot if one stays at the level of operational definitions. Not only do operational concepts narrow the range of inquiry; they also confront the scientist with the possibility of unresolvable gaps in his explanation and theory—and, more likely, with the possibility that he will not be able to derive an explanation at all. The scientist thus finds himself in the embarrassing position of having to deny the existence of certain phenomena because his operations are unable to measure them or because he is unable to devise operations to do so. For example, the physicist P. W. Bridgman, one of the staunchest advocates of operationalism, is forced to state: "Time, as defined by Newton, in terms of properties, does not exist because it cannot be measured."[14] For the operationalist, what cannot be measured, cannot be analyzed —and, moreover, does not exist. This brand of science is decidedly limited and incomplete.

This is not to say, however, that all operationalism is without merit. On the contrary, the problem is only that it does not go far enough. As Levinson has pointed out, there is in scientific research today an imbalanced concern for measurement at the expense of conceptualization. More time and concern are devoted to measurement than to conceptualization. There seems to be a certain reluctance, particularly on the part of those researchers who stop at operationalism, really to engage in theorizing. Lazarsfeld's attempt to add an element of reality to the traditional operational definition by way of probability inference proposes a solution to this problem. His procedure gets away from traditional operationalism, or rather improves upon it, by adding the notion of probability—thereby implying an element of reality, since the concept is defined by the probability of the occurrence (or the existence) of a given phenomenon. Clearly, this is a step in the proper theoretical direction.

All of these questions of conceptual definition have their fundamental consideration in the process by which concepts are introduced into scientific activity. At what point in the theoretical process do concepts make their appearance? This seems to be a problem area that might be the cause of much of the unfortunate state of affairs in which we find ourselves. Does one begin with concepts, terminate with them, or, perhaps, find them somewhere within the course of scientific investigation? Our proceedings offer two seemingly opposing views—put forth by Levinson and Lazarsfeld respectively.

Levinson advocates the need for clearly and precisely defined concepts *at the outset* of the research process and suggests that these then be translated into terms that will facilitate empirical observations and measurements. Is it possible, however, to have phenomena so well defined in advance of empirical investigations? Clearly not, answers Lazarsfeld. Such concepts are the objective, and not the premise, of scientific activity. Indeed, if it were possible to begin with precisely defined concepts, there would be no need for much of the research process, since conceptualization is the pivotal segment of the entire process of explanation. Nevertheless, both Levinson and Lazarsfeld are correct in one sense—the *kind* of concept being discussed. Levinson is quite right, of course, in demanding precision at the outset of the theoretical process. Precision is imperative in every phase of science; its compromise should not be tolerated at any point in the research process. What is implicit in Levinson's position, however, is that precise *nominal* concepts are desirable at the beginning of the research process, because they delimit and generate the ensuing research. As Sherif tells us, it is imperative to know the nature of the analytical situation before one can denote the behavior within it. Clarity should characterize the universe of discourse. Nonetheless, as Lazarsfeld rightly maintains, "precision" in the initial stages of the research process is tentative and therefore subject to refinement and verification.

Nominal concepts, as methodological concepts, are given at the outset of the research process. One begins, as Lazarsfeld has pointed out, with "broad imageries" (descriptions) which migrate through a process of refinement and specification into a more precise nature. This "conceptual imagery," as Lazarsfeld calls it, orientates and directs the research process toward a specification and refinement of the conceptual apparatus. *Real* concepts are not given at the outset of inquiry; they result only from empirical investigation of the phenomena in question. As Bierstedt points out:

> It is necessary to rely upon investigation itself in order to determine whether or not the properties the definition ascribes to the concept actually do belong to it, whether to put it bluntly, the *definiens* does in fact define the *definiendum*, whether, in short, the definition is "true."[15]

Here, indeed, is the crux of Levinson's concern for why scientists do not spend more time measuring concepts of "broader significance"—that is, real and substantive ones, rather than those that are implicit in "conceptual imagery." Such concepts—the substantive ones of theoretical significance—cannot be measured while they still exist as nominal and methodological elements in the phase of generating ideas. Only when the migration process has been completed can measurement of a substantive nature be performed. Herein is the distinction that Lazarsfeld draws between the "interpretative" use of a concept and its use as a "classificatory" device. The distinction seems to be a respective parallel between nominal and real concepts. The research process—more specifically, conceptual analysis—begins with descriptive and nominal elements. It terminates, hopefully, with interpretative and real elements. Precision is a matter of degree throughout.

Scientific explanation cannot terminate at the descriptive level of nominal concepts. The gap between the poles of "imagery" and "definition" in the migration process is wide and crucially significant. Concepts need to have not merely descriptive power; ultimately, and from a theoretical point of view, they also need to have interpretative power, and they need to be fruitful in a predictive sense. It is not possible to use imaginary tools to construct theoretical explanations of real things. If we are looking for laws of human behavior, then our concepts must be more than sets of operations, or of mathematical formulas, or of logical realities, or of sheer descriptions. They must have empirical, and not merely rational, implications. Reification of our conceptual/ theoretical abstractions is a major scientific hazard in the process of conceptualization. Nominal concepts do not correspond to real phenomena. Consequently, when used in an explanatory context, they may produce conceptual schemes and theoretical systems that are not ontologically true. Concepts with no empirical meaning can serve no explanatory function. The ultimate goal of all scientific inquiry is to produce substantive theory—a theory which is propositional and whose propositions are assertions about reality. Only a conceptual scheme that is constituted of real concepts—those that have referents in the empirical world— can produce substantive theory.

Problems of concept formation and definition are related to problems of measurement and empirical verification. The resolution of the one problem necessarily involves the resolution of the other. This is our next consideration.

Measurement and Empirical Verification

Measurement refers to the procedures by which empirical observations are made in order to represent symbolically the phenomena and the conceptualizations that are to be explained. With the major exception of Lazarsfeld's contribution, this Symposium has been little concerned with the question of measurement. Perhaps the lack of this concern is another indication of how our symposiasts perceive and define the topical problem of conceptual definition. Of course, some of them quite frankly are not directly interested in these aspects of scientific explanation. Yet, as Lazarsfeld states in the opening sentence to his paper, problems of concept formation, of meaning, and of measurement necessarily fuse into one another. The measurement of concepts presents an indispensable consideration which the theorist cannot avoid—however much he himself may not be interested in the empirical task. All too often the theorist fails to indicate how one demonstrates the validity of his conceptualizations and the exist-

ence of their empirical referents, or how one measures them
scientifically. The consideration of measurement is all the more
significant for the behavioral sciences because the nature of their
phenomena (their time-boundness and complexity, for example)
presents special problems of measurement.

This question of measurement necessarily involves consideration of the empirical verification of conceptual formations and of
theoretical explanations. Science—more specifically, behavioral
science—is empirical; if its conceptual and theoretical formulations are to be of any significance in scientific explanation, it is
imperative that they be subjected—successfully subjected—to
empirical verification. To propose an unverifiable theory, or
theoretical system, is to make no significant contribution to the
scientific explanation of reality. As Sherif has warned, theorizing
must not be unbridled speculation. It needs to be controlled and
validated in terms of the ever-increasing data derived from
empirical investigations. An enormous mass of data has already
been uncovered in all the fields of behavioral science—and this
situation undoubtedly will witness a geometric growth in the
immediate years ahead. These developments are going to make
more demands on both the experimenter and the theorist. Many
scientists, as Sherif alleges, fail to take inventory of these stock-
piles of data, as well as of the theoretical developments, not only
in their respective fields particularly, but also in the tangential
disciplines. And, more specifically, these theorists do not examine
their own pursuits in the light of these scientific developments.
Empirical verification of a theoretical system—including such
considerations as locus problems, analytical boundaries, and the
particular methodology of a theoretical system—shows the degree to which that system is efficient and productive, or the
circumstances under which it is distorting and sterile.

The validity of a theoretical system, and of its conceptual
apparatus, is obtained by means of empirical confirmation. Such
verification requires an empirical correspondence, which is
achieved with the success of the entire explanatory scheme and
with its consistency. Empirical confirmation alone is sufficient
evidence of the reality of the phenomena under investigation

(particularly regarding the latent property space and its structure) and of the validity of the explanatory scheme. Nobody has ever seen an attitude or a value, just as nobody has ever seen an atom or an electron; yet these concepts do "work" theoretically as explanatory elements of the empirical phenomena to which they relate. They work not so much because of the intrinsic logic which they provide, but rather because their validity has been confirmed empirically by means of successfully predicted phenomena. As we have seen, a theoretical system, and therefore its conceptual apparatus, need to have predictive power. Successful prediction on the basis of a theoretical system and its conceptual apparatus is sufficient evidence of an empirical confirmation. The empirical specification of a theory in the form of prediction is a sufficient test of its validity. Successful prediction requires an essential correspondence between conceptual/theoretical and phenomenal elements—which prediction, as such, offers sufficient evidence of the reality of the phenomena. As long as the correspondence continues, as predicted, then the theory is confirmed; if and when it disappears, the explanatory scheme needs to be modified or abandoned.

One fundamental problem in measurement and verification is caused by an unrealistic dichotomy of interests in the scientific process which results in one's neither perceiving nor respecting the fundamental unity of theoretical explanation. In an extreme sense, the division obtains between the staunch theorists and the die-hard methodologists. It seems that the latter constitute the scientific majority. Conceptualization, as Levinson has suggested, has been conceived predominantly in terms of measurement, which has outstripped the work on conceptualization. Obviously, what is needed here is a balance of interests and a respectful concern for the reciprocal and complementary role which these two phases of scientific research constitute for theoretical explanation. Just as the methodologist and the experimenter have to face up to the role of theory and its considerations in the scientific process, so too the theorist has to face up to the role of empirical measurement and verification. All too often the specialized behavioral scientist fails to recognize and to appreciate the relationship between substantive problems and methodological analysis. Lazarsfeld has attempted to clarify this problem for us. His treatment of "inferential concepts" shows the combination of the steps of conceptualization and measurement, and the effectiveness—of course, even the necessity—of following through to unite these two phases by means of the migratory process of conceptualization.

Even more besetting than the split between conceptualization and measurement is the fact, as Levinson further points out, that wherever problems of measurement have been handled, the greater concern has been evidenced for the reliability rather than for the validity of the measuring procedures and techniques. The fact is that as a consequence of the methodological procedures used in formulating theoretical explanation, measurement and experimentation may introduce distortion by altering the true nature of the phenomena. Accordingly, the validity of measurement procedures and techniques should be of as much concern as their reliability.

This concern for the validity of measurement is a specific application of the general concern for the role of "scientific interference" in the explanatory process on the part of the scientist. To what extent does he invent or create—rather than discover—reality by his methods of measurement? In the behavioral sciences the vast majority of concepts and theory are derived from the indirect observation of phenomena; the validity of the methodological procedures and techniques that are used for the formation and application of such concepts and theory is a greatly neglected problem. Decisions have to be made as to how precisely inferences from concrete observations to concepts are to be drawn—how one moves methodologically and analytically from the manifest property space to the latent property space—if we are to develop a consistent and integrated system of concepts and theory. All of this requires empirical measurements that are not only reliable, but more especially valid, instruments. As Sherif suggests, we need to evaluate the appropriateness of the techniques that are used to gather our data and to evaluate our theory. Tools cannot be effective unless they are also appropriate. One has to question, moreover, the general influence of the modes of research on the research process itself. As Lazarsfeld points out, a slight modification in this respect may result in significantly different conceptual and theoretical consequences.

The sad state of measurement—and therefore of verification— in the behavioral sciences is revealed in Lazarsfeld's demonstration of the inconsequential effect which is produced by an arbitrary selection of empirical indicators to measure behavioral phenomena. This lack of precision and specification in measurement is directly reflected in, and subsequently reflective of, the degree of precision and specification of theoretical explanation in the behavioral sciences. Concepts, theory, models, measuring techniques—in short, both the conceptual and methodological apparatus—need to be validated. All too often much of this just does not take place. Many scientists prefer just to "theorize." The theorist is too theoretical, and the experimenter is too experimental. What we need here is an "intradisciplinary" collaboration. Just as the methodologist must become theory-conscious, so too must the theorist become empirical-minded with regard to verification. Measurement is indispensable for empirical verification, and verification is the *sine qua non* for scientific validity.

Scientific Convergence

Synthesis versus specialization is by now a somewhat old, yet ever current, theme in scientific pursuits. These orientations vie constantly for influence in directing the course of scientific activity. The latter usually dominates; provincialism is found extensively in many quarters of science. Nonetheless, if our symposiasts seem to be in agreement about anything, it is a need for an interdisciplinary perspective in behavioral science research. Their plea for scientific convergence is not new. Its cries, however, are neglected much too often; and the implicit problems—those of achieving adequate, complete, and comprehensive theory—are becoming especially acute as scientific specialization becomes more and more inevitable and extensive as a consequence of the never-ending growth of knowledge.

All knowledge is one. The single discipline in isolation is just as artificial as the single fact in isolation. We frequently seem to forget that the divisions of the behavioral sciences into separate disciplines, as with divisions in all other areas of knowledge, are arbitrary and, even at best, considerably indefinite. Assuming, heuristically, a closed chain of knowledge, the individual disciplines may be envisioned as constituting interlocking links. Thus, to illustrate, culturology may be seen to interlink with sociology, which interlinks with psychology (constituting social psychology), which interlinks with biology (constituting physiological psychology), which interlinks with anthropology (constituting physical anthropology), and so on, until the chain is closed to represent the oneness of truth and reality. Several of our symposiasts appeal for a recognition of and a respect for this unity of knowledge. We must fix our attention on this fundamental principle—of the systemic nature of reality, and therefore of knowledge and truth as its reflections. Moreover, we must not lose sight, as Sherif cautions, of the established principle that a system, either of reality or of knowledge, determines the nature of its parts. Research has to put this principle to its logical applications in the research process. If the diverse phenomena being studied, as Sherif points out, are parts of one system of reality, there has to be a composite analysis, such that the different parts are fitted together theoretically as they are in the empirical system. The different types of approach that are found in various disciplines, and the different levels of analysis, should, if they are valid, supplement rather than contradict one another.

Our symposiasts protest very strongly against reductionism. Ackerman and Parsons's general theory of action approach, accounting as it does for the interpenetration of three systems, is clearly intended to counteract reductionism. White speaks adamantly against the exclusively psychological explanations which have been offered for cultural phenomena. Particularly vocal about this type of reductionism is Sherif, who, as we have seen, has labeled such things "untenable solipsism." He speaks strongly against such restricted research interests, which often are elaborated as "approaches." Clearly, we are as strongly opposed as these other symposiasts to attempts to reduce all patterns of social organization and culture to human behavior (or to any single explanation)—and vice versa. "Personality" is not an isolated phenomenon and "interaction" is not a pure process, devoid of content and context. The delimitation of these elements for analytical purposes must be recognized as scientific distortion.

Sherif and Levinson, as we have seen, want to study individual behavior in its social and cultural settings, and they want to study society and culture in terms of individual behavior. Sherif, for example, asserts that "what is needed today is a conception of the individual in his group and cultural setting, and a conception of group and cultural setting relative to its members." Levinson is of similar orientation, as may be seen in his discussion comment, in that he feels that White is excluding the role of people—and, therefore, of personality—in influencing the dynamics of culture. He pleads, in the words of Ackerman and Parsons, for a consideration of the "interpenetration" which seems to be involved between the personality system and the cultural system. Each of these symposiasts argues against a sharp demarcation of the disciplinary boundaries of analysis on the grounds that this does not reflect the empirical situation. Sherif pleads for a framework of fundamental orientations in the behavioral sciences. We endorse his strong exhortation that, rather than to wrangle over prerogatives of function and scope, the individual disciplines need to complement and to supplement one another. The instances are many and frequent when scientific evidence gained in one domain is very relevant for theoretical explanation in another, and when the same major conceptual and theoretical structures are found to underlie fields that seem to be quite disparate.

There is, of course, much heed paid to "interdisciplinary" research. It seems almost profane to deny either the legitimacy or the imperativeness of such an approach in science. But what in fact has been the nature of interdisciplinary activity by and large? As Sherif points out, mere discussion about the same or related problems by scientists in different disciplines does not constitute interdisciplinary research. Sherif tells us that much lip service is given to an interdisciplinary orientation; but, in the *de facto* process of research, its implications are forgotten. The fact of the matter is that much interdisciplinary scientific activity has remained to a large extent provincially specialized. Often this fact is disguised by a merely hyphenated brand of "interdisciplinary" undertaking which is actually nothing more than an unintegrated combination of specialized interests.

Many in the behavioral sciences recognize the multi-faceted nature of behavioral phenomena; and, nearly all scientists seem to acknowledge the legitimacy of other fields and approaches. Some openly appreciate the contributions of other disciplines, and even admit the need for them and their dependence upon them. Nevertheless, they contend that they cannot be analytically responsible for all behavioral phenomena, and thus hope that this assistance will be forthcoming from other researchers somewhere along the line. This *modus operandi*, some argue, creates rather than annihilates distortion. From a methodological point of view, perhaps research can be done more readily and more effectively within the confines of single disciplines. From a theoretical point of view, however, it is not methodological expediency that holds the premium. Whenever necessary, this should be sacrificed for theoretical precision. Incomplete theoretical explanations, however valid in themselves, should not be sufficiently comforting rewards for methodological purity. Why are we, as Lazarsfeld suggests, only at the pre-theoretical stage of research in the behavioral sciences? His answer is that our concepts do not form a logically closed system. Why not? One reason for this absence of adequate closure may be a consequent of the lack of synthetic orientations in the behavioral disciplines. Human behavior, as Sherif points out, cannot by its nature be studied in a series of vacuums. Its components interpenetrate too intimately, and these must be synthesized on the theoretical level for an adequate and complete explanation.

Academic scientists in particular seem to be especially conservative about interdisciplinary activity; much more progress along these lines has been made in non-academic circles. Apparently, there is much fear of losing an identification with a particular discipline—which is not as much of a problem in non-academic environments, such as industry, where these traditional disciplinary identities often are not made as finely, nor do they have the same signification and function in these contexts. This "identity anxiety" has been singled out by many as the fundamental ailment of multi-disciplinary activity. Yet, what is overlooked is that this psychological malady need not perpetuate itself. Interdisciplinary research does not imply that the entirety of one discipline needs to be related to or converged with the totality of another. Certainly, there are areas in each discipline that neither overlap nor interpenetrate. Many phases of any discipline will always remain outside the boundaries of any interdisciplinary enterprise. This is reflected in our heuristic chain of knowledge. Social psychology and demography, for example, would be cases in point. Specialization, moreover, need not be sacrificed. In fact, it may be demanded even more precisely as science continues its seemingly endless course of increasing the human fund of knowledge. But, more importantly, interdisciplinary research does not necessarily imply, nor does it require, physical collaboration or collective activity on the empirical level. Some of this, to be sure, is demanded—and all of it is welcomed. We are appealing for only the serious assumption, and a more widespread one, of an interdisciplinary *orientation*, particularly at the theoretical level. Sherif describes a multi-faceted research program that illustrates such an integrative research orientation. His program delineates a definite and orderly sequence of procedures (at least for studies in the area of individual-group relationships), one which attempts to eliminate the distorting influence which inevitably results from the division of research into specialized interests and perspectives. An explanatory synthesis is what we are primarily seeking, a meeting ground of concepts and theory—not mere physical collaboration.

What steps would be in the direction of establishing interdisciplinary orientations? There are a host of answers, many of which have been suggested implicitly in these proceedings. Obviously, the first thing that is needed is an awareness of what is going on in the neighboring and related disciplines—with particular attention to the relevance of this activity for one's own theoretical interests. Many scientists simply do not apprise themselves sufficiently of the research activity that is taking place in different disciplines on the same or similar analytical problems. One specific thing that needs to be done is to develop a sensitivity to convergence—to recognize, to strive to recognize, where the several disciplines do, and must, come together theoretically, and to facilitate such a union. We need to focus more closely on the arbitrariness of disciplinary boundaries and to give more attention to their interpenetration. This requires removing the ambiguity which inevitably characterizes these conventional lines of analytical demarcation. These steps toward interdisciplinary orientations constitute analytical loci of the most urgent priority for all of the behavioral sciences. Their consideration would contribute toward resolving many of the epistemological and explanatory questions that have been discussed in this chapter.

Fortunately, the need for interdisciplinary effort has been recognized to some extent for sociology and psychology. Earnest attempts at fulfilling this need for these disciplines have been quite effective. The outcome of this activity, however limited, may be seen in the expanding field of social psychology, and in the contributions it has made to the construction of more fruitful theoretical explanations for each of the parent disciplines. Explanations in social psychology assume a comprehensiveness which is more reflective of the complexity of the phenomenal situation that they explain than are strictly sociological and strictly psychological explanations. This has been demonstrated by the contributions of the psychologists represented in this Symposium. Levinson, in particular, has devoted much of his theoretical activity to effecting a convergence between sociology and psychology; his paper in this Symposium, which refers to a "new" social psychology, reflects these efforts to show the necessary integration of the two disciplines. Sherif's perspective is, of course, along similar lines. More pursuits of this type are needed for all of the disciplines in the behavioral sciences. We need, for example, a dynamic resurrection of culture and personality studies; they hold much hope for more comprehensive explanations in the fields of anthropology and psychology. Whenever possible and necessary, each of these separate fields must incorporate, in its own theoretical pursuits, the theoretical perspectives and contributions of the others, retaining what is fruitful and rejecting what is sterile or distorting. We need more complex conceptions of personality, of society, and of culture; we need more complex theory of human behavior to reflect the complex nature of human behavior. To this end our explanations become more comprehensive and more complete.

The several disciplines, in many instances, deal with the same phenomenon in formally different ways. Research of this type, of course, is imperative; many questions can be answered only by such specialized approaches. At a further point, however, lies the question of the relationship of these several perspectives to one another. Postulating the oneness of reality, these individual perspectives must be congruent with one another and, at an "ultimate" point, must converge into one comprehensive explanation. Scientific explanation must work toward this theoretical integration. Ackerman, for example, has shown this concern for convergence when he offers Parsons's AGIL paradigm as a general model of the empirical specifications presented by each of the other symposiasts. His attempt to apply this conceptual scheme of action theory to those from other disciplines is the kind of thing that must be done. What is needed in particular, therefore, are attempts such as those by Ackerman and Parsons to develop general and synthetic theory which endeavors to bridge the arbitrarily delimited boundaries of analysis. Complementation and convergence, rather than contraposition and divergence, should be the desired perspective and course of action.

Another specific thing that must be done has reference to our previous statements in Chapter I, in which we call for a common scientific language for the behavioral sciences—and, wherever possible (such as in methodology), for all scientific disciplines. It is most difficult to make scientific progress with the persistent use of common, everyday language whose ambiguous vocabulary with its multiple connotations is a chief impediment. The physical and biological sciences, in the development of their specialized vocabularies, were able to avoid such problems, partly because no generally accepted terminology existed for much of their phenomena. The behavioral sciences have not been so fortunate, but much of this handicap is due to their own reluctance to rectify the problem. To avoid the ambiguity of ordinary language, and to avoid its irrelevant and confusing connotations, we need a standardization of scientific concepts and scientific language. We have this unity in many aspects of methodology, and we should have it, wherever possible, for all common areas of science.

Conceptual consensus among the behavioral sciences, then, is obviously a necessary step for scientific convergence. By partly fulfilling Sherif's plea for "a framework of fundamental orientations," it would contribute much to solving the major problem of communication, which has been a fundamental handicap in facilitating scientific interchange among the several disciplines. Yet, first of all, as we remarked in Chapter I, it is necessary to establish conceptual consensus within the single disciplines. The state of explanation in the behavioral sciences is reflected in the fact that even the basic definitional problems have not gone beyond the stage of controversy. These fundamental problems of conceptual definition must be resolved by each of the individual disciplines before much success can be expected for scientific and theoretical convergence.

No scientific discipline of whatever type is a law unto itself. This is particularly true of the behavioral sciences, which are mutually dependent upon one another. Their analytical boundaries necessarily are delimited less sharply than those of other categories of science; their phenomena interpenetrate much more intimately. We repeat again our exhortation that the arbitrary lines which delimit our separate disciplines must be transgressed whenever such boundaries restrict, or tend to distort, scientific inquiry. Synthetic explanations, compatible with the phenomena of reality, demand such action.

Conclusion

Our focus in this concluding chapter has been on a few selected issues that seem to comprise the central questions of the preceding contributions. We have delineated those problems which appear to form, in part, the crux of further progress toward theoretical explanation in the behavioral sciences. We have made no attempt, of course, to resolve these issues—nor do we pretend to have penetrated the depths of the many problems that have been suggested—but simply to put them into focus and in some manner to lay bare their wounds for further treatment. The issues that we have selected for consideration are not mutually exclusive ones in regard to their content. This no doubt was apparent in our treatment of them. Our inclusion of specific topics in any one rather than another of the several major issues was, in many cases, an arbitrary decision. One thing, however, that has not been mentioned, and which may not be too obvious, is the interdependence of these major issues upon one another. We have in fact tried to show a logical continuity among them as progressive steps of the research process.

Although we have tried to show their particular application to the behavioral disciplines, many of the issues we have considered are not specific to the behavioral sciences, since by and large they are fundamental problems of scientific methodology. These methodological issues are ones which, judging from the preceding presentations, need to be confronted with some serious determination before significant progress toward explanation in the behavioral sciences can be expected. Our emphasis on these issues is not intended to imply that the most serious problems confronting the behavioral sciences are methodological ones—and that their solution is the panacea for scientific success in the theoretical explanation of human behavior and of our world of socio-cultural reality. What we have tried to say, however, is that progress in scientific explanation for the behavioral sciences rests in part—but in great part—on the resolution of the methodological problems that have been discussed in these chapters. These questions are fundamental considerations which show a logical priority in the scientific process. Before substantive issues can be subjected to scientific analysis, methodological questions must be resolved and placed in proper perspective. The state and quality of substantive analysis are reflected directly in the state and quality of methodology.

The knowledge produced by the behavioral disciplines should

belong epistemologically among the sciences and not among the humanities. It is time that the "underground" of the behavioral sciences—those that refuse to admit that the behavioral disciplines are, or can be, methodologically scientific—face up to scientific tenability, even though they themselves refuse to subscribe to it. The hassle is already quite old that, since the behavioral sciences differ from other scientific disciplines in content and subject matter, they should differ in methodology. While this argument has been debated many times, it is still unresolved to the satisfaction of everyone. It remains to handicap and to impede the progress we are seeking. Certainly, non-scientific perspectives for the analysis of human behavior should be welcomed—as indeed they are. They have a contribution, however limited, to make to all of the behavioral disciplines. But, to assume a cynical and dogmatic attitude of anti-science for the behavioral disciplines is, to say the least, unsophisticated scholarship. Too narrow a dogmatism will always defeat itself. Fundamentally, this question of what the proper methodology of the behavioral disciplines should be is a scientific one, and thus one that cannot be resolved unless one assumes a scientific mentality and orientation.

Theoretical explanation in the behavioral sciences has been somewhat slow in its maturation. One of the biggest problems is the strain after scientific precision. Compared to other scientific disciplines, we have very few established principles on which to base scientific predictions. If we intend to narrow the gap between ourselves and these other scientific disciplines with regard to the successful formulation of theoretical explanations, then it is not time alone that we need. As Kaplan tells us: "The trouble with behavioral science is not that it has not arrived, but that often it seems unwilling to get going."[16] Hopefully, the considerations of this chapter—and, more particularly, those of the preceding ones—have provided a clarifying and impulsive step toward explanation in the behavioral sciences.

NOTES

1. Albert Einstein, "Albert Einstein: Philosopher-Scientist," in Paul A. Schlipp (ed.), *The Library of Living Philosophers* (Evanston: Northwestern University Press, 1949), VII, 683–684.

2. Arthur Eddington, *The Philosophy of Physical Science* (Ann Arbor: University of Michigan Press, 1958), p. 7.

3. *Ibid.*, p. 55.

4. Abraham Kaplan, *The Conduct of Inquiry* (San Francisco: Chandler Publishing Company, 1964), p. 258.

5. Benton J. Underwood, *Psychological Research* (New York: Appleton–Century–Crofts, 1957), p. 1.

6. Quoted in Kaplan, *op. cit.*, p. 27.

7. Abraham Edel, "The Concept of Levels in Social Theory," in Llewellyn Gross (ed.), *Symposium on Sociological Theory* (New York: Harper and Row, 1959), pp. 172–175.

8. See R. B. Braithwaite, *Scientific Explanation* (New York: Harper and Row, 1960), pp. 367–368; and Eddington, *op. cit.*, pp. 106–113.

9. Robert Bierstedt, "Nominal and Real Definitions," in Gross (ed.), *op. cit.*, pp. 141–142.

10. F. S. C. Northrop, "Toward a Deductively Formulated and Operationally Verifiable Comparative Cultural Anthropology," in F. S. C. Northrop and Helen H. Livingston (eds.), *Cross-Cultural Understanding: Epistemology in Anthropology* (New York: Harper and Row, 1964), p. 195.

11. Franz Adler, "Operational Definitions in Sociology," *American Journal of Sociology*, LII (1947), 441.

12. See George A. Lundberg, *Foundations of Sociology* (New York: David McKay Company, 1964), p. 65.

13. John G. Kemeny, *A Philosopher Looks at Science* (New York: D. Van Nostrand Company, 1959), p. 131.

14. P. W. Bridgman, *The Logic of Modern Physics* (New York: The Macmillan Company, 1928), p. 14.

15. Bierstedt, *op. cit.*, p. 125.

16. Kaplan, *op. cit.*, p. 352.

SUGGESTED READINGS*

Adler, Franz. "Operational Definitions in Sociology," *American Journal of Sociology* (1947), 52:438–444.

* See also Suggested Readings following Chapters I through VIII.

Berelson, Bernard (ed.). *The Behavioral Sciences Today.* New York: Harper and Row, 1963.

———, and Steiner, Gary A. (eds.). *Human Behavior: An Inventory of Findings.* New York: Harcourt, Brace and World, 1964.

Bierstedt, Robert. "Nominal and Real Definitions," in Llewellyn Gross (ed.), *Symposium on Sociological Theory.* New York: Harper and Row, 1959.

Bidney, David. *Theoretical Anthropology.* New York: Columbia University Press, 1953.

Braithwaite, R. B. *Scientific Explanation.* New York: Harper and Row, 1960.

Braybrooke, David. *Philosophical Problems of the Social Sciences.* New York: The Macmillan Company, 1965.

Bridgman, P. W. *The Logic of Modern Physics.* New York: The Macmillan Company, 1928.

Cohen, Morris R., and Nagel, Ernest. *An Introduction to Logic and Scientific Method.* New York: Harcourt, Brace and Company, 1934.

Craik, Kenneth J. W. *The Nature of Explanation.* Cambridge: The Macmillan Company, 1943.

Eddington, Arthur. *The Philosophy of Physical Science.* Ann Arbor: University of Michigan Press, 1958.

Edel, Abraham. "The Concept of Levels in Social Theory," in Llewellyn Gross (ed.), *Symposium on Sociological Theory.* New York: Harper and Row, 1959.

Einstein, Albert. "Albert Einstein: Philosopher-Scientist," in Paul A. Schlipp (ed.), *The Library of Living Philosophers.* Evanston: Northwestern University Press, 1949.

Furfey, Paul H. *The Method and Scope of Sociology.* New York: Harper and Brothers, 1953.

Gross, Llewellyn (ed.). *Symposium on Sociological Theory.* New York: Harper and Row, 1959.

Hempel, Carl G. *Aspects of Scientific Explanation.* Glencoe: The Free Press, 1965.

Kaplan, Abraham. *The Conduct of Inquiry.* San Francisco: Chandler Publishing Company, 1964.

Kaufmann, Felix. *Methodology of the Social Sciences.* New York: Oxford University Press, 1944.

Lazarsfeld, Paul F. "A Conceptual Introducion to Latent Structure Analysis," in Paul F. Lazarsfeld (ed.), *Mathematical Thinking in the Social Sciences.* Glencoe: The Free Press, 1954.

——— (ed.). *Mathematical Thinking in the Social Sciences.* Glencoe: The Free Press, 1954.

————. "Problems in Methodology," in Robert K. Merton *et al.* (eds.), *Sociology Today*. New York: Basic Books, Inc., 1959.

————, and Rosenberg, Morris (eds.). *The Language of Social Research*. Glencoe: The Free Press, 1955.

Levinson, Daniel J. "Toward a New Social Psychology: The Convergence of Sociology and Psychology," *Merrill-Palmer Quarterly of Behavior and Development* (1964), 10:77–88.

Lundberg, George A. *Foundations of Sociology*. New York: David McKay Company, 1964.

Madge, John. *The Tools of Social Science*. New York: Doubleday and Company, 1965.

Margenau, Henry. *The Nature of Physical Reality*. New York: McGraw-Hill Book Company, 1950.

Merton, Robert K., *et al.* (eds.). *Sociology Today*. New York: Basic Books, Inc., 1959.

Nagel, Ernest. *The Structure of Science*. New York: Harcourt, Brace and Company, 1961.

Northrop, F. S. C. *Logic of the Sciences and Humanities*. New York: The Macmillan Company, 1947.

————, and Livingston, Helen H. (eds.). *Cross-Cultural Understanding: Epistemology in Anthropology*. New York: Harper and Row, 1964.

Sjoberg, Gideon. "Operationalism and Social Research," in Llewellyn Gross (ed.), *Symposium on Sociological Theory*. New York: Harper and Row, 1959.

Underwood, Benton J. *Psychological Research*. New York: Appleton–Century–Crofts, 1957.

Notes on the Contributors

CHARLES ACKERMAN is an Assistant Professor of Sociology at Cornell University. One of his major areas of specialization is the "General Theory of Action." He previously served as an instructor at the University of California at Los Angeles, and as a research associate at Harvard University where he received his graduate training.

ALAN ROSS ANDERSON is Professor of Philosophy at the University of Pittsburgh. His main field of interest is mathematical logic, and its application in the philosophy of mathematics and science. He was formerly Professor of Philosophy at Yale University, where he received his undergraduate and doctoral training; he has also served as a Fulbright Lecturer at the University of Manchester in England.

GORDON J. DiRENZO is an Associate Professor of Sociology at Indiana University (South Bend Campus). He formerly served as Assistant Professor of Sociology and Social Psychology at Fairfield University. His major field of research interest concerns the functional relationship between personality structures and social systems. He received his undergraduate and graduate training at the University of Notre Dame and is the author of a forthcoming volume entitled *Personality, Power, and Politics*.

DORIS C. GILBERT is a Visiting Associate Professor of Psychology and Director of the Child Study Center at the University of Denver. Previously, she was a member of the faculties of the Medical Center at the University of Colorado, Harvard University, and Wellesley College; she also served as a member of the staff at the Massachusetts Mental Health Center.

PAUL F. LAZARSFELD is Quetelet Professor of Social Science at Columbia University, where he served as Chairman of the Department of Sociology for ten years until relinquishing the post in 1962. During that time he established the well-known Bureau of Applied Social Research. He is a former president of the American Sociological Association.

DANIEL J. LEVINSON is Professor of Psychology in the Department of Psychiatry at Yale University. He formerly was Director of the Center for Sociopsychological Research at the Massachusetts Mental Health Center and a member of the Department of Psychiatry of the Harvard Medical School. One of his current theoretical interests is the development of a social psychology that combines dynamic personality theory with sociological and anthropological elements. He is one of the co-authors of the now-classic study of *The Authoritarian Personality*.

OMAR K. MOORE is Professor of Social Psychology at the University of Pittsburgh. His many publications have spanned the disciplines of sociology, anthropology, psychology, logic, and the philosophy of science. He has held professorships in sociology at Yale University, Northwestern University, Washington University, and Rutgers University.

TALCOTT PARSONS is Professor of Sociology at Harvard University. One of his major scientific preoccupations is the development of a systematic theory of social behavior. He is the author of *The Structure of Social Action* and *The Social System*, among a host of other sociological writings, and was formerly president of the American Sociological Association.

MYRON R. SHARAF is an Assistant Clinical Professor in Psychiatry at Tufts Medical School. Among his current research interests is a series of studies on "intraception" in connection with the recruitment and training of professional personnel in the field of mental health.

MUZAFER SHERIF is Professor of Social Psychology at the Pennsylvania State University. He was formerly Director of the Institute of Group Relations at the University of Oklahoma. He is a major contributor to reference group theory. Among his recent writings are *Reference Groups: Exploration into Conformity and Deviation of Adoles-*

cents and *In Common Predicament: Intergroup Conflict and Cooperation*.

LESLIE A. WHITE is Professor of Anthropology at the University of Michigan, where he formerly served as Chairman of the Department for twenty-five years. He received the Viking Medal and Award from the Wenner-Gren Foundation in 1960 for outstanding contributions in the field of anthropology, and served as president of the American Anthropological Association in 1964. His books *The Science of Culture* and *The Evolution of Culture* are widely known.

Index